BEHIND THE SCENES

In South Dakota

by

Joyce L. Vander Lugt

ThinkPrint Publishing Company
Sioux Falls, South Dakota 57105

104°
A
103°
B
102°
C
101°
D
MONTANA
Missouri
Little
46°
Bowman
Cedar
Mott
Cannonball
Cr.
N.
Hettinger
NORTH DAKOTA
STANDING
ROCK
Ft. Yates
IND. RES.
La
Oa
Missouri
Lemmon
McIntosh
McLaughlin
Fork
Shadehill
Res.
Grand
River
1
Buffalo
S.
Fork
HARDING
Bison
CORSON
N.
Fork
PERKINS
Thunder Butte
Timber Lake
Isabel
Trail City
D-E-W-E-Y
Moreau
CHEYENNE
45°
BUTTE
S.
Fork
Dupree
Eagle Butte
RIVER
La Plant
Maurine
Faith
IND. RES.
+ Geographical Center
of the United States
Cherry
ZIEBACH
Belle Fourche
Res.
Newell
Cr.
River
Lake
Belle Fourche
MEADE
Cherry Creek
Oahe
Spearfish
Sturgis
Belle
Cheyenne
O
D
2
Central City
Ft. Meade
Lead
Deadwood
Fourche
R.
Milesville
Ft. Pierre
LAWRENCE
B
L
A
C
K
Rapid
City
HAAKON
BLACK
ELLSWORTH A.F.B.
44°
New Underwood
Wall
Philip
Bad
Midland
R.
JONES
Harney Pk.
7,242
Hill City
PENNINGTON
BADLANDS NAT'L
MON.
JACKSON
Murdo
Newcastle
Keystone
MT. RUSHMORE
NAT'L MEM.
Kadoka
Belvidere
White
JEWEL CAVE
NAT'L MON.
Custer
CUSTER
S
WIND CAVE
NAT'L PARK
WASHABAUGH
(UNORGANIZED)
Wanblee
MELLETTE
White River
H
I
L
L
S
3
Hot Springs
River
PINE
White
RIDGE
River
INDIAN
Kyle
RES.
White R.
Woo
Cheyenne
Angostura
Res.
Allen
Parmelee
Mission
Edgemont
Igloo
SHANNON
(UNORGANIZED)
BENNETT
Martin
S.
ROSEBUD IND. RES.
St. Francis
FALL
RIVER
Pine Ridge
Fork
D
TODD
(UNORGANIZED)
43°
Chadron
NEBRASKA
Valentine
SOUTH DAKOTA
Niobrara
River
WYOMING
MILES
0
10
20
40
60
80
KILOMETERS
0 10 20
40
60
80
State Capital
County Seats
104°
A
103°
B
102°
C
101°
D

(c) Hammond Incorporated, Maplewood, New Jersey, license # 10,208.

Grateful acknowledgment is made for use of all source material and permission to quote from the following:

Robert F. Karolevitz, *Douglas County: The Little Giant,* copyright 1983 by the author and quoted with his permission.

Celda Lundin, *Revillo: A Century on the Prairie,* copyright 1984; by permission of the author.

E. Mandat-Grancey, *Buffalo Gap,* translated by Phyllis Gorum, edited by Keith Cochrane and published by Lame Johnny Press, 1981; by permission of Dave Strain.

Joseph N. Nicollet on the Plains and Prairies: The Expeditions of 1838-39 with Journals, Letters, and Notes on the Dakota Indians, translated and edited by Edmund C. Bray and Martha Coleman Bray published and copyright 1976; by permission of the Minnesota Historical Society Press.

Kathleen Norris, *DAKOTA: A Spiritual Geography,* copyright 1993; by permission of Houghton Mifflin Company/Ticknor & Fields.

History of Faulk County, South Dakota 1919-1982, copyright 1982; by permission of the Faulk County Historical Society.

South Dakota Magazine quoted by permission of Bernie Hunhoff.

South Dakota's Ziebach County, History of the Prairie, copyright 1982 by the Ziebach County Historical Society; with permission of Jackie Birkeland.

From *Summer '93 Magazine* published by the Black Hills, Badlands & Lakes Association of South Dakota; by permission of Bill Honerkamp.

The South Dakota map was used with permission of Hammond, Incorporated, Maplewood, New Jersey, license # 10,208.

Dedication

To Karel, Ellen and Bill

and

To the memory of Spot,
who increased our joy
on so many South Dakota hikes.

Paula Bylsma's quilt: Something Old; Something New.

PREFACE

BEHIND THE SCENES in South Dakota captures some of the color of South Dakota, past and present. The book is somewhat like a comfortable quilt constructed of varied pieces, old and new. This is a sampler and not intended to be a guidebook or history. The reader will undoubtedly think of places, events or stories that should have been included and will be right in thinking so. I can't give it all away, and so you are left to discover for yourself some of the many interesting people and unique places in South Dakota. Generalizations are risky, particularly when writing of South Dakota, and although I have lived in the state for more than 25 years, I don't presume to have a handle on it. So, I encourage you to explore, to see for yourself, and to experience life in this "Land of Infinite Variety."

This book presents vignettes of communities from Aberdeen to Zell, in alphabetical order. Each place has stories to tell, and I have drawn on those which I found representative, varied and interesting. Population figures, based on the 1990 United States Census numbers, are given for most towns and cities. Figures are unavailable for unincorporated communities, except by township; although these are usually small, there are exceptions such as Piedmont which has a population of about 500. Places such as White Rock and Tinton are categorized by others as ghost towns, but I hesitate to use that term when people live there. A list of places with counties of location and topics appears at the end of the book.

Many provided help on this adventure, and I thank those who contributed information in visits and telephone conversations. I am especially indebted to my family who believed in the project from the start and gave encouragement and support for which I am immeasurably grateful. Amy Johnson was exceptionally helpful in editing; Ellen Vander Lugt and Carol Dalebout critiqued parts of the manuscript; Paula Bylsma read proof copy. Their work is appreciated. Professor Tom Shields provided helpful cover consultation. Thanks to Bill Vander Lugt for the "Behind the Scene" drawing of Mount Rushmore. I have drawn from the work of many who have written about people and events in South Dakota, and I am particularly appreciative of the work of county historical societies, local groups and individuals who have preserved a record of our past. My thanks go to those who gave permission to use quoted material. Finally, I acknowledge any errors as my own.

Joyce L. Vander Lugt

Sioux Falls, September 1994.

A Selected South Dakota Chronology

1743	The Verendrye brothers placed a lead plate near present Fort Pierre, claiming the region for France.
1750	(approximately) The Lakota (Teton Sioux) moved into the plains area, eventually driving out the Omaha and the Arikara.
1780	(approximately) The Nakota (Yanktons and Yanktonais) were forced to move from Iowa and settled in the James River Valley.
1803	France sold the Louisiana Territory to the United States.
1804-1806	Lewis and Clark and their Corps for Northwestern Discovery explored the Upper Missouri River area as they traveled to and from the Pacific northwest.
1808	The St. Louis Fur Company organized fur trade on the Upper Missouri.
1831	Steamboat travel on the Upper Missouri River began with the trip of The Yellowstone to Fort Tecumseh, near present Fort Pierre.
1838	Nicollet and Fremont explored what is now eastern South Dakota.
1839	Father De Smet did missionary work among the Native Americans and returned on subsequent trips.
1856	Fort Randall was built to assert military control on the Northern Plains.
1857	Settlers came to Sioux Falls, Flandreau and Medary.
1858	The Yanktons signed a treaty relinquishing land between the Big Sioux and Missouri Rivers.
1861	The Organic Act established Dakota Territory, which included present day South Dakota, North Dakota and more.
1862	Some Minnesota Santees resorted to violence, causing settlers to flee to Yankton.

1868   The Great Sioux Reservation, covering most of the western half of present South Dakota, was established by the Fort Laramie Treaty.

1872   The first railroad in Dakota Territory arrived at Yankton.

1874   Custer's expedition found gold in the southern Black Hills.

1876   News of gold in Deadwood Gulch brought gold seekers there. Custer and his 7th cavalry troops were killed at Little Big Horn.

1877   The Great Dakota Boom began.

1880   A terrible blizzard occurred in October.

1881   Joseph Ward established Yankton College, the first institution of higher learning in Dakota Territory.

1882   The University of South Dakota was established.

1883   The State Agricultural College opened in Brookings.

1888   A November blizzard took many lives.

1889   North Dakota and South Dakota became the 39th and 40th states. The Great Sioux Reservation was reduced to six small reservations.

1890   Troops killed innocent Native Americans at Wounded Knee. Settlers rushed for 11 millions acres of former reservation land.

1910   The Capitol building was dedicated.

1927   Gutzon Borglum started work on Mount Rushmore.

1946   Pick-Sloan program was adopted for Missouri River control.

1947   Korczak Ziolkowski began work on the Crazy Horse Monument.

1975   The American Indian Movement group took over Wounded Knee.

1993   Governor George Mickelson and seven other state leaders died in an airplane crash.

. . . .May I not be permitted, in this place, to introduce a few reflections on the magical influence of the prairies? It is difficult to express by words the varied impressions which their spectacle produces. Their sight never wearies. To look at a prairie up or down; to ascend one of its undulations; to reach a small plateau, (or, as the voyageurs call it, *a prairie planchè*,) moving from wave to wave over alternate swells and depressions; and, finally, to reach the vast interminable low prairie, that extends itself in front, -be it for hours, days, or weeks, one never tires; pleasurable and exhilarating sensations are all the time felt; *ennui* is never experienced. Doubtless there are moments when excessive heat, a want of fresh water, and other privations, remind one that life is a toil; but these drawbacks are of short duration. There is almost always a breeze over them. . . .all, everything, is calculated to excite the perceptions, and keep alive the imagination. In the summer season, especially, everything upon the prairies is cheerful, graceful, and animated. . . .It is then they should be visited; and I pity the man whose soul could remain unmoved under such a scene of excitement.

Joseph N. Nicollet, 1839

(A footnote states: "The modern reader may see such a view on S. Dak. state highway 10, between Sisseton and the Minnesota border.")

Reprinted with permission from *Joseph N. Nicollet on the Plains and Prairies: The Expeditions of 1838-39 with Journals, Letters, and Notes on the Dakota Indians*, translated and edited by Edmund C. Bray and Martha Coleman Bray, published and copyright 1976 by the Minnesota Historical Society Press.

INTRODUCTION

The Inside Scoop

South Dakotans have it all -
Summer, winter, spring and fall.
We have plains; we have Hills.
We have rocks; we have rills.
We have cities; we have places.
We have country; we have spaces.
Our pulsebeat is measured by Native American drum
While wheels of progress and business hum.

Travelers often emphasize making time on interstate highways, but it is rewarding to take time to travel state roads which offer encounters with friendly people, home-cooking in small cafes and views that would otherwise be missed.

In South Dakota, there are old friends to see and new friends to meet. Hazel, Opal, Ramona, Ravinia, Bradley, Erwin, Kyle, Marty, Victor, Virgil and Ward will welcome you. We have Frankfort, Stockholm, Vienna, Florence and Naples in addition to Bristol, Bath, Chester, Chelsea and Stratford. Travelers with more exotic tastes might want to visit Columbia, Lebanon or Alexandria. History buffs might want to think about Virgil, Tolstoy, Dante, St. Francis, Custer, Madison, Monroe or Jefferson. As with any travel, one needs to approach such a trip with a certain sense of adventure and exploration. But there are many friendly folks to help you in any situation. The hospitable Native American people of the nine reservations in South Dakota extend a welcome, too.

More than fifty thousand Native Americans live in South Dakota, and although they are collectively called Sioux, they are Dakota, Lakota and Nakota people. The three groups have different languages and geographic areas: The Teton (western) Sioux speak the Lakota dialect; the Yankton (central) Sioux speak the Nakota dialect; the Santee (eastern) Sioux speak the Dakota dialect. Because Sioux was derived from a Chippewa word meaning "snake in the grass," some would like to abolish use of that word, along with the term "Indian." Dakota means "friend" or "ally."

Three of the reservations are open with no set boundaries. These are the Yankton Sioux, the Flandreau Santee Sioux and the Sisseton Wahpeton Dakota. The other six reservations, of which Pine Ridge is the largest with a population of 11,166, have defined boundaries. The Rosebud Reservation is second largest with 8043 people. The Cheyenne River, Crow Creek and Lower Brule Reservations are home to approximately 7500 people in total. Although most of the Standing Rock Reservation is in South Dakota, its headquarters are in North Dakota. The people of the reservations have their own governments and judicial systems and sovereignty within their borders. They welcome visitors to their reservations, particularly those who respect and seek to understand Native American culture.

South Dakota Is Not a Southern State!

Misconceptions abound regarding South Dakota. Although South Dakota follows South Carolina in the atlas, that's the extent of our proximity. There are days, however, when we feel like we are a southern state. Few places on earth have the temperature extremes that we South Dakotans experience, with temperatures below zero in winter and above 100° in summer. The highest recorded temperature was 120°F at Gann Valley on July 5, 1936, and the lowest temperature recorded was -58°F at McIntosh on February 17, 1936. Life in South Dakota isn't for the fainthearted; some say that the weather sorts out the riff-raff.

Winter weather is invigorating, and we enjoy sledding, skiing, sleighing, tobogganing, ice skating, snowmobiling, ice fishing. Don't feel too sorry for the ice fishermen, some of whom have shanties with comforts beyond belief. There are some times, fortunately not too many, when it's unfit for human or beast to be outside, and then we just settle in with hot chocolate and a good book or Gurney's seed catalog.

You can't really appreciate spring if you haven't experienced winter. As one asked, "When winter comes, can spring be far behind?" The changing seasons bring a certain joy and expectancy and speak to us of the seasons of life.

The Secret Is Out

When a newcomer told his grandmother in the East that he was moving to South Dakota, she paused as she tried to visualize the location without a map and said, "Oh, one of the squaa-ah states!" Well, we're not quite square. Although we sometimes resent a pervasive ignorance, we like keeping secret the quality of life in our state. South Dakotans had mixed feelings when Sioux Falls was named the number one city in the United States by *Money* magazine in 1992. It's not that we don't want visitors and newcomers, but we like what is good and wholesome about our state, including our wide open spaces. And if forced to admit it, we are somewhat resistant to change.

Some would ask what there is to see and perhaps think only of the attractions of the larger cities or the colossal mountain carvings at Mt. Rushmore and Thunderhead Mountain. In contrast, the beauty of the prairie is subtle. As the eyes search, the discerning viewer is rewarded with a distant butte, a small prairie flower, an eagle or a sea of prairie grass waving in the wind. Father DeSmet, an early Jesuit missionary said, "Solitude seems to give scope to man's intellectual faculties, the mind seems more vigorous, the thought clearer. . . ."[1]

Great Faces, Great Places and Great Spaces

Milo Dailey, editor of the *Yankton Daily Press and Dakotan* thinks of our state as "the most stretched out city of 700,000 people in the world." "The Missouri River is our fishing hole.

The Black Hills are our park. Pierre is our City Hall, and Deadwood is the risque part of town."[2] Sioux Falls is the downtown; Huron is the fair ground; playgrounds and shopping centers are spread about. More than 90 percent of the state is farm or ranch land.

Overpopulation is far removed from the experience of most South Dakotans, many of whom live a considerable distance from their neighbors and welcome human interaction. Sioux Falls is the only South Dakota city with a population of over 100,000. Rapid City has about half as many people with 54,523. Aberdeen has almost 25,000 people. There are seven towns that have between 10 and 20 thousand people: Watertown, Brookings, Mitchell, Pierre, Yankton, Huron and Vermillion.

Fifty-four percent of South Dakotans live on farms or ranches. Many of us identify with small towns where:

> You don't use turn signals because everybody knows where you're going.
> You're born on June 13 and your family receives gifts from the local merchants because you're the first new baby of the year. You dial a wrong number and talk for 15 minutes anyway.
> You can't walk for exercise because every car that passes offers you a ride. . . .
> You write a check on the wrong bank and it covers for you anyway. . . .
> You missed church on Sunday and the preacher sends you a get well card.
> Someone asks how you feel and spends the time to listen to what you have to say.
>
> Excerpted from "Thank God for Small Towns."
> Author unknown.[3]

Don't underestimate South Dakotans. Linda Stephen, a co-publisher of the *Nation's Center News* in Buffalo said, "You can't be a dummy and live here. It just won't work."[4] We are thinking people and have an independent streak which confounds politicians. Even in remotely located rural communities, there is global interest demonstrated in discussions and deeds. Communities respond to global needs by sending money, supplies and volunteers.

Country style was popular in South Dakota long before it became fashionable elsewhere. Folks who have grown up in boots think there is nothing in the world more comfortable. An easy-going informality allows one to be comfortable in a sport coat and western tie worn with jeans and boots at South Dakota events where more sophisticated fashions are also present. South Dakotans have known what fun country dancing is for many years and are amused as their two-steppin' urban friends put on western duds. Many light-on-their-feet country dancers learned their steps at small town dances which were and are a focus of community social activity.

As a state with a strong agricultural interest, meat and potatoes are "soul food" here! Most of us grew up on good home cooking which still can be found in restaurants in South Dakota towns. Native American fry bread and Indian tacos are hard to beat. We enjoy a variety of ethnic foods that those who came to the state brought with them, including Norwegian lefse and lutefisk, Danish ebleskiver, German sausages, Greek gyros, Czech kolaches, Dutch olieballen and Polish pierogi.

Thinking Big

What's **big** in South Dakota? Well, first there were **big** dinosaurs. Later there were **big** buffalo herds. Then, in 1803 the United States made a **big** land purchase which included almost all of South Dakota and more. That was followed by a **big** expedition of Lewis and Clark to explore the upper Missouri River as they sought river routes to the Pacific Northwest. Later, Wall Drug began as a struggling drug store that became a **big** tourist attraction. Today, the sculptures of the four Presidents at Mt. Rushmore and Crazy Horse at Thunderhead Mountain come to mind when we think of **big**. The Sturgis Motorcycle Rally is an incredibly **big** phenomenon, too. **Big** business has come to the state. And we can tell some **big** fishing and hunting stories, without lying!

Although entitled to some bragging rights, South Dakotans display a tendency toward understatement. "Pretty good!" is about as good as anything gets! A compliment to a cook might be, "That's not bad!" Our state flower, the pasque flower, peaks through prairie grass in early spring and seems to represent the understatement which prevails in South Dakota. This pale purplish flower grows low to the ground and is a small bloom that many have not seen or appreciated.

See For Yourself

The incredible diversity of South Dakota's people, scenery, weather, geology and politics makes it hard to characterize the state and its people. Feel the freedom of the vast expanse of the plains. Hike or bike some trails. Sit in on a cattle auction. Go to a county fair and enjoy the plate supper at a local church booth. Get off the highways, to visit the small towns where folks are friendly. It doesn't take much to break the ice while enjoying coffee and homemade pie at a small town cafe. State senator Bernie Hunhoff who publishes *South Dakota Magazine* gives this advice, "You can argue religion and politics all day long and not offend a South Dakotan. But don't ask how many acres a farm or ranch family owns. Also, avoid conversations on gambling, property taxes, teacher salaries and cholesterol."[5]

Max Rittgers, a Florida resident, chose an unusual way in which to experience South Dakota when he bicycled across his native state on a ten day trip in November of 1993. The weather was nippy, especially for a Floridian, but Rittgers said, "This is a precious place. It's been a thrill, the best thing I've ever done. People are wonderful here."[6]

FROM ABERDEEN TO ZELL

ABERDEEN, 24,927

One, two, three, four, five. Quintuplets! Sakes alive!

The Aberdeen quints born in 1963 were the first surviving quintuplets in the United States. Four days before their babies were born two months prematurely, the parents, Mary Anne and Andrew Fischer were told they would have triplets. Mary Ann and James Andrew arrived as surprises along with Mary Magdaline, Mary Catherine and Mary Margaret. In celebration of the special event, a creative Aberdeen bartender came up with the "quintini," a double martini featuring four olives and an onion. President Kennedy sent congratulations, and Pope Paul VI sent a gold medallion for each of the babies. The Fischers built a seventeen-room home west of Aberdeen for their family of eleven children and attempted to live a normal life outside of the glare of publicity.

In 1991, more unusual birth news came from Aberdeen when librarian Arlette Schweitzer gave birth to her grandchildren. Because her daughter Christa was born without a uterus, Arlette Schweitzer acted as a surrogate mother. Eggs from Christa Uchytil's ovaries were fertilized with the sperm of her husband, Kevin, and implanted in Schweitzer. On October 12, 1991, the surrogate mother delivered twins, Chad and Chelsea Uchytil, a story portrayed on television as "Labor of Love: the Arlette Schweitzer Story." Schweitzer had a bit part in the movie as, appropriately, a librarian. A reviewer wrote of the film, ". . .it lets us meet fine people. If these folks are typical, we'll all want to move to South Dakota. . . ."[7]

AGAR, 82

Agar was without its own high school after 1984, but the Prairie Economic Development Academy opened as an alternative for Agar high school students in 1993. Agar residents decided to use the money they would otherwise have sent to a neighboring district to run their own experimental school 215 days of the year, 40 more than the usual in South Dakota. The small school demonstrates a can-do spirit that exists in Agar. It relies totally on local tax dollars to support the school which has a limit of eight students per grade. The school opened in the Agar school building in the fall of 1993, with five freshmen, one junior and one senior. Classwork in a variety of subjects is done at computer terminals which make it possible for students to do college prep study. To meet graduation requirements at Prairie Economic Development Academy, students must develop a business with help from local business people. Townspeople hope that the unique graduation requirement will be a stimulus to growth after a 41 percent population decline in Agar from 1980 to 1990.[8]

AKASKA, 52

Akaska is #2 on the "Best of the Rest" list of a newspaper publisher with a sense of humor. Chuck Cecil's "tongue in cheek" list named the top ten towns and cities in South Dakota overlooked by other publications. Cecil described Akaska as "populated with flourishing off-spring of some of the...ah...shall we say...ah...slower men who left the US of A for the great Gold Rush in Alaska in the 1800's but became confused after eating spoiled lefse in Des Moines, Iowa, and ended up farming the dirt around Akaska."[9]

ALCESTER, 843

Alcester was home to a Civilian Conservation Corps camp in the 1930's. A camp usually consisted of 200 single men between the ages of 17 and 25 who worked on various projects as part of a federal work-relief program. The workers received food, clothing and pay ($30 a month of which $25 was sent to the parents) in addition to medical care and educational, recreational and religious programs. The group based in Alcester worked on conservation and prevention of soil erosion; they built stock dams and planted shelterbelts. In 1937, they planted 7050 trees which are enjoyed by visitors to Union County State Park park today. An historical plaque in Alcester tells how the C.C.C. provided work for 31,087 jobless men in the state from 1933 to 1942 when there were 43 C.C.C. camps in South Dakota.

ALEXANDRIA, 518

The C.O.B. was one of the most interesting clubs in the town's history, and although the exact name is unknown, it might have been the Comaraderie of Bachelors or the Chartered Order of Bachelors. The group of unmarried men held dinner meetings in the dining room of the Alexandria House at the turn of the century. Their motto was, "Not in favor of the Single Standard, but do favor the Double Standard; By Agreement." When a bachelor married, he was fined $10 and dropped from the club. The menus of the C.O.B. resembled those of a gourmet club. [10]

ALLEN

In 1891, Chief Luther Standing Bear administered the school at Allen, and of his experience there, he wrote, "The Government furnished nearly everything, and I was getting along splendidly. . .The children were anxious to learn." Adults were interested when Standing Bear organized a group who shared a meal and then discussed questions such as "Which is more useful - salt or tobacco?" Standing Bear wrote, "These debates brought up all sorts of topics. As the whites say nowadays, 'We got a great kick out of it.'" That small group led to a larger meeting to discuss tribal matters, treaties and ways to improve the life of the Sioux. [11]

ALPENA, 251

A statement from 1909 "School Notes" in the *Alpena Journal* might raise some eyebrows today. "More farm boys will register for school as soon as farm work gets lighter. They will

C.O.B. MENU

THANKSGIVING 1890

SOUPS
Oxtail, Oyster or Bean

OYSTERS
Blue Point, on the half shell, fried or scalloped

MEATS
Turkey with cranberry sauce
Chicken, baked and fried
Mallard ducks with Champaigne sauce
Quail on toast
Rabbit, fried, gravy a la Seitz
Young pig, roasted
Mutton stew
Salmon baked
Tongue
Ham

And from a 1901 C.O.B. menu:

VEGETABLES
Mashed potatoes, Sweet Potatoes
Turnips, Cabbage, Parsnips
Tomatoes, Corn, Lima Beans

SALADS
Potato, Chicken, Salmon

BREADS
Brown, Cream, Rolls and Rusk

DESSERT
Pies: Apple, Mince and Pumpkin
Plum Pudding
Assorted Fruits and Nuts

BEVERAGES
Coffee, Tea, Chocolate, Milk

be good athletic timber and it is hoped they will not let their studies interfere with their track work."[12]

In the same year the *Alpena Journal* ran a little piece called "The Devil's Corner."[13]

> These chilly days cause Alpena's sages to gather in some shop about town where there is a warm fire going. Then that fraternal body, inspired by woolen underwear and buckwheat slapjack diet, give vent to profound convictions. They have settled the women's rights question. They believe in women's suffrage. They will let the women keep their feet to themselves these cold nights and suffer the same as the men.

ALTAMONT, 48

The Altamont Prairie Preserve is one of ten South Dakota preserves owned by the Nature Conservancy. The Conservancy is working to restore the 62 acres near Altamont to its native state as tallgrass prairie. Although it has never been plowed, weeds and non-native grasses have encroached. To eliminate leafy spurge and other unwanted plants, farmers have loaned 136 Angora goats and 73 sheep in exchange for free grazing. The goats and sheep munch happily on the preserve as part of a plan to use them for 45 days twice each year for five years. A black donkey prevents coyotes from preying on the goats which are separated from the sheep by an electric fence. Conservationists hope that big and little blue stem, Indian grass, side oats and wild rye will comprise fields like those found by the prairie settlers. In addition, they hope to preserve two endangered butterfly species, the Regal Fritillary and Dakota Skipper, which suck nectar from the native flowers.[14]

AMHERST

A unique reunion of Amherst graduates took place in 1993. Although the school closed in 1966, an alumnus organized a "mail reunion" of classmates scattered from Sacramento to New Guinea.

ANDOVER, 106

Railroad graders called it Station 88, but the town that developed was given a proper name: Andover, taken from Andover, Massachusetts. There were high fallutin' ideas, with a Waldorf Hotel - not the Waldorf Astoria, mind you, but it was considered the finest hotel between Aberdeen and Minneapolis. On Saturday nights, the "modern public baths" with local artesian water were busy, and the tonsorial needs of gentlemen were met. An orchestra came from Minneapolis to play for dinner each Sunday, and strict dress code was in effect.

ARDMORE

The Buffalo Gap National Grassland covers the far southwestern corner of South Dakota, where Ardmore is located. This is ranch country where one cow needs 25 acres to graze. Ranchers are happy to see their neighbors when they gather to worship in the little church at Ardmore. Because there is no daily mail or newspaper delivery, students bring these with them when returning home from school in Edgemont, 30 or 40 miles away.

You don't have to go to the South Pole to be part of a select group of explorers and adventurers! In a remote location southeast of Ardmore, a fenced marker designates the point where South Dakota, Nebraska and Wyoming meet. If you get there, sign the guestbook contained in a metal cabinet since not many people do. Only eight people were recorded for 1993.[15]

ARLINGTON, 908

When Rand McNally left Arlington off the state map in 1985, there was a hootin' and a hollerin' that let the map-making firm know that Arlington is very alive. Because of the error, Rand McNally made a donation of $1000, used for a community picnic. The people of Arlington organized a three-day "Put Arlington Back on the Map Day" festival and circulated the phrase, "I Found Arlington!" on posters and buttons. We won't forget them, and they won't let us![16]

After the California earthquake of January 1994, the Arlington Development Corporation placed an ad in the *Los Angeles Times* that read, "Tired of living on the fault-line? Relocate to South Dakota. Affordable housing and quality of life." The telephone line was jinglin' on the Monday after the ad appeared, and ten-minute videos of Arlington were distributed to quake and crime weary Californians. The Arlington Development Corporation has been busily responding to inquiries.[17] Life-long Californians Ken and Vicky Russell visited the Arlington area and were so impressed that they made plans to move. The Russells look forward to life in a small, quiet midwestern town with their two young sons.[18]

ARMOUR, 854

Philip Danforth Armour, for whom the town was named, was the president of the Chicago meat packing company and a member of the board of directors of the railroad which came to Armour. Townsite promoters in 1886 knew all about hype as the following ad indicates:[19]

WESTWARD THE STAR OF EMPIRE TAKES ITS WAY,
AND
ARMOUR, DAKOTA, IS TO BE THE NEW
STAR OF BETHLEHEM

Located in the best region for Stock and Agricultural purposes in all Dakota. The land is the best; of the quality of soil there is none better. It is a delightsome land. . . .

It may fairly and truthfully be said that this section of Dakota "Takes the Cake," and it is to the everlasting good of thousands of wise, pioneering people who have found it out, and have anchored here to build homes and raise fat children and happy families.

Douglas County is the place to buy a farm, and ARMOUR is the town for Live Men. LIVE MEN MAKES LIVELY BUSINESS, AND LIVE BUSINESS MAKES LIVELY MEN. . . . The coming year will largely add substantial improvement, and choice locations for business will be eagerly sought for.

> Those wanting Choice Lots at the present Bargains
> should not delay the matter too long. First come,
> first served. For information as to location and prices,
> address or call on
>
> J. E. DAVIS, Townsite Agent
> ARMOUR, DAKOTA

ARTAS, 28

Recollections of a one room school teacher provide insights of life in the Artas area in the thirties:

> My year in Campbell County near Artas, South Dakota, as a beginning teacher in the "dirty thirties" introduced me to the normal tasks of the teacher. I learned to start a fire every morning as an introduction to teaching 26 pupils in eight grades. I learned to cope with dust storms so severe classes had to be suspended while the children sat huddled in their desks with wet handkerchiefs over their faces. I learned to teach current events without a single newspaper in the district. I learned that character was not learned from books, but by example.[20]

ARTESIAN, 217

In 1884, long before Henry Ford's first auto, an Artesian resident fashioned a motorized carriage which was driven 20 miles to Woonsocket. It reached a top speed of 15 miles per hour and used five gallons of kerosene and ten gallons of water. Modest South Dakotans are just slow to claim fame.

ASHTON, 148

James Norwood, an Ashton dairy farmer from 1895 to the 1930's, built a round barn. The circular structure stands today as an Ashton landmark, one of fewer than 3000 round barns in North America. Regretably, the old barns that grace the country scene are slowly disappearing. The replacement metal pole structures are functionally fine but lacking in interest when compared with the old barns. Whether painted red or displaying wood that has weathered over years, the barns of yesteryear have a quality of character unmatched by the new structures. In a forward to a book called *Barns,* Bill Lacy

**Do they round dance in round barns
and square dance in square barns?**

wrote, "A man's barn bespoke his worth as a man. It expressed his earthly aspirations and symbolized the substance of his legacy to his children."[21]

ASTORIA, 155

"Oh, Ole!" will likely bring a response in Astoria. If you happen to be among the few who haven't heard a Scandinavian Ole and Lena joke, Ole is pronounced "O-lee" with the accent on the first syllable and is usually a nickname for Olaf or Olav, but sometimes refers to an Olsen or Olson. Many Oles have come and gone on Togstad Street over the years. Ole Rogness, Ole Odney, Ole Dahle, Ole Solem, Ole Bakken, Ole Anderson, Ole Lunde and Ole Hanson are among the list of Oles who have lived in the Astoria area.[22] One Olson, an Astoria area state's attorney, was linked, according to a local source, "to some strange plant pots, or vas dey pot plants? Vel, I don't know! Oh, Ole!"[23]

ATHOL

The president of the Chicago and Northwestern (sometimes called the Chicago and Norwegian) Railroad visited Dakota Territory in the 1870's and decided it would be good business to extend the railroads. By 1880, railroad lines entered the state and reached the Missouri River. To promote railroad traffic in the Territory, posters advertised: "2,000,000 farms of fertile prairie land to be had free," and "30,000,000 acres of most productive grain lands in the world." Claim seekers and immigrant cars came in great numbers during the years from 1878 to 1886, during the Great Dakota Boom.

Winter weather sometimes brought a halt to railroad travel, until a plow cleared the tracks. After one three-day "blow" in Athol, huge drifts had to be removed north and south of the depot. The depot agent had instructions to board up the windows of the station when a snowplow was ordered out on the tracks. The waiting room was packed with people. "The train made better time than was expected, and one of the men opened the door at the wrong moment just as the plow whizzed by. A dozen men inside the station fell all over themselves, knocking down the waiting-room stove, and digging snow from their eyes, ears, pockets, collars."[24]

AURORA, 619

Highway 14, or the "Chicago to Black Hills and Yellowstone Park Highway," which became known as the "Black and Yellow Trail," passed through Aurora for over 20 years. The road was marked out in 1913, and to minimize hazards, it became illegal to tie horses and cows on the roadway or near the sidewalk. The marshall purchased a stopwatch to better enforce the 12 mile per hour speed limit. Many travelers took the trail which, in places, consisted of raw gumbo that stuck to wagon wheels and cars. In bad weather, wayfaring strangers sought lodging at homes along the route. This important east-west highway was graveled in the 1920's, but Aurora was left off the trail when Highway 14 was rerouted in 1936.[25]

AURORA CENTER

In the bleak years of the Great Depression, the National Geographic Society sponsored a scientific manned balloon flight, called Explorer 2. Long before the days of the Mercury and Apollo and other space programs, scientists yearned for information that could be obtained from above earth. On November 11, 1935, the stratosphere balloon Explorer 2 was launched in the Black Hills (a year after the ill-fated attempt of Explorer 1 when the balloon ripped while 11 kilometers high, forcing the men aboard to parachute to safety). Two captains, in a chamber that looked somewhat like today's space modules, made a record ascent of over 13.7 miles in 8 hours and 13 minutes. The *New York Times* reported, "Two men in a metal gondola are hurling down through the South Dakota skies from a height of 72,000 feet. At the same time they are talking to a newspaper office in London." The two-man crew landed in a field west of Aurora Center at 4:14 p.m. on Armistice Day, November 11, 1935, with instruments intact and new information about atmospheric conditions, cosmic rays and high altitude photography. Five thousand people from several states soon converged on the area.[26]

AVON, 576

The *Avon Clarion,* first published in 1901, is one of approximately 7000 small-town newspapers in the United States, and if you haven't read a paper like it, you're missing out on an interesting part of American life. "Obituaries are regularly run on the front page, as are articles on Girl Scout cookie sales and the most recent snow storm," but the paper also takes on controversial issues such as property taxes, school bond issues and the landfill. The local newspaper makes a distinct contribution to the life of a community as it keeps a finger on the pulse of local activity. One reviewer wrote of the weekly newspapers and editors, "They have front-row seats on our society under exceedingly intimate circumstances. They inform, they guide, they cajole. The small-town weekly newspaper is the kind of publication that the Founding Fathers were thinking of when they considered the merits of a free press."[27]

Clair Brodeen, a traveling salesman, bought the *Avon Clarion* in 1956 so he could spend more time with his family. Brodeen handled most of the news gathering and printing, and his wife made the weekly calls for social news. The paper was run on an old Linotype, the "dinosaur of the printing business." Forty inches of copy an hour was the most a good typesetter could do since each letter had to be picked up singly. Time brought changes to the paper which Jack Brodeen bought from his dad in 1992, but the *Avon Clarion* continues to publish the good news of its community and the bad.[28]

BADGER, 114

Nobel prize (1979) winning economist Theodore Schultz grew up in the area on a farm still operated by his family. Schultz was the oldest of eight children and learned about agricultural economics at an early age when his family took livestock to Badger. He recalled a time when his father drove some wayward hogs cross country to the railhead at Badger. The animals went "hog wild" and had to be rounded up by Ted Schultz and others who quickly learned about profit and loss. As a student, Schultz practiced his oratorical skills in the fields and became locally known for the Fourth of July orations he delivered in Badger. At South Dakota State College, Ted Schultz excelled in debate and oratory, skills which later served him well as an economist at Iowa State University and the University of Chicago.[29]

BALTIC, 666

> Dis Baltic am one fine good place
> Believe me ven I say
> Dat near dis grand place I vas born
> Undt here, you bat, I'll shtay.
> From "Poem About Baltic" by "A Local Friend"[30]

One can still hear Norwegian accents in Baltic, originally named St. Olaf. Although the community dropped its Norwegian name, the Scandinavian heritage has been preserved in the community, as you might guess from the verse.

BANCROFT, 30

In 1915, residents decided they needed a community hall and raised money by selling shares. The hall, dedicated in January 1916, became a center of community life. It provided a place for dances, school programs, P.T.A., roller skating and basketball games. Silent movies were shown in hall while Charlie Barber provided background music, playing the same tune for a half-hour. Hoot Gibson, Tom Mix, Henry Fields, Harold Lloyd and Rin Tin Tin appeared on the screen in the Bancroft hall. The old hall served the town well until 1960 when it was replaced by a new facility, and the old building went to rest on an area farm.[31]

BARNARD

This little community is not much bigger today than when it was the site of the Colin Campbell Trading Post, established by Campbell for the Columbia Fur Company in 1822. A monument marks the site of the stockaded post where traders did business from 1822 to 1828.

BATH

Bath was the railroad station for fashionable visitors going to the nearby resort at Tacoma Park. The people of Bath tried to present themselves in the best possible way and inspected the board sidewalks daily so protruding nails would not catch the hems of ladies' dresses. From 1890 to 1930, Tacoma Park was a popular attraction with "carnivals, chautauquas, nightly dances and summer theater, accompanied by the customary stands and a merry-go-round." Interest in Tacoma Park decreased as the 1930's brought hard times and recurring floods, along with new entertainment forms and the automobile.[32]

BELLE FOURCHE, 4335

Belle Fourche (Bell foosh) was a flourishing cowtown in the early 1890's and had the world's record for range cattle shipping in 1893. Cowboys drove herds of cattle, some as large as 3000 head, from Texas to the Dakota range on the Black Hills and Canadian trail. Ruts left by these herds can still be seen along the Belle Fourche River. According to one old timer, "We'd take skinny longhorns from Texas,....turn 'em on that buff'lo grass, and in six weeks every one of 'em was so fat they had double chins and dimples on their knees."[33] As the railroad extended into the range country, the long cattle drives were eventually eliminated.

The Western South Dakota Stock Growers Association, which exists today, was formed in 1892 to provide rules for working the range and safeguards against rustlers and predators, in addition to inspection of cattle shipments. In the 1890's, approximately 50 cattle outfits were running herds on the open lands. Cattle were branded with registered marks to designate ownership under regulations that began with the first round-up in Dakota Territory in 1881. Roundups occurred twice a year with calves being "cut" - that is, separated from the herd, in cowboy jargon - for branding at the spring roundup. In the fall roundups, the mature animals were separated for shipment to market. The last of the large roundups was in 1904, with sixteen different sites so that all of the range could be covered as quickly as possible. After that, homesteaders moved in and forever changed the cattlemen's domain.

More than 21,000 different brands were in use in 1968, and in cases where the same brand was used by different ranchers, the brand was placed on a different part of the animal. Belle Fourche is still an important center for livestock auctions and wool shipping and retains an aura of the Old West. Each Fourth of July since 1918, the town has celebrated its heritage with the Black Hills Roundup. The roundup originated with cowboys who came into town and showed off their riding and roping skills. A bronze sculpture, Lasting Legacy by Tony Chytka, in Centennial park is a tribute to all the daring and colorful cowboys.

BELVIDERE, 63

In 1989, senior citizen Esther Serr published a 58-page booklet entitled *The Belvidere Cemetery* which lists 418 graves in alphabetical order and provides information about those buried there. The best-known person interred in Belvidere cemetery is Governor Tom Berry who came to South Dakota when Mellette County was opened for homesteading in about 1913. Having dreamed of a ranch of his own, Berry borrowed a wagon to which he hitched a couple of broncos to take his bride and belongings to their homestead on Blackpipe Creek. They eventually built a 16 by 30-foot log house in which happy evenings of neighborhood dancing took place. Tom Berry was elected to the state legislature in 1922 and served as governor from 1933 to 1937. The cowboy governor had a Will Rogers resemblance with a broad grin and shock of hair showing from under his cowboy hat.[34]

BERESFORD 1849

The Go Getters Extension Club is a group of homemakers who organized in 1965 "to provide a more abundant life for ourselves, our families, and our community." After a program on parties, the club decided to share their ideas and put together a 135 page book called *Party Potpourri* published in 1981. The book is full of ideas for various kinds of parties with games, menus, recipes and songs, including a bowling banquet song to be sung to the tune of the "Battle Hymn of the Republic"! The Bridal Shower section provides advice for the new farm wife:

> When he says: Could you help me for a couple of hours today?
> He really means: He has two days of plowing he'd like you to do.
> When he says: It's been a tough spring. I've put in long hours on that planter, but I'm caught up on the work now.
> He really means: His neighbor buddies want him to go fishing with them this weekend.
> When he says: (In a menacing tone) If that tractor gives me trouble just one more time!
> He really means: You'd better forget about that new refrigerator.
> When he says: (Tenderly) You certainly have a way with animals, dear, especially the little ones.
> He really means: He wants you to help give the baby pigs their iron shots.
> When he says: (Sheepishly) That wind really picked up this afternoon. It was darn near a gale.
> He really means: He was burning cornstalks and burned down most of the fence posts before he finally got the fire under control.
> When he says: You always were a whiz at math and book-keeping, weren't you, honey?
> He really means: He's got the record books in a mess and he needs you to straighten them out.
> When he says: The cattle seem to be off-feed lately. I'll have to watch them pretty closely for the next few days.
> He really means: That trip to your mother's has been called off again.
> When he says: Why don't you just take the car and go shopping today.
> No translation needed: Better pack your bag and head home to mother. You'll probably never find out what he's done. . . but you can be assured it must be serious![35]

Facing the Wind

BIG STONE CITY, 669

To the northwest of Big Stone City is Hartford Beach State Park, the site of an early trading post. In 1819, Hazen Mooers established that fur trading post which continued in operation for several decades. An 1845 inventory recorded the following: "795 buffalo robes, 10,307 muskrat, 117 mink, 77 raccoon, 12 otter, 2 bear, 2 beaver and 21 fisher."[36]

BIJOU HILLS

The hills were named for fur trader Joseph Bijou who established a post on the Missouri in 1812. French explorer Joseph Nicollet traveled the area in 1839 as he and his party took a steamboat called the Antelope up the Missouri River. Nicollet noted in his journals, "Hills on fire from 1833 to 1837. Sulfurous fumes." The explorer coined the term "pseudo volcanoes" to describe a burning phenomenon attributed to "the decomposition of iron pyrites in damp shale" in the area of Bijou Hills. In Bijou Quarry, Native Americans found green quartzite which they used for making tools and weapons.[37]

BISON, 451

The town got its name from a large pile of bison bones found by a settler. The large shaggy animals once roamed the plains in great numbers, causing the plains to look black and in motion. An estimated 40 million bison roamed the plains in 1800, but the number of animals steadily diminished to near extinction.[38] The American buffalo are Bison bison in scientist's terms. These animals were symbols of self sacrifice for the plains Indians, providing for almost every aspect of life. No more were killed than were needed; the Native Americans used every part of the bison. The hide provided blankets, tipis, clothing and moccasins. The flesh was eaten, and bones provided utensils and implements as well as needles for which the sinews provided thread. Rib bones were used for snow sleds and horns for ladles. The intestines were used for war charms, and the scrotum was used for a vessel. Sadly, by the middle of the 1870's, most of the buffalo had been killed by the whites who wanted mainly skins and tongues, a delicacy when pickled. By 1887, only 300 bison roamed wild, ending the way of life that Native Americans had known. When most of the bison had been killed, piles of bones remained to be collected by homesteaders who sold them for up to $12 a ton until about 1890. The bones were shipped eastward for use in refining sugar and the manufacture of bone china and fertilizers.[39]

BLUNT, 342

In 1883, Mentor Graham, a retired teacher, moved to Blunt to be with his son Harry Lincoln Graham in Dakota Territory. They ran a boarding house in a modest two-story home which has been restored as a memorial to Mentor Graham, an important man in the life of Abraham Lincoln. The young Lincoln lived in the Graham's home for six months while a grocery store clerk in New Salem, Illinois. Mentor Graham encouraged Lincoln's pursuit of knowledge and perhaps planted the idea of public service as they discussed issues of the time. When Lincoln ran unsuccessfully for the Illinois legislature, Mentor Graham assisted him in drafting a speech and platform. Years later, Graham was invited to Lincoln's Presidential Inaugural. Because of hearing loss, Mentor Graham sat close to the front, and upon seeing him, Lincoln invited his mentor to be seated on the platform. Graham continued teaching for several years after Lincoln's death and then moved westward to spend the last three years of his life at the home of his son in Blunt where he died.

BONESTEEL, 297

Rosebud land opened for settlement in 1904 when several million acres of land previously allocated to Native Americans were made available. Bonesteel was the gateway to the much sought land to the west. A lottery system was used to determine who would get the 2500 claims of 160 acres each at a price of four dollars per acre. Excitement was in the air, and claimseekers waited in long lines to participate in what could be thought of as the first big South Dakota lottery. Prospective settlers were required to register for the land rush, and 35,176 people filed in Bonesteel. The carnival like atmosphere in July of 1904 deteriorated as a wild and lawless group engaged in gambling, drinking, stealing and brawling. Law-abiding citizens united in an effort to restore order. The good guys took charge after a July 20, 1904, shooting stand-off known as the "Battle of Bonesteel," in which one gambler was killed and others were wounded. Of the many thousands of people who filed to obtain land, 1 in 46 got the desired claims.

BOWDLE, 589

During the blizzard of 1888, a homesteader became lost and disoriented while returning home. He burrowed into a haystack for survival during the night and got up and ran around the stack whenever he thought he might fall asleep, not knowing he was only a half-mile from home.

Bowdle has been a community of German accents. However, Spanish was heard when cattlemen from the Mexican states of Sonora and Chihuahua came to inspect South Dakota breeding stock in September of 1993. The Mexicans found a fine Charolais herd at Bowdle on their MIATCO (Mid-America Agri-Trade Council) trade mission. The history of livestock trade between South Dakota and Mexico goes back almost a century when Mexican longhorns traveled northward by trail drive and cattle car. In 1907, two South Dakota buffalo, destined for a bullring, traveled to Mexico in a railroad car lined with hay.

BOX ELDER, 2680

Nearby Ellsworth Air Force Base, which opened in 1950, is home to a B-1 Bomber Squadron. Until recently, it housed the 44th Missile Wing responsible for 150 Minutemen II missiles in western South Dakota. Under terms of the START nuclear disarmament agreement with the former Soviet Union, President Bush ordered removal of the warheads in 1991. Using large TE's (transporter-erectors) to convey the 60 foot long and 39 ton missiles, parts of the weapons were transported to Texas for likely use as booster rockets in the space program.[40]

BRANDON, 3543

Brandon area mounds present evidence of people who lived along the Big Sioux River and Big Stone Lake area from approximately 500 to 1500 A.D. The so-called Mound Builders hunted, gathered, and raised crops such as corn, beans and squash. They left 38 mysterious mounds. Excavation of five of the mounds revealed remains of two people in one mound and as many as 56 skeletons in another, in addition to food and weapons. From a location about a mile south of Brandon, a chain of hills extends about 15 miles to the southeast, and the mounds rise on the crests of the hills.

BRANDT, 123

The town was founded in 1884 and named for a minister, Rev. P. O. Brandt. The pious founders inserted a clause in each deed, forbidding the sale of intoxicating liquor on the premises for 50 years. They didn't want booze sold in Brandt in their lifetime.[41]

BRENTFORD, 69

Not far from the present Brentford is an island in the James River first known as Drifting Goose Island and later called Armadale. The island, containing 100 acres, was home to Drifting Goose and his band of Yanktonais who camped there until 1897. Drifting Goose was highly respected by his people and others as a man of intelligence, integrity and understanding.

The land ceded to the United States government by the Native Americans in the Laramie Treaty of 1868 included the James River Valley in which Drifting Goose and his people lived. The chief said he had not agreed to give away the land of his fathers and resisted the surveyors and settlers. On June 27, 1879, President Hayes attempted to placate Drifting Goose and his band by setting aside three townships for them. The chief and his people, however, wanted the settlers out of the area and terrorized the the valley, without taking lives, in an attempt to get them to leave. Railroads changed their route to avoid confrontation with Drifting Goose. The hostile demonstrations ceased after Drifting Goose went to Washington and was compensated for land. The Native Americans then moved beyond the Missouri.[42]

BRIDGEWATER, 533

George Anderson lived in Bridgewater until he was nine and has fond remembrances of his hometown where he enjoyed hunting pheasants. You're wondering, "Who's George Anderson?" The Sparky Anderson athletic complex in Bridgewater honors this baseball great and long time manager of the Cincinnati Reds and Detroit Tigers, the fourth winningest manager in baseball. Sparky fondly remembers growing up in Bridgewater and said, "I was able to grow up in a place where it was safe and you didn't have to worry about anything." One of Sparky's first teachers, Delila Dettmer, recalled a "show and tell" experience and asked, "Do you know what Sparky brought? - a bat and a ball."[43]

BRISTOL, 419

The Milwaukee railroad reached Siding 70 which became Bristol in 1880, and for a while, that was as far west as one could go on the Milwaukee Railroad, if one heeded the call to "Go West!" The Railway Townsite Company laid out the town, named for Bristol, England. After building a hotel to serve the railroad workers, R. P. Brokaw decided to stay in Bristol. Some of the family were still running the old Brokaw Hotel when Tom Brokaw, now the well known N.B.C. news anchor, was born in the area in 1940. Because Bristol didn't have a hospital, he was born at in Webster. When Red Brokaw took a job at the U.S. Ordnance Depot, he and Jean moved their young family to Edgemont. The Brokaws later moved to Pickstown and Yankton where Tom attended high school before studying at the University of South Dakota.[44]

BRITTON, 1394

On Main Street, a plaque marks the Continental Divide. You might expect an East-West divide, but in this case it marks division between waters that flow northward to the Hudson

Bay and those that flow southward to the Gulf of Mexico via the Mississippi River. This Continental Divide became very important in a big, international land transaction. After England and France fought and settled their differences over territories in North America, England claimed all lands draining north into Hudson Bay. The land south of the Continental Divide became part of the Louisiana Purchase of 1803 when the United States bought 831,321 square miles of land from France for $15 million which amounted to less than three cents an acre. That parcel, which doubled the size of the United States, extended from the Mississippi River to the Rockies and from the Gulf of Mexico to British North America. The northeast corner of present South Dakota has a unique history since it was not a part of the Louisiana Purchase. A South Dakota area north of Highway 10 was in British territory from 1763 to 1818, when the present Canadian boundary was established.

BROOKINGS, 16,270

Brookings is the home of the South Dakota State University "Jack Rabbits." Begun originally as an agricultural college, the university provides higher education for 15,000 students in a variety of fields, and it's not all corn or beans. McCrory Gardens on the campus of S.D.S.U. has been described as the prettiest 70 acres in South Dakota and is ranked among the top 10 small botanical gardens in the United States. There are 14 theme gardens including the centennial prairie garden, the rock garden, the chidren's maze, the rose garden, the pharmaceutical garden, the presidents' garden and others.

Brookings boasts some very nice parks, one of which is the original tree claim of a Norwegian settler. Under terms of the Timber Culture Act, a homesteader could establish a holding by planting and growing ten acres of trees on any 160 acres of unsettled land, and at the end of eight years, the land would belong to the settler. Martin Christianson was one of the area's early homesteaders, and his tree claim is now Hillcrest Park in the city of Brookings.

The first white men known to have visited the area were Joseph N. Nicollet and J.C. Fremont, "the great pathfinder," who studied and mapped the area between the Mississippi and Missouri Rivers. Nicollet wrote in his journals on July 8, 1838:

> We passed a bad night; the mosquitoes devoured us. As we have only a short distance to travel today, I let the men and the horses rest longer than usual. . . .
>
> . . . In an hour and a half, after 8 miles, we reached the summit of a beautiful treeless hill, situated in the middle of a magnificent group of eight lakes (Oakwood Lakes), all of the most beautiful proportions. We pass the rest of the day studying these lakes, and the evening in determining the geographical position of the camp at the summit of the hill.
>
> . . . The country is full of grandeur and beauty. . . .The Sioux only come at a certain time of year to fish and hunt the abundant game. They name these lakes Titanka he - the place of the great lodge.[45]

A winter gathering known as the "Frozen Foot Rendezvous" has taken place in recent years in early January at Oakwood Lakes near Bruce. It began more than a decade ago when a couple of fellows wondered what winter living was like in frontier days. Says one participant, "Potatoes get real hard when it's 9 below. It takes an axe to crack an egg. . .You have to think opposite of summer. Instead of ice, we pack the groceries in the grub box with warm rocks!"

If you are thinking about participating, consider the following:

> They learned one good buffalo robe was warmer than 30 pounds of goosedown and that you needed as much bedding underneath as on top. This winter camping adventure has grown into a full-fledged event....patterned after the rendezvous of the 1830's. A favorite event is the wild game cooking contest featuring dishes ranging from cormorant stew to fried squirrel. The wild game cook off is judged first on the tastiness of the meal. The second critieria is more important - the cook's tale about getting the critter together with the cooking pot, allowing for plausible prevarication.[46]

In 1890 B.A. Carey was appointed as pound master. He was to see that no hogs, cattle, horses, mules, sheep, geese or poultry were permitted to run at large in the streets, alleys, or public places within the corporate limits of Bryant.

The first fire fighting equipment, which included ladders, one dozen buckets and three axes, was purchased in 1893. . . .

In June, 1893, an ordinance was read and passed which probibited the running of bicycles, tricycles and velocipedes on the sidewalks of Main Street, and providing punishment for such offenses.[47]

BUFFALO, 488

Buffalo is 55 miles west of Bison on Highway 20 in the scenic northwest part of the state. At last count, Harding County had 28 sheep for every one person and three cattle.[48] If you see what appear to be monuments of piled stones atop hills, they are probably "stone Johnnies," the work of sheep herders who occupied time by piling the stones while watching their sheep from the hilltop.

Many have dreamed of being a cowboy or going West to find their fortune, but Archer B. Gilfillan, a short bespectacled Phi Beta Kappa Ivy League scholar of Latin and Greek, was not a likely cowboy. After graduating from the University of Pennsylvania in 1910, he worked on a cattle ranch in the Black Hills and soon hankered to strike out on his own. Gilfillan attempted to homestead a section of land on which he built a cabin, and with family money, he bought some sheep and horses. His ranching venture, however, was a financial disaster! Feeling called to the ministry, Archie Gilfillan went to a seminary for almost three years but abandoned that plan. Then, he again went west, taking the first job offered to him as a sheepherder on the AD ranch near Buffalo in 1916 and planning to stay about a year. He stayed 16 years and spent a lot of lonely hours in the sheepherder's wagon reading and writing. Gilfillan kept a diary and wrote some short pieces for a travel magazine and an article called "The Sheep Herder" for the *Saturday Evening Post* in 1924. His book, *SHEEP, Life on the Dakota Range,* was published in 1929 and fills a special niche in the literature of the West.[49]

BUFFALO GAP, 173

An account of ranch life at Buffalo Gap was written by an adventurous French baron who visited the Black Hills several times and in 1889 published a book in Paris entitled *La Breche Aux Buffles*. The translation of the book, *Buffalo Gap,* was completed by Black Hills resident, Phyllis Gorum, in 1978.

When Baron de Grancey made his third trip to the Black Hills, his French chef and several prominent Frenchmen accompanied him for a six-week visit at the Fleur de Lis horse ranch in 1887. The baron wrote candidly, "Here, thank God, there are no mosquitoes and no bedbugs, but I believe that all the flies in creation have made rendezvous here. . . .There are not only flies. There are also wasps by the hundreds."[50]

Baron de Grancey wrote of the envisioned boom resulting from the discovery of gold which would bring prosperity and growth to the town. Building sites were expected to skyrocket in price as Buffalo Gap became a "fashionable resort," and the baron wondered "if Pine Street will be able to contain all the banks which will accumulate there." No such problem developed.[51]

The Frenchman explained the origin of the name of Buffalo Gap, situated at the edge of the great prairie. Three or four gaps (breches) provided mountain passages well known by Native Americans who found large herds of buffalo and gave the area a name meaning Buffalo Gap, which the Frenchman translated as Breche aux Bulles. Native Americans fought over hunting rights for the area where three or four thousand buffalo were sometimes slaughtered in a day.

BUFFALO TRADING POST

This crossroads locale has been a gathering place since it opened in 1927 and the first customer bought a pound of Prince Albert tobacco. Eggs, cream, hides and other goods could be traded for merchandise from the store, and this trade continued until sometime after World War II. Nowadays, the trading post is a filling station. All that's traded is local news, but you can fill a vehicle with gas from the single pump out in front and also fill up on real meat and home-made mashed potatoes at a daily lunch special, priced at $3.00 in 1993 - and this included apple pie and ice-cream for dessert. One of the regulars who comes in about four times a week said, "Yup, it's always this good. Generally, you can hardly get in here. It's most times full."[52]

BULLHEAD

Sitting Bull Park, where the great leader's home still stands near Bullhead, honors the memory of one of the most colorful, controversial and powerful leaders of the Hunkpapa Sioux. Legends surrounding the life of Sitting Bull make it hard to separate fact from fiction, but he was ambitious, intelligent and committed to protecting the interests of his people and stopping the encroachment of whites in the land of the Sioux. A reviewer of a recent biography of Sitting Bull said, "Sitting Bull was a model of Lakota bravery and generosity. In fact, his life was a model that all people should study."[53]

Sitting Bull believed he had been divinely chosen to lead and protect his people. Although reluctant to wage war against non-Indians, he was provoked by injustices and indignities to killing. Enduring the Sun Dance in 1876 when he was about 45 years of age, he had a vision of victory if the Sioux and Cheyenne would stand their ground. As spiritual leader and tactician, Sitting Bull played a key role in the defeat of Custer. After that, he spent time in Canada with 2000 others of his band and subsequently was imprisoned at Fort Randall. He returned to the Standing Rock Reservation in 1883 and led the last organized buffalo hunt of the Teton Sioux on record. He traveled with Buffalo Bill Cody's Wild West Show and then decided to settle down in a cabin near his birthplace close to Bullhead where he continued to be a spokesman for his people. He opposed relinquishment of land and led a struggle for better conditions on the reservation. Officials, especially uneasy with the Ghost Dancing at the time, determined that Sitting Bull should be arrested as a leader of the resistance to Federal authority. Sitting Bull was killed on December 15, 1890, in a tragic confrontation between Indian police sent to arrest Sitting Bull and his loyal warriors who panicked. Seven followers died with him and are buried in a mass grave on the site, although Sitting Bull's remains are interred at Mobridge. [54]

BURKE, 756

Burke is thinly disguised as Kirk in a novel written by Oscar Micheaux, an African-American poet and writer who wrote of his pioneer days in Gregory County in *The Conquest: The Story of a Negro Pioneer,* published in 1917. The actual towns of Gregory, Burke and Herrick became Megory, Kirk and Hedrick in the book. Micheaux was a Pullman porter who decided to stake a claim in South Dakota and spent nine years in the state. After writing the book telling of his homestead experience, he established a company in Sioux City to distribute his first book and two other novels that followed. He formed a film company to make a movie of his book called *The Homesteader* and became very successful as a movie producer and owner of Micheaux Movie Productions. He is widely recognized for his film achievements, and the Oscar Micheaux Awards Ceremony today honors outstanding African-American artists in the Black Filmmakers Hall of Fame.[55] [56]

BUSHNELL, 81

Main Street was once such a rowdy place that residents passed laws to prohibit "throwing away fruit peels, tying up stud horses, and landing planes there. . . ."[57] Today, Bushnell is a quiet place where, surprisingly, the store is only open on Sunday, but 40 customers have keys so they can transact business on their own. Bushnell residents experience true community: "If anybody catches a fish, they have a fish fry. And if anybody shoots a pheasant, they have a pheasant fry."[58]

The town has attracted some artists. Dave Huebner makes Dakota Stoneware in one of Main Street's old buildings which has an extraordinary history. Built as a store, it housed the post office in the 1890's. Later, it was a depot, restaurant, grocery store, billiard hall, boxing ring and boarding house.

The Wagon Men

The building had a hidden bar during Prohibition. The exterior of the building served as a movie screen in the silent movie era while the local folks viewed from their cars and buggies. That may have been one of the first drive-in movies, right there in Bushnell.

CANISTOTA, 608

For 84 years, Sport Days have been held annually in Canistota where good fun and competition take some unusual forms. In the greased pig scramble, a well-greased little "porker" is released and chased by those wanting to take the piggy home to raise on the family farm. And there's the cow chip plop, too. It doesn't require any active participation except by the cows who just "do their thing." Organizers divide a field into marked areas on which a cow is free to roam. Dollar bets are placed with hopes the cow will unload on the selected square. If you don't think that sounds like fun, you can listen to the Sweet Adelines who sing barbershop harmony.

CANNING

The Rousseau brothers came to the area in 1860, and Marcel Rousseau ran a fur trading post on Medicine Creek. Posts were usually established in areas with good access to transportation (a river) and trade with the Native Americans. The community that developed in Medicine Valley was described in 1883 as "composed of thoroughly stirring people."[59] Close to the sorghum mill was a large still which provided brew for the saloons of Canning. The three Canning hotels of 1883 went out of business as traffic bypassed Canning and residents drifted away.

CANOVA, 172

Watch out for the Canova Gang, a baseball team that does battle in the Corn Belt League. Dave Gassman, the "Ace of Diamonds" who heads the gang, is a veteran of 29 amateur seasons. When he is not pitching, Gassman manages the team. In his 45 years, the baseball standout has set a state record for victories and strikeouts. The Canova Gang has been in the state tournament for 20 out of the last 21 seasons, and they are tough to beat.[60]

CANTON, 2787

Early discussion about the name of the town resulted in a decision to name it for the opposite area on the globe. The Chinese "Kwang-Tung" was adapted to become Canton. But don't expect to find a Chinese restaurant in Canton.

Despite a Chinese name, Scandinavian influence prevailed. Augustana College of Sioux Falls has its roots in "The Literary and Theological Institute of The Lutheran Church of the Far West." This college of Norwegian background found its way to Canton in 1884. As ski jumping became a popular sport, the Augustana Athletic Association sponsored competition based on distance and style in 1912. World War I and the move of Augustana College to Sioux Falls brought competition to a halt until the Sioux Valley Ski Club was formed and sponsored a tournament in 1923. Canton hosted the national competition in 1925 when 15,000 spectators brought by special trains came to watch the 20 competitors on the Big Sioux River bluffs east of Canton. More spectators came in 1930 when Canton again hosted the national event in which two of the top three skiers were members of the local club. The winter of 1931 was very warm, and it was necessary to truck 400 to 600 tons of snow from Lake Okoboji in Iowa for the Central United States Ski Tournament. Winter Olympic trials of 1932 were held at Canton, and three of the team of six sent to Lake Placid were from the local club. Caspar Oimoen placed fifth in the Olympics, with three Norwegians placing ahead of him. The years that followed brought a disastrous combination of bad weather and poor economic conditions, and the club was bankrupted. Old-timers still remember the thrill of the competition as the Norse ski jumpers took to the air with snoose coming out of the corners of their mouths as they went for the perfect jump.[61]

CAPA

Although still on the map, not many people go to Capa unless they are looking for ghost towns. Originally known as Capa

City, it is said to have received its name in 1907 when the NorthWestern railroad began running freight cars through this section of the west-river country. The word "capacity" on the sides of the box cars was divided by the doors to read "capa city." This makes a good story, but an alternate version says the name was taken from the Sioux word "capa," meaning beaver, since many lived along the Bad River.[62]

CAPUTA

Kevin Costner's Academy Award-winning film, "Dances With Wolves," was filmed entirely in South Dakota at various locations. The Fort Hays set at Caputa contained the fort, the headquarters where Lt. Dunbar received his orders and also a sod house, horse barns, warehouse and buffalo killing field. Promoters decided to offer the set as a tourist attraction, first at Caputa and later in the Rapid City area which had more tourist traffic. Moving poorly constructed and stapled set structures had some problems, but the Fort Hays set was reassembled near Rapid City, although you could say the buildings were somewhat "Caputa."

CARPENTER

Family quilts are special, but all the more so when the community family puts together a quilt, which is what they did for Carpenter's centennial celebration in 1994. Each family was asked to contribute an 8 inch by 8 inch square (no polyester!) highlighting the family's history. The result was a king sized quilt pieced from 120 squares. The highest bidder of $700 took home a very special remembrance after the July 2, 1994, centennial celebration.[63]

CARTER

From Carter comes the story of mail carrier Carl Tideman who was 107 hours behind schedule. When the mailman heard a big blizzard was headed toward the area on a January day in 1952, he tried to beat the storm:

> It was a poor race on my part. I didn't even make it to the next mail box, which was less than a mile, before I was

enveloped in a furious and blinding blizzard. . . .I couldn't
see, but knew I was in the road, as I could feel the front
wheels jerk when they hit the snow bank on either side of
the road. . . I was getting stuck. Fortunately I had an army
blanket and seven-foot wool, knitted scarf in the cab. I would
wrap the scarf around my head and chest, put the blanket
over me Indian style and start out, but after several hard
falls I went back to the cab. One time the blanket opened up
like a parachute and carried me 25 or 30 feet until I let go
of it. I recovered it and went back to the jeep and tried to
shake some of the snow out of it. . . .The most trouble I had
was to keep my feet warm. I knew if I fell asleep, they would
freeze. . . .Well, I waited. Yes waited! until 3:00 or 3:30
next day when the storm seemed to be relenting a little. It
had turned colder too. I knew I couldn't spend another night
there. . . .I decided to go to John Brickman's by following
the fence as it was not under snow. I started out along the
north side of the fence, but that didn't work very well as the
wind soon blew me into the fence. The blanket got tangled
in the barb wire. . . .I made it to the Brickman farm and
stopped in the barn for a while. . .full of cows, calves and
some hogs. All together they made it warm and steamy inside.
. . .It was a great relief for me just to be. . .out of the storm
and to know the worst of that ordeal was now behind me.[64]

CARTHAGE, 221

A fifteen year-old lad named Alfred crossed the Atlantic
in 1887 and came to Carthage where he found work on a farm
and good people to help him. He lost his way as he sought
the farmhouse in the fury of a blizzard in January 1888. Alfred
and a friend wandered miles, trying to reach a location actually two-and-a-half miles from where they began. The exhausted young men fell asleep on the frozen prairie in what was
Alfred's last night on this earth. The friend survived, frost-
bitten so badly that a leg and part of the other foot were ampu-
tated.[65]

CASTLE ROCK

This area takes its name from one of the biggest buttes in
Butte County, Castle Rock, which has an elevation of 3741

feet. The buttes were often given names based on their form such as Antelope, Deers Ears, Owl, and Haystack Buttes. An exception is the Geographic Center of the Nation Butte located to the west of Castle Rock. When, Alaska and Hawaii came into the Union, the geographic center shifted from Smith Center, Kansas, to a location due west of Castle Rock and 21 miles north of Belle Fourche. To be precise, it is at 44 degrees and 58 minutes North and 103 degrees and 46 minutes West.

CASTLEWOOD, 549

"Operator! Operator!" The first telephone service came to Castlewood in 1899. Doc Vaughn was the first subscriber, and the magnetic switchboard with six pairs of cords was located in the drug store. (That drug store also contained the lending library and was the source of much community information.) The first long distance line was constructed in the area in 1905, linking Castlewood with Watertown. In 1923, the telephone operation was moved to a residence for the convenience of the operator and improved service to customers. Dial operations began in 1955.[66] Further changes in 1993 left farmers fuming because they weren't able to phone from the barn to the house as they had previously been able to do. After their protests, the old barn to house service was restored for a one-time $10 charge. Newer isn't always better.[67]

CAVOUR, 166

Because railroad builders in the United States were impressed with the great builder of railroads and prominent Italian statesman Cariello Benno, the Count of Cavour, the town was named for him. The Count became premier of Sardinia and was instrumental in the unification of Italy in 1861 when the King of Sardinia, Victor Emmanuel II, became king of all Italy.[68]

CENTERVILLE, 887

Some Chicago lawbreakers thought Centerville was an ideal spot to "hang out" in the early 1930's. This quiet town became known as Little Chicago. On one occasion, Baby Face Nelson and John Dillenger rolled dice in the card room of The Bloody Bucket, a Main Street establishment where the specialty of the house was baked beans. As a witness to the event described it, "Three men sat, rolling dice, with a pile of money between them. There was also a knife and an awful big gun on the floor beside one." They were drinking "near beer" spiked with something from another bottle. "After a time, Baby Face Nelson seemed to notice the stove for the first time and asked what was cooking. Beans, Fred told him. Then he says, 'Well let's flavor them up!' and he fired his gun right into the stove, Bang! Bang! Bang!"[69]

The Bloody Bucket no longer stands, and the site is now a parking lot for the local Ford garage. But if you stroll down Main Street and stop in a local establishment, some can still tell you about Baby Face Nelson and John Dillenger.

CENTRAL CITY, 185

Central City in Deadwood Gulch is quiet today, perhaps still recovering from a time when it was "the gold mining center of the region and the richest, wildest, rootin' tootin', hell raising town in the entire west. . . . Without a doubt, safely locked in the mountains surrounding Central, there exist vast deposits of precious metals that would make the Fort Knox hoard look like the pennies in baby's piggy bank."[70] When an old prospector came along and eyed a rock used as a doorstop for many years, he realized it was a piece of "high grade." The rock that had been picked from the side of the road contained a 2.75 oz. "pure gold nugget shaped exactly like a little kettle with three legs and a handle."[71]

Jewelry made of gold from the area was first manufactured in Central City after the grape and leaf pattern was brought from California's gold country in 1876. Black Hills Gold is traditionally patterned in delicate grape and leaf designs of pale pinks, greens and yellows. Gold is alloyed with copper to produce the pink shades and with silver to produce the green coloration. The crafting of the fine jewelry continues in the Black Hills today although the manufactory in Central City is no longer in operation.

CHAMBERLAIN, 2347

In the 1890's, the railroad ran special Sunday excursion trains from Iowa to Chamberlain so visitors could experience the "wild and woolly West." The people of Chamberlain tried not to disappoint and provided a variety of amusements, including ball games and horse races. One enterprising fellow had a gramophone with six sets of tubes that, for a nickel, could be used to listen to a tune or a lecture being played.[72]

When the land west of the Missouri was opened for settlement in 1890, settlers had to cross the river by a ferry that operated during limited hours or by travel on ice when the river was frozen. An unsafe pontoon bridge came into use in 1893, made so that one end floating on a flatboat could be released to accommodate river traffic. A railroad bridge was built in 1905, but other traffic continued to use the pontoon bridge. After nine children were orphaned in 1920 when their parents died in an accident on the pontoon bridge, a movement to construct a permanent bridge for automobile and wagon traffic gained momentum. In 1923, the legislature approved construction of five bridges across the Missouri; one of them was in Chamberlain.

CHANCELLOR, 276

German immigrants, many from the East Friesland area of Germany, named the townsite for Chancellor Von Bismarck of Germany, the first chancellor of the German Empire. The town originated at the Vermillion Crossing which provided sloping banks and a firm river bed for wagons crossing the Vermillion River on the trek westward. When the railroad track was laid a few miles east, the townsite moved from the river crossing to be on the railroad line in Germantown Township.[73]

CHERRY CREEK

The name of Cherry Creek came from the abundant wild cherries, plums, gooseberries and currants. The new Takini school west of Cherry Creek serves the children of that area on the Cheyenne River Sioux Reservation. "Takini" means "survivor," (even though you might be told it means lost government surveyor) and many of the students are descendants of Wounded Knee survivors. Most of the 260 students are bussed daily, and many of the staff live in housing next to the school where Lakota language and culture are integrated into the curriculum. Students begin a typical day in a circle with a traditional ceremony of burning of sage or sweet grass. Almost half of the 32 teachers and all of the support staff are Native American. A rodeo ring next to the school is the sight of the annual Skyhawk Stampede at the end of May. Students wanting to further their education on the reservation have the opportunity to attend the Cheyenne River Community College in Eagle Butte, one of five institutions of higher learning on reservations in South Dakota.[74]

CHESTER

A banker, a missionary, a merchant and two saloon keepers were founding fathers of Chester. Most towns of the state celebrated their centennials in the twentieth century, but Chester didn't get its start until 1905.

Chester's pride is demonstrated by students who volunteer to spruce up the school on Pride Day one weekend every May. They happily fix bleachers, paint, trim the yard and do a variety of chores to have the school looking its best for their graduation.

CLAIRE CITY, 85

The Trail of the Spirits, a registered National Recreation Trail, winds along a pretty stream through the floor of Sica Hollow State Park, southwest of Claire City. A second trail, the Skyline Trail, provides a climb up the side of the Coteau des Prairies, the hills of the prairie. One can enjoy hiking, horseback riding and cross country skiing on 13 miles of trail in the park.

But Sica Hollow is also the mysterious place of a legend. The story has a familiar sound as it tells of evil, a flood, and one who was spared:

> Sica Hollow once protected many peaceful Indian camps.
> Its trees blocked the North Wind, but then a stranger came.

The young girls grew afraid. The old women wished to send him away. The old men said, 'When it is warm again, outside the Hollow he will go.'

The sly stranger, Hand, did not leave when the Sun returned to the north. Instead he taught the young boys to strike and kill. Blood flowed. The old men sought help from Wicasa Wakan, Medicine Man. 'What shall we sacrifice to make our Hollow as it was long ago?' they asked.

Wicasa Wakan returned to his lodge and waited for Wakantanka, the Great Spirit, to reply. Soon Wakantanka sent his messenger, Thunderer, who brought a cloud that rained over the Hollow. Madness seized Hand. He tried to run, but vines encircled his ankles. The water filled his screaming mouth. Thunderer's talons ripped out his eyes so he would never see the Happy Hunting Ground.

Of all the people in the Hollow, only a raven-haired maiden called Fawn was saved from the rising water. She fled to the top of the highest hill and sang her grief and remorse to the Great Spirit. Then she slept many days. When she awoke, the Hollow was clean and bright. Yet the memory and the evil name - Sica Hollow, Bad Hollow - linger.

Even today, Sica Hollow remains mysterious. Small waterfalls moan and groan as trapped air escapes. Swamp gas makes stumps glow in the dark. Indians see water and moss, colored rusty-red by iron deposits, as the blood and flesh of their ancestors.[75]

CLARK, 1292

Beside a railroad track out on the prairie in the vicinity of Clark is the grave of an unknown boy who lived over a century ago. The boy, thought to be about 14 at the time of his death, lived in a railroad camp with his parents, and always waved when the train carrying his friend, Brakeman "Big Bill" Chambers went by. The railroad men grew accustomed to the daily greeting of the boy and looked forward to his wave, just as the little fellow looked forward to the coming of the train. One day in 1888, the brakeman missed the regular wave from his friend, and soon there was a grave beside the track. The boy died of smallpox and was buried by his grieving parents in an unmarked grave on the prairie, not far from the tracks.

Big Bill, the brakeman, faithfully visited the grave on Decoration Day for 42 years. When Chambers died in 1931, the conductor of Train 106 and Chambers' family kept the tradition going. The railroad company sent flowers to the grave in the 1940's and 1950's, and the national media broadcast the story. In 1950, the railroad stopped passenger service in Clark, and in 1981, all railroad traffic in Clark ended. The Rotarians decided to preserve the tradition of the Memorial Day tribute to the memory of the boy and the faithful brakeman.[76]

CLEARFIELD

A skunk who snuggled under a farmhouse in January of 1952 delivered a "stink bomb" that prompted the residents of the house to try anything they could think of, including orange peels, talcum powder, and burning rags in an effort to eliminate the powerful odor. When those attempts failed, the family went to town to buy Air-wick, but while they were away, a storm worsened and made the five mile trip home impossible. When they finally reached home, they found a remarkable scene in their barn.

Mrs. Paul Zimbelman reported:

> Our stock had taken better care of themselves than we could have had we been there. They had broken down the gates and got into the barn for shelter and to the hay stack by the barn for feed. The fresh milk cows had somehow managed to get the calf pen open and their baby calves had taken care of the milking for us. The hogs had gotten out of their pens and into the barn. There was one grand mix-up in the barn - horses, cows, calves, hogs, and some chickens that didn't get back to the chicken house.
>
> We scooped our way into the house. With the bed room windows open and the wind and snow blowing through, the house had had a good chance to air. We didn't need the Air-wick now, two days later.[77]

CLEAR LAKE, 1247

The Crystal Springs Ranch rodeo was born in 1945 when a Clear Lake cowboy drained a duck pond in his pasture, put up some corn cribbing and announced a rodeo on a Sunday afternoon. If one has a good horse, riding ability, and the grit to "hang in there," rodeo participation might be the sport of choice. It is a collegiate sport for men and women at South Dakota State University. In the South Dakota Rodeo Association circuit, participants compete in bareback riding, saddle bronc riding, bull riding, calf roping, steer wrestling, team roping, barrel racing, goat tying, breakaway roping and team penning. Winners are rewarded with saddles, gold buckles, cash and reputation. Many South Dakotans enjoy rodeo as a family oriented sport. Little duffers from four to seven years of age compete in what is called mutton bustin' - getting on a sheep and hanging on for dear life.

COLMAN, 482

Although many think bigger is better, community leaders in Colman have been happy to be small and to suffer fewer headaches than larger cities. When the 1980 census results were published, Colman's population was first reported at 501, but upon recount, it was 499. Officials were glad to be under 500 because it saved them changing bookkeeping procedures and complying with many state regulations, including fluoridation of water. A decade later, the population still numbers under 500.[78]

COLOME, 309

Communities such as Colome know all about togetherness. Memories include organized shoot-outs in years when the rabbits were over-abundant. The community divided into hunting teams, and after the hunt, the losing team provided stew (not rabbit stew, but oyster stew) for all. Neighbors visited and played cards while waiting for the stew to be served.

Necessity reinforced family togetherness. The Taggert family of ten lived in a four-room house that had two enclosed porches to provide additional space. Mary Taggart Hammon described life in the Taggart household:

> It was crowded but we were happy. Then came the dust storms and the grasshoppers. I will never forget that. I remember

how it was to be poor. Had it not been for WPA and surplus
commodities, I don't know how we would have stayed alive.
As it was, we were never hungry. We may have had corn
meal mush three times a day, but we had three meals. I also
will never forget Corn Flakes - we fought over the boxes
every morning to see who got the box to cut up and put in
the bottom of their shoes to cover the holes for that day.

Of her parents and family, she wrote:

They taught us to love and to share, to be good Christians
and good neighbors. The whole family went to church every
Sunday in a Model T Ford, that was togetherness, ten of us
in a Model T. Sometimes the Model T didn't have enough
power to get us over the hill, so we kids would get out at
the bottom and walk up and our parents would ride up and
wait for us at the top.[79]

COLTON, 657

Ole Edvard Rolvaag came to South Dakota in 1896 after his
uncle, who farmed near Elk Point, sent a ticket for his trip from
Norway. Rolvaag was a fisherman in Norway, but he had aspirations other than fishing or farming. His mother laughed when he
said he wanted to be a poet or professor, but her son Ole eventually pursued his dream. After studies at Augustana Academy
in Canton and St. Olaf College, he became a professor and writer.

Rolvaag had a great appreciation of his heritage and a com-
mitment to preserving the best of that heritage to nourish the
souls of immigrants and enrich life in America. He learned about
early settlement from his in-laws who had settled in the Garretson
area. When Rolvaag wrote his acclaimed classic, *Giants in the
Earth,* he chose Colton for the locale, adding features that he
had observed elsewhere in South Dakota. The novel was first
published in Norway as two books, *I de Dage (In These Days)*
and *Riket Grundlaegges (The Kingdom is Founded).* After Lincoln
Colcord translated the work from Norwegian into English, it was
published in the United States in 1927 as *Giants in the Earth.*
Rolvaag's sensitive and realistic portrayal of immigrant life has
made thousands of people think of that settlement at Colton and
the price paid by the immigrants who settled there and elsewhere.

COLUMBIA, 133

"Hail, Columbia!" The future looked incredibly bright in 1882 for this gem in Dakota Territory. Columbia had aspirations of being the territorial capital and was, for a while, the county seat. Sailboats, steamers and yachts plied Lake Columbia formed by a dam on the James River. The four-story Grand Hotel was the center of social activity and hosted many balls and dances. Before the turn of the century, the town grew at a phenomenal rate, but declined almost as quickly when the railroad built its line further south. The Milwaukee Railroad had planned to make Columbia a crossing point, but the Town Site Company asked for a right-of-way payment and a drawbridge, prompting the railroad to change its plans. The town fathers looked "penny wise and pound foolish."

CONDE, 203

One of the most touching immigrant stories is that of James Beechey born in the slums of Bristol, England, in about 1860. His father, a habitual drunkard, deserted the family, leaving four children under 12 years of age and a wife dying of cancer. The oldest child disappeared, and the three younger children, including James, were placed in an orphanage where the head master did not spare the rod. At the age of 12, James was one of a shipload of boys sent to an orphanage in Canada from which he and his brother ran away after a number of whippings. James worked on farms and went to school whenever he could. As young men, the Beechey brothers went to St. Paul, Minnesota, and eventually took the stage coach to Dakota Territory. After becoming a United States citizen in 1883, James Beechey filed a claim north of Conde where he built a sod house and made it through a winter with the help of good neighbors, without whom he would have starved. A musical man, he learned to play the harmonica, accordion and organ, and the instruments brought pleasure on long winter nights. After marriage, Beechey was joined by his English wife in singing hymns by lamplight as they shared life in Spink County.[80]

B.C. - Before Cars

CORONA, 118

"All aboard for Corona!" You can take the "choo-choo" to Corona during Milbank's yearly Train Fest Celebration which has become a three-day event. It doesn't take that long to get to Corona from Milbank, mind you, but this is an extraordinary ride with train robbers and bums trying to hitch rides. Conductors, hostesses and dining car waiters in 80 year-old Milwaukee Railroad uniforms add to the color as The Whetstone Valley Express crosses the Coteau des Prairies for a memorable trip on the old train.

CORSICA, 619

Hollanders prevail in this community, home of Wooden Shoe brand cheese. The Dutch have traditionally taken their religion seriously, but in Corsica they also take their baseball seriously. That caused a conflict in 1950. The Corsica American Legion team lost their first game of tournament play on a Saturday. They were scheduled to play on Sunday but refused for religious reasons, believing it would not allow them to properly honor the Sabbath. Some claimed the Corsica team should be ousted for a forfeit, but a newspaperman wrote an editorial that was influential in giving the Corsica team the opportunity to play on Monday. -And play they did! They beat Redfield; they defeated Hot Springs; finally, they won the third game of the day against Elk Point to become the State Class B Champions![81]

CORSON

You can sometimes see red rails in the sunset if you look westward toward the "prairie skyscraper," that is, the Corson grain elevator alongside the railroad tracks. A sense of humor exists in this community which is home to the "The Mighty Corson Art Players" and a summer riding lawn mower competition. In 1994, lawn mowers with blades removed were painted and numbered for competition on a figure eight course in Corson where participants revved up low-power lawn mower engines of eight horsepower or less to earn a berth in national competition in Illinois. Said one observer, "It's stupid, but it's fun!"

COTTONWOOD, 12

An historic marker in the area says, "You're in cow country now mister. If you had a cow for every brand that run critters on Cottonwood Creek, Midas would turn green with envy." The old Ft. Tecumseh to Ft. William trail ran a dozen miles north of Cottonwood at Pineau Springs, and many furs and Indian trade goods passed that way. With the discovery of gold in the Black Hills, traffic on the old trail picked up as millions of tons of freight traveled westward on that route in wagons pulled by oxen.[82]

CREIGHTON

A verse from the area tells about "Old Finnegan,"

> Old Finnegan came from "Alkali,"
> A place you all know well.
> He came down to Ash Creek
> Where the people are raising Hell.

Arthur Finnegan, a full blood Irishman, had been in the Black Hills from the start of gold mining and operated a saloon in Galena, the only thing he was sorry for and ashamed of in his life, he said. The bachelor moved to the Ash Creek area where he became a cattleman whose stock was branded 26. An old cowman remembered the Irishman warmly:

> A good old man he was - he was good to me on several occasions and I loved him. Once I was a "night hawk" on the fall round-up with the Pedro Pool wagon. Arthur Finnegan came to the outfit to take a good look at his steers in that beef herd. . . .I was sick and feverish and chilling and that old man took my place and took that remuda out and herded them through the night. . .while I stayed in my bed roll all night. [83]

CRESBARD, 185

Clark Thorne met his sweetheart, Maud Dunsmore, at the Dunsmore school which they both attended in the present day Cresbard area. Clark took a fancy to that plucky prairie girl who learned to ride and drive a team as a youngster, and they were married on Maud's 18th birthday in 1902. Believing in

the future of Cresbard, Clark Thorne unloaded the first shipment of lumber on the townsite. Maud was the first woman to
live in the town, and the couple lived in a horse shed until their
house was finished. The family was getting nicely established
when Clark contracted smallpox, and then his wife and two
small children also became infected. One old neighbor kept
the family going, bringing milk from his cow and groceries
and supplies from the store, leaving the provisions outside the
door of the quarantined home. Fortunately, the Thorne family
survived the dreaded disease.[84]

The old-timers celebrated with Old Settler's picnics held
for many years at the Miller grove. The day-long celebrations
included speeches and music and a ball game. A row of buggies lined up at the ball game in 1904, and one can only imagine the friendly visiting and chatter that took place as friends
and neighbors gathered. Lemonade was sold from a barrel and
children gathered around the candy stand. A steam-powered
carousel which was shipped to Faulkton and then hauled by
horse drawn wagon to the grove wowed the crowd. That was
quite a shindig, and those early settlers deserved to celebrate.[85]

CROOKS, 671

There aren't any! There are no crooks, nor are there Crookses
in the town, although the town was named in honor of an early
resident who ran a general store and was postmaster at a time
when the town was called New Hope. New Hope embodies so
much of the spirit of the early settlers that we wish that name
had endured.

CUSTER, 1741

BIG!!!! In 1947, Korczak Ziolkowski began the largest monument in recorded history on Thunderhead Mountain north of
Custer. Henry Standing Bear had suggested the idea of a monument to the Sioux people and proposed a sculpture of Crazy
Horse, the great warrior who gave his people hope and unified
them in their struggle as they tried to preserve their land and
way of life. Ziolkowski, a self-taught sculptor who worked on
Mount Rushmore in 1940, pursued the vision of a colossal

sculpture of the charismatic leader. Tons of rock were blasted from the mountain to prepare the site on which Ziolkowski worked until his death in 1982. Ziolkowski is buried near the mountain carving, but the project continues under the supervision of his wife, Ruth. Other family members also work to carry out the dream of Korczak Ziolkowski. After receiving an honorary degree at Black Hills State College in 1981, the sculptor gave the commencement address. These were his words to the graduates: "It is said that when the legends die, the dreams must end. . . When the dreams end there is no more greatness. My friends, never let your dreams end."[86]

A tourist once asked a grizzled old-timer if the mica particles that sparkle in Custer's broad Main Street were gold, he replied, "Yes, they are, ma'am - the genu-wine article. But there's something mighty pee-culiar about this gold. It's been exposed to the sun so long it's lost all commercial value." The old-timer was "tickling the tenderfoot."[87]

DAKOTA DUNES

It takes a stretch in one's thinking to envision dunes in South Dakota since they are not among the geologic features generally attributed to the state. Developers found a choice parcel of land on the far southeastern border along the Missouri River and named it Dakota Dunes. Of the name, *South Dakota Magazine* said, "If that wasn't the brainstorm of an advertising agency, we've never seen a watermelon at Forestburg. We like it though. It seems to go well with the sort of businesses and institutions every town needs. Dakota Dunes Donuts; Dakota Dunes Noon Spoons; Dakota Dunes Burial."[88] Seriously, Dakota Dunes is a 2000 acre master-planned community that boasts a spectacular golf course and tax incentives that make the Iowa folks across the river want to pack up and move.

DALLAS, 142

Not long after Lawrence Welk's marriage to Fern Renner in Yankton, South Dakota, his band played some gigs in Dallas where the young bandleader spent one of the worst nights of his life. A band member spoke for all of the players, telling Welk they were going to leave him because he was holding them back. The disgruntled player said Welk couldn't even speak English and would not succeed as he bounced around in a barn dance style. The band put on smiles and stayed together to finish that engagement. After that, they split up, and Welk hired new musicians to play with him.[89]

DANTE, 98

Various stories surround the name, one claiming the town was named for a favorite author. According to another version, when the railroad refused the name "Mayo," the owner of the townsite, H.T. Mayo said, "Call it Dante's Inferno, for all I care," and the name stuck.[90]

DAVIS, 87

On Main Street you'll find the Down Home Cafe and the Country Roundup Store among other businesses. This is a country place, and the *Quick 'N Easy Country Cooking* magazine comes right out of Davis. A hometown enterprise called Parkside Publishing began putting out the magazine in 1987. Drawing on the appeal of country that represents a simpler life to stressed out Americans, this magazine features good recipes and a country emphasis that seeks to nourish body and soul. Recipes predominate, but the magazine contains a potpourri of articles, poetry and thoughts.

You can learn all you need to know to make a great apple pie: the secret is to use the right apples inside a crust made of flour, lard, cold water, and a pinch of salt and baking powder.[91] This confirms part of a story about two ladies in church who began conversation during offertory organ music. As the organ volume swelled, their conversation also increased in volume. When the music suddenly stopped, the women were caught by surprise, and one was heard to say, "Well, I always make it with lard!"

DEADWOOD, 1830

With the discovery of gold in Deadwood Gulch in 1875, Deadwood became the rowdiest and most raucous gold mining town in the West. Leander P. Richardson, who arrived on a Sunday afternoon in July of 1876, wrote an article for *Scribner's Monthly Magazine* called "A Trip to the Black Hills." It provided this description:

> Our train finally halted in Deadwood City, and we were immediately surrounded by a crowd of miners, gamblers and other citizens, all anxious to hear from the outer world. It was Sunday afternoon, and all the miners in the surrounding neighborhood were spending the day in town. The long street was crowded with men in every conceivable garb. Taken as a whole, I never in my life saw so many hardened and brutal-looking men together, although of course there were a few better faces among them. Every alternate house was a gambling saloon, and each of them was carrying on a brisk business. In the middle of the street a little knot of men had gathered, and were holding a prayer-meeting, which showed in sharp contrast to the bustling activity of wickedness surrounding it.[92]

Seth Bullock isn't as well known as Wild Bill Hickock and Calamity Jane, but he was an important resident of the old mining camp. Bullock was a horse rancher, businessman, gold miner, U.S. Marshall and first sheriff of Deadwood who tried to bring law and order to the wild town. He built a hotel on Main Street in 1895 which is still in business today. Some are convinced that the spirit of Seth Bullock still roams the corridors, and stories are told of unexplained slamming doors, moving furniture, floating clothing, and shadowy apparitions. He seems to like the third floor and especially bathrooms. According to the owner, "We had a lady come down one night and say she'd seen a tall cowboy in her room." The desk clerk said, "Oh yeah, that would be Seth" The television producers of "Unsolved Mysteries" filmed a segment there and brought a psychic from England by the name of Sandy Bullock who confirmed that the spirit of Seth Bullock is indeed present in his old hotel. The present owner says, "I think he's got a good sense of humor."[93]

DEERFIELD

Gen. George A. Custer's expedition of 1874 passed through this area as they explored possibities of gold and a military site. Custer and his 1000 troops started out at Fort Abraham Lincoln in North Dakota with 110 wagons, 1000 horses, 300 cattle and a variety of support staff (teamsters, herders, blacksmiths, saddlers, etc.). They were charmed by the beauty of the valley area with wild flowers blooming in profusion and named it Floral Valley. As they paused to enjoy that beautiful place, the soldiers decorated the horses with flowers while the military band played. Everyone was impressed, including Custer who wrote in his "Report of the Expedition to the Black Hills":

> In no private or public park have I ever seen such a profuse display of flowers. Every step of our march that day was amid flowers of the most exquisite colors and perfume. So luxuriant in growth were they that men plucked them without dismounting from the saddle. Some belonged to new or unclassified species. It was a strange sight to glance back at the advancing columns of cavalry, and behold the men with beautiful bouquets in the hands, while the head-gear of the horses was decorated with wreaths of flowers fit to crown a queen of May. Deeming it a most fitting appellation, I named this Floral Valley.[94]

DELL RAPIDS, 2484

Dell Rapids is located in such a scenic place that it is little wonder that the first concrete road in the state (constructed in 1923, with the aid of federal funds, of course) ran from Sioux Falls to Dell Rapids. One can enjoy a pleasant hike along the Dells where the Big Sioux River cuts through the pink quartzite quarried in the area. The handsome pink granite buildings on Main Street have aged gracefully and indicate the connectedness of the city to its surroundings.

DELMONT, 235

The saloon was a popular place for swapping stories. When the railroad crew of about 250 came in 1886, the drinking establishment required a daily replenishment of its otherwise ample stock. The railroad workers were amazed to see what appeared to be "a nudist colony for crazy people." Delmont residents were hopping in the streets. In fighting a lice infestation, itchy inhabitants shed their clothing which was dipped in boiling water and hung on a fence to dry. Wearing little or nothing, people ran about and moved their arms vigorously in an attempt to keep warm in the crisp autumn air.[95]

DE SMET, 1172

This is "The Little Town on the Prairie" which many have come to know through the books of Laura Ingalls Wilder. Railroad timekeeper Charles Ingalls was asked to become stationmaster at a site selected for the town. Laura Ingalls Wilder's father worked for the railroad until he established his claim and could make his living from the land. When she was 65 years of age, Laura Ingalls Wilder, submitted a manuscript called *Pioneer Girl,* that told the story of her early years. After publishers rejected the work, her daughter resubmitted some of the stories under the title *Little House in the Big Woods.* It was immediately successful and is a much-loved book enjoyed by children today.

Visitors to DeSmet can see the surveyor's shack in which the Ingall's first lived upon their arrival in the area. The shanty was moved into De Smet and furnished according to Laura's description. One can also see the house Pa Ingalls built for his family in 1887, containing many items crafted by Charles Ingalls. An outdoor pageant is presented near the site of the Ingalls homestead the first weekend in June and the first two weekends in July.

The cottonwoods Pa Ingalls planted still grow near the site of their homestead where a plaque states:

SITE OF THE INGALLS HOMESTEAD 1880
THIS IS THE HOMESTEAD SITE OF
CHARLES AND CAROLINE INGALLS
AND THEIR DAUGHTERS
MARY, LAURA, CARRIE AND GRACE
. . . . Here Pa planted the cottonwoods that still
stand, and Ma made a home for her family. After

the October Blizzard they returned to town to spend "The Long Winter" (1880-1881). One of the schools Laura was to teach was a mile south of this site. In "These Happy Golden Years," she told of her romance and marriage to Almanzo Wilder and their life in a claim shanty two miles north of De Smet, where their daughter, Rose Wilder Lane, journalist and author, was born. Mrs. Wilder died Feb. 11, 1957, aged 90, at the farm in the Ozarks near Mansfield, Mo., where they had lived since 1894.[96]

DIMOCK, 157

This town was the Star of Dakota Territory, named after Star Township, and became known as Dimock in 1922. When the German settlers came to the area, they soon built a church and a cheese factory. The Star Catholic Church burned down in 1908, but tragedy turned into triumph when the parish built a brick structure so beautiful that it attracted visitors from a large area. In 1985, St. Peter and Paul Catholic Church observed the centenary of the Dimock parish.[97]

Loyalties are strong in the small communities, and one of the area farmers, Bill Ripp, says, "I've been to 20 other countries, and there's no other place I'd live. In Dimock or Parkston, I know everybody and I trust my neighbors. How do you put a value on that?"[98]

DOLAND, 306

When the late Vice-President Hubert Horatio Humphrey, Jr. was in second grade, his family moved to Doland where his father bought a drugstore and served as mayor. The young Humphrey enjoyed sports and played the baritone horn. As a high school student, Hubert Humphrey was active in debate and dramatics, talents which served him well in his political life. He was valedictorian of the graduating class of 1929, and then studied pharmacy, following in his father's footsteps. When the Depression forced an interruption in his studies, Humphrey returned to Doland to run the pharmacy temporarily while his father went on the road to sell a pig serum he had developed. As Hubert Humphrey's interests shifted, he earned a master's degree in political science and became active in political life, serving as mayor of Minneapolis, Senator from Minnesota and Vice-President of the United States under President Lyndon B. Johnson.

DRAPER, 123

Draper is the real "Prairie Home," having had a Prairie Home School in which the Prairie Home Literary group was organized in 1906 and held meetings every Friday night. The community enjoyed recitations, entertainment and debates of various topics such as "Resolved, there is more pleasure in anticipation than in realization," and "Resolved; the bachelor is more benefit to the community than the old maid." Garrison Keillor should find his way to the true roots of Prairie Home country in Draper, once home of the Prairie Home Farmers Union, The Prairie Home Threshing Machine Company, the Prairie Home Ladies and the Prairie Home Museum which preserved the past in the old twelve by sixteen-foot Drury claim shack and the Spears School house. Keillor could probably find enough material in Draper to last a lifetime.[99]

DUPREE, 484

Dupree was named for frontiersman Fred Dupris, an old Frenchman of the American Fur Company who married a Cheyenne woman and settled in the area. Thomas Riggs wrote of stopping at the Dupris ranch after participating in one of the last buffalo hunts:

"Fred Dupris, an old employee of the American Fur Company, and another Frenchman greeted me in true earlyday manner with tears, laughter, curses and prayers curiously intermingled. Fred called to one of the boys, 'Take Tom's hawse; put de hawse on de stable; put hay on de hawse; and Tom come in de house and put your feet on de stove!'"[100]

Dupris and his son Pete are credited with saving buffalo from near extinction by urging a policy of preservation and turning five buffalo calves loose with their cattle. The buffalo in the Dupris herd increased to 57 animals by 1901, when they were purchased by Scotty Philips, who moved them to his ranch north of Fort Pierre. The buffalo introduced at Custer State Park came from the herd begun by Dupris. [101]

EAGLE BUTTE, 489

The name of the town comes from the nearby butte where Native Americans dug pits to lay a trap for eagles. After covering the pits with light branches on which a rabbit was laid for bait, an alert trapper hidden in the pit could grab an unsuspecting eagle coming to get the rabbit.

The eagle is of special significance to Native American people, who proudly wear eagle feathers awarded for significant feats. A wise and distinguished tribal elder taught for many years on the Pine Ridge reservation and was awarded an honorary doctoral degree which many would be proud to receive. But Agnes Ross said she was more honored when Chief Fools Crow tied an eagle feather in her hair. Traditionally, the eagle feathers were awarded for feats of bravery in battle, but today they are awarded for other important accomplishments in life. [102]

EDEN, 97

This must be paradise. Well, the town of Paradise was actually 12 miles west of Eden, but it doesn't exist on the map any more. As the story goes, it got its name when a homesteader named Adam had a claim next to a homesteader named Eve. Alas, they both left their homesteads and didn't get together. Paradise didn't make it either.

EDGEMONT, 906

Edgemont has a long been identified with weapons from primitive to high tech. Native Americans quarried stone to get material for weapons and tools from an area that came to be called Flint Hill by white settlers. Many prehistoric artifacts have been found at the site which provided a silicified sandstone used for arrows and other weapons. In the twentieth century, many came to the area as employees of the Black Hills Ordnance Depot which operated seven miles south of Edgemont from 1942 to 1967.

Prairie Homestead

EGAN, 208

Roscoe, founded in 1876, was the important site of a mill and also the best ford of the Big Sioux River in many miles. When Roscoe was bypassed by the railroad in 1880, Egan came into existence nearby. Ordinances provide glimpses of life in that community. An 1881 ordinance stated, "It shall be unlawful for a person or persons on Sabbath day, commonly called Sunday, to engage in any game of ball, croquet, horse racing, or other amusement within the corporate limits of the village of Egan to the annoyance or disturbance of any of the citizens thereof." An 1883 ordinance stated, "It shall be unlawful for any persons to undress and bathe or go swimming in the Sioux River within view of any highway or bridge within the village of Egan." Female harassment was addressed at the turn of the century: "Any male person who shall, in the city of Egan, make an impudent, insulting or licentious advance or salutation to any female person upon the street, or in any store or other public place, shall upon conviction thereof, be fined in any sum not exceeding fifty dollars." However, they also addressed "lewd women": "It shall be unlawful for any lewd woman or girl of bad character to enter any saloon or other place except drug store where intoxicating liquors are sold at retail within the city of Egan." [103]

ELK POINT, 1423

Native Americans gave the name to the area where a trading post was established by 1755. Lewis and Clark camped in the vicinity on August 22, 1804, after crossing the Big Sioux River. Sergeant Charles Floyd had died of what was called "biliose chorlick" (thought to be a ruptured appendix) the day before, and while camped at Elk Point, the party elected Private Patrick Gass to be the new sergeant. Member of the expedition hunted buffalo near the present site of the town where Eli Wixson built a home in 1859. Several years later, a log hotel was built to serve as a post office and stage stop. In 1873, Elk Point was the biggest town in South Dakota.

ELKTON, 602

When hard times made money scarce in 1893, some enterprising Elkton businessmen contracted with a Minnesota firm to have coins made from aluminum. They actually used and circulated them, about $15,000 worth, and thought it was a great idea - until a government inspector came by one day. That ended the "funny money!"

There was no shortage of good ideas in Elkton. In 1896, Henry Heintz got a patent on an aircraft. With Henry Wulf of Aurora, Heintz built a flying machine which performed somewhat like a helicopter. Amazed spectators watched it lift off the ground briefly on a trial flight and quickly return to earth. It never got the forward thrust, and there is no record of further attempts. [104]

EMERY, 417

Folks have been coming and going in Emery since the early days of the old Sioux Falls - Black Hills Trail when they came with oxen and prairie schooners through virgin prairie land with grass three feet high and slough grass taller than they were. Obtaining food was difficult until the settlers were established, but an ample supply of prairie chickens provided meat in the Emery area. "All you had to do was stick your gun out of the door of the claim shack in the morning and shoot one." [105] Some pioneers pushed farther westward, but some settled in Emery. The Fahy family started an inn, The Emery House, in 1884. The building still provides food and lodging as a Bed and Breakfast Inn, but the barn and livery service have long been gone. [106]

ENNING

One of the dinosaurs that lived in what is now South Dakota was the Ornithominus, a creature about 13 feet long which thrived in swamps and forests. Scientists identified a single partial skeleton from Enning as Ornithominus, a creature that is part of the same branch of the dinosaur family tree as the Velociraptor. The Ornithominus roamed the area from the later part of the Jurassic Period and into Cretacious Period over 100 million years ago. [107]

EPIPHANY

At the turn of the century, Father William Kroeger served in Epiphany and was widely known as a priest-healer. He was a medical college graduate who practiced medicine a few years before studying to become a priest. He came to South Dakota in 1893 claiming reasons of health, but he perhaps wanted to make a new beginning, having accrued substantial debts while building a large parish in Elkhart, Indiana. Father Kroeger practiced healing of body and spirit in Epiphany and became famous for his medicinal remedies which he dispensed at $1 per flask. Many patients came to the priest, and six years after leaving Elkhart, Father Krueger began sending checks to pay his debts in full. In 1899, demands for his services as a physician forced resignation of his priestly duties, although he was reinstated before his death in 1904, when he left a fortune of $200,000. [108]

ESTELLINE, 658

A letter from Estelline written by Eva Sutton in 1881 describes the life of a young woman hired to teach there, when standards were somewhat less than those today. (She had been taught by her mother, and no examinations were required.)

Estelline, D.T. September 6, 1881

My Dear Brother:

Don't it seem just awful to be so far from home? Well here I am further away from home than you are. I am living six miles from Estelline teaching school in a sod house. I board in the same house where the school is. Mr. Dick owns the house and his wife and two children live here too. She is a nice woman but he is just awful and I don't see how she stands it to live with him. While our house is made of stone this house is about as big as ours and has two rooms instead of one but it is all above the ground which makes it nice. I sleep in the room we use for school but that does not make much difference for there are not many scholars. How many do you think there are? Well I will tell you. Four signed up but only three have come so far. Another is coming next week and this will make five. The table I use for a desk is round and covered with green cloth. Mr. Dick says it was used to play poker on back in Minnesota where he ran a saloon. There is a hole in the top and a drawer on one side.

Mr. Dick filled some sacks part full of wheat and we use them for chairs, really they are better than chairs for they can be made any height we want them. Mattie the littlest girl has hers almost full because she is so small. Today there is no school for we have no fire but Mr. Dick says he will haul in some hay this afternoon and then we can have a fire tomorrow. I hope he twists it for I don't like that job, it cuts my hands so. I wish we had wood here like we do down home. [109]

ETHAN, 312

On a day in 1910, a farmer left his field to go home for his noon meal and found his three children standing on the porch. His wife had left with the horse and buggy found tied to a post by the railway station later in the day. She had boarded a passenger train, never to return again. [110]

EUREKA, 1197

Although it may be hard to think of Eureka as a commodity capital, it was the largest primary wheat market in the world from 1887 to 1902. Two-thirds of the world's wheat crop was shipped from this town in 1897. Thirty-six grain elevators were used to hold some of the thousands of bushels of grain from area farms that fed the dinner tables of the world. Some of the grain found other uses, too, as this city is reputed to have had a powerful thirst, especially for German beer. Prohibition must have been a hardship for the people of Eureka who at one time had 18 saloons for a population of about the same size then as now.

FAIRBURN, 62

A trip to this little town could be rewarding because it is home to the Fairburn agate, the gemstone of South Dakota. This semi-precious stone, a favorite of rock collectors, is used in making jewelry. Before becoming too hopeful, however, you should know that they are scarce and have become almost impossible to find.

FAIRVIEW, 73

Fairview got off to a shaky start when the Spencers who owned the townsite ran into financial difficulties in the early 1890's and disappeared, leaving the residents without clear title to the land on which they lived and worked. An enterprising Iowa banker offered lots at a townsite called Elm Springs across the Big Sioux River in Iowa. Fairview residents were attracted, and the community relocated. They celebrated their move with a reinactment of the Biblical march around Jericho. "The walls of Fairview did not fall down, but many of its residents may have, for each of the seven circlings of the town was punctuated by a stop at the local saloon for refreshment." Elm Springs enjoyed a heydey from 1896 to 1898, until the Spencers returned to Fairview, paid off debts and provided clear title to land. Elm Springs buildings were moved on the ice across the river to Fairview, and the South Dakota town came back to life. Thus, the residents of Fairview were spared from being Iowans.[111]

FAITH, 548

In summer of 1940, an anonymous woman, who said she had always wanted to visit the town named for her, left an envelope containing $100 to be used in the best interests of the community. Although accounts differ, the name seems linked to the daughter of a railroad man. Some say, however, the name was chosen because faith is needed to live on that semi-arid land. A highway marker claims that on the vast prairie "deceit finds no place to hide and man is known for his true stature." This is cowboy country with wide open spaces, and the historical marker states, "Our grass is unsurpassed anywhere, producing beef, the backbone of our existence."[112]

FARMER, 23

The lush land looked like a farmer's paradise to an early settler. Josephine Gottsacher Schladweiler witnessed the transformation of the prairie into cultivated fields yielding good crops in her life of more than 99 years. She attributed her longevity to working hard and eating what she enjoyed: onions and a slice of home-made bread.[113]

FAULKTON, 809

In 1889, Major John Pickler, a Faulkton resident, was elected the state's first Congressman. The ambitious Civil War veteran and University of Michigan Law School graduate moved to Faulkton. The Pickler home began as a claim shanty and underwent a series of expansions from 1882 to 1894, including the addition of a former hotel to become a 20-room mansion described in *Historic Sites of South Dakota* as "ostentatious beyond any purpose."[114] The Victorian "Pink Mansion" on Main Street is open today to visitors who may ascend the tower and also visit the many rooms which include a 2000 book library, a music room with hand-carved panels of wood, and a secret room in the kitchen closet used for shelter during storms and Indian attacks. Theodore Roosevelt and Susan B. Anthony were overnight guests at the house.

The *Faulkton Times* of February 10, 1884, reported, "The Chautauqua Circle with invited guests to the number of nearly half a hundred, met at the residence of Major Pickler on Friday evening last, to celebrate the birthday anniversary of the Scottish poet, Burns, by appropriate literary and musical exercises."[115] The celebration included Scottish music played on organ and violin, a biographical sketch of Robert Burns, songs and poetry, concluding with "sentiments by the Circle" and the singing of "Auld Lang Syne."

With an appreciation of the arts that was fostered early in Faulkton's history, it is appropriate that an opera was performed on a Faulkton farm in the summer of 1993. Opera on the farm? Yes, a University of Minnesota touring company brought to a South Dakota farm setting Aaron Copland's *The Tender Land,* which tells the story of a farm girl graduating from high school in the 1930's.

FIRESTEEL

Firesteel got its name from the lignite coal in the area which the Native Americans called "rock that burns." This community was close to the junction of two important trails: the Jimtown Trail which first brought mail to the James River Valley and the Ft. Thompson Trail heavily traveled in Gold Rush days.

Although a post office and grocery store are all that remain of this Cheyenne River Reservation community, residents rose to the occasion of the 75th anniversary in 1987 with a special calendar that portrayed livelier coal mining days when Firesteel was a community of several hundred people. The lignite from Firesteel was of a poor grade but provided a source of fuel in the thirties.

Other fuel sources were put to use, too. Cow chips burned well, but so quickly that one was kept busy feeding the stove and hauling out the ash. Mike Barondeau wrote of the fuel of the thirties:

> For the heating stove, sheep manure was a much longer lasting fuel. The flock of sheep would not be provided with much bedding and when spring came the sheep barn floor was packed and leveled. We took an axe and cut the manure in square blocks to fit the stove. These were set on end outside the door to dry. They provided a much longer burning fuel than the cow chip and compared very closely to the lignite coal that many burned.[116]

FLANDREAU, 2311

A coffee group, who began calling themselves the "West Inn Garden Club," gathers weekdays at a local cafe. The early birds come in at 6 a.m., and anyone overhearing their conversation might mistake them for a Rush Limbaugh support group. The group grows to about 18 at the peak of morning discussion, covering everything from weather to local issues and politics. Participants posted ground rules: "Daily meetings. Subjects discussed: human relations, behavior, gambling, animal husbandry, law and order, the Chicago Board of Trade, politics, taxes, critiques of the school board and city council meetings, weather, garbage service, farm programs. Number of members unknown." Good natured bantering takes place, but it is a forum for issues. If you want to test an idea, put it on the table at the Flandreau "Garden Club" where opinions are freely expressed.[117]

FLORENCE, 192

South of Florence is Medicine Lake, called Minnepejuta by the Sioux. It is spring fed and contains minerals which give it healing quality. The mineral content is so great that bathers float easily with no risk of sinking, and the water is clear and uncontaminated by bacteria. Animals avoid the bitter water, and geese and ducks quickly fly away if they land there. Native Americans made use of the water, long before entrepreneurs bottled and sold it far and wide, claiming it brought relief from skin eruptions and irritations.

FORESTBURG

Forestburg melons are first and foremost in the minds of those who know this melon mecca. The soil along the Jim (James) River in this area is very conducive to the growing of tasty watermelons and cantaloupe. In late summer, roadside stands with mounds of melons prompt motorists to interrupt their travel.

FORT PIERRE, 1854

This town on the Missouri River has a long and colorful history as the oldest continuous white settlement in what is now South Dakota. In 1743, the Verendrye expedition claimed the land for France and left a lead plate found by children in 1913. In the Louisiana Purchase of 1803, the United States acquired the land, explored by the Lewis and Clark expedition the following year.

Fur traders established a trading post in 1817, and boats took goods to and from Saint Louis. In 1831, a specially built steamboat traveled the upper part of the Missouri River to Fort Tecumseh, at the site of present Fort Pierre. Pierre Chouteau, Jr., a leading operator of the fur trade and promoter of steamboat transport of pelts, made the trip to inspect the American Fur Company post and to observe the steamboat operation. Chouteau became impatient when low water caused a several day delay, but after some cargo was removed to other boats, the Yellowstone continued and reached the trading post. Four weeks later, the boat returned to St. Louis with a cargo of furs, buffalo robes and 10,000 buffalo tongues. When the Yellowstone made the trip the following year, Pierre Chouteau, Jr. was again a passenger, and a newly built trading post was named for him. Fort Pierre was the name that became attached to the area.

The Missouri River presented challenges, which included shallow water, sandbars and snags; 20 steamboats were wrecked during a half century of steamboat travel in South Dakota. At first sight, the smoke belching steamboats frightened the Native Americans, who called them "fire canoes" and sometimes attacked the boats. Eventually, however, some Indians traded furs for passage and cut wood for the boats which burned a cord an hour. On early trips, crews chopped down shoreline trees, but as river traffic increased, woodhawks sold wood in seasons of river travel and trapped furs in winter.

The 1832 trip of the Yellowstone brought interesting visitors, including painter George Catlin and German Prince Maximilian, a student of natural history. Catlin wrote,

> The Missouri is, perhaps, different in appearance and character from all other rivers in the world; there is a terror in its manner which is sensibly felt, the moment we enter its muddy waters from the Mississippi. . .
>
> . . .the shores of this river (and, in many places, the whole bed of the stream) are filled with snags and raft, formed of trees of the largest size, which have been undermined by the falling banks and cast into the stream; their roots becoming fastened in the bottom of the river with their tops floating on the surface of the water, and pointing down the stream, forming the most frightful and discouraging prospect for the adventurous voyageur.
>
> Almost every island and sand-bar is covered with huge piles of these floating trees, and when the river is flooded, its surface is almost literally covered with floating raft and drift wood; which bids positive defiance to keel-boats and steamers, on their way up the river.
>
> With what propriety this "Hell of waters" might be denominated the "River Styx," I will not undertake to decide; but

nothing could be more appropriate or innocent than to call
it the River of Sticks.

The scene is not, however, all so dreary; there is a redeem-
ing beauty in the green and carpeted shores, which hem in
this huge and terrible deformity of waters. . .[118]

FORT THOMPSON, 1088

The pressures of settlement caused much frustration among
the Minnesota Santees. In 1862, some of that band resorted
to violent action, and the government responded by reloca-
ting the Santees. As punishment, 38 were hung, and 300 were
imprisoned. Over a 100 died before 1306 Santees (mostly old
men, women and children) were transported by steamboat to
the bleak and drought stricken Crow Creek agency in May of
1863. Fort Thompson, the administrative center of the Crow
Creek Reservation, was named for the Minnesota colonel instrumental in this relocation which led to the deaths of over 300
Santees due to malnutrition and exposure in the winter of 1863-
1864.

FRANKFORT, 192

Fisher Grove State Park is a pleasant place on the Jim River
where settler Frank Fisher, a lawyer from Indiana, stopped
while traveling down the James River in 1878. Nearby, one
can see traces of an old rocky ford used by Native Americans
and settlers in crossing the James River. That point was first
known as Fisher's Ford and later as Belcher's Ford. The town
that was established was to have been named Frankford, for
Frank's Ford, but an error in Washington (Would you believe
that?) resulted in the name Frankfort.

FREDERICK, 241

Frederick is a fine and friendly farming community where
Finnish families have flourished. The Savo Lutheran Church
was named for a Finnish province, and the Savo Monument,
northeast of Frederick, honors Finns who came to the area.

The Finnish and Bohemian immigrants led the consumer
cooperative movement which promoted locally shared ownership to establish fair markets for goods and reduce the cost of

supplies. Although some were suspicious of such organizations, members saw it as an opportunity to address the market with a unified effort. Early in the 1900's, several cooperatives were established in the Frederick area, the first of which was the Finnish Cooperative Creamery in 1901. Other cooperative organizations followed with the Co-Op Telephone Company established in 1910, the Equity Exchange Elevator in 1915, the Cooperative Mercantile Company in 1918, The Frederick Shipping Association in 1920, the Co-Op Oil Company in 1926 and the Co-Operative Credit Union in 1950.

FREEMAN, 1293

Freeman is home to the Schmeckfest which has gained national publicity in the 35 years of its existence. The women's auxiliary began the event as a fundraiser for the Freeman Academy, an institution of the General Conference Mennonite Church. Residents of the community prepare and serve hearty German food, family style, to a capacity crowd in Pioneer Hall on each of several nights at the end of March. On the menu is nudel suppe, dampfleishch (stewed beef), gebratene kartofflen (fried potatoes), salat, sauerkraut, grune schauble suppe (green bean soup), bratworst, kase mit knopfe (cheese buttons), geschmache (relishes), dried fruit sauce, fruit pockets, poppy-seed rolls, kuchen, and of course, kaffe. Yum! Cheese making, caning, soap making, quilting, weaving, spinning and sausage making are demonstrated. Tempting homemade goodies are offered for sale. Music is a big part of life in Freeman, and winter nights are spent preparing for a musical performed during the Schmeckfest.

FRUITDALE, 43

Fruitdale has the #3 spot on South Dakota "Best of the Rest" list, a spoof compiled with a chuckle. According to Chuck Cecil, Fruitdale has a "plan to advertise its existence in some of the so-called 'niche' newspapers in and around the San Francisco, Cal. Bay area." The advertising idea has some merit. Arlington and Wessington have attracted new residents as the result of advertisements placed in West Coast newspapers.[119]

FULTON, 70

One Fulton resident has been here and there and decided that "here" is best. Veterinarian Dr. Kay Hall grew up in the area, and after going out to New York to get a degree at Cornell University, she set up a veterinary practice in the little town of Fulton. Besides Hall's busy veterinary clinic, the town has a grain elevator, post office, bank, beauty salon and a craft shop. The local high school is just a memory, and one has to travel to a neighboring community to shop, but Dr. Kay Hall appreciates life in a small town. She says, "Given any opportunity at all, young South Dakotans would ignore the big-city lights for life in the small towns they knew growing up."[120] Similar thoughts were expressed by astronaut Chuck Gemar, who grew up in Scotland (40 miles south of Fulton). Gemar said, "You spend the first eighteen years of your life trying to figure out how to get out of this state, and the next eighteen years trying to figure out how to get back into it - how to make a living out here."[121]

GANN VALLEY

In 1939, Gann Valley had the world's tallest sheriff in seven foot three inch August Klindt who weighed 325 pounds and wore size 14 shoes. The amiable fellow was a good story teller who once worked for a circus. As sheriff, Klindt never carried a weapon, but he did use his size to advantage. "If a couple of guys got into it, he'd pick 'em up by the backs of their necks and bounce their noses together. When he put 'em down they'd take off."[122]

GARDEN CITY, 93

Railroad workers stayed in the Carpenter home and gave Mrs. Carpenter the honor of naming the new town in appreciation for her hospitality. As a lover of flowers, Mrs. Carpenter chose to call the town Garden City. The township was appropriately called Eden. Millions of bushels of potatoes have been produced in the Garden City area.[123]

GARRETSON, 924

This pleasant town on the banks of the Split Rock River is home to some colorful legends. The Native Americans believed that a tomahawk hurled by a god from the spirit world cleaved the area known today as the Palisades. The sheer red cliffs are a noted feature of the area where rock climbers often come to practice. Jesse James and his brother Frank are said to have come through the area on horseback when eluding a posse after the James gang robbed a bank in Northfield, Minnesota, in 1876. North of Garretson, the brothers temporarily split. Frank rode on the west side of the river, and Jesse traveled on the east side, not knowing he would come to a natural chasm, known today as Devil's Gulch. The hidden canyon forced Jesse James to make a quick decision, whereupon he spurred his horse to make the leap over the gorge at least 20 feet across and 50 feet deep while the posse watched him ride away in awe. The James brothers rendezvoused near the present site of beautiful Palisades State Park where they rested in a cave for a few days before going on into Nebraska. Six years later, Jesse James was killed by a member of his own gang when a reward of $10,000 was offered by the governor of Missouri for his capture, dead or alive. Today, a footbridge crosses the chasm where the jump is said to have occurred. Visitors wonder how much of the quartzite has eroded since 1876 because the gap seems greater than any horse could leap.

GARY, 274

A cattle drive moves down Main Street on the last Saturday in October. It's the best way to get 200 cows and 150 calves approximately 15 miles from summer pasture to winter quarters. A dozen riders on horseback drive the herd 15 miles in about six-and-a-half hours. Traffic is rerouted, and, yes, there is a "poop scoop" detail in the end.

GAYVILLE, 401

The Yankton County town of Gayville should be called "Hayville!" If you like the sweet smell of freshly cut alfalfa, be there in July for Hay Day. Area residents roll bales of hay

**The Palisades

in competition down Main Street and then enjoy an old fashioned barbecue and country dancing. They "make hay" in a variety of forms seen around Gayville. Besides traditional haystacks and two by four-foot bales, there are large five-foot diameter spools and other stacks that take the form of giant loaves of bread.

GEDDES, 280

Sports rivalries have traditionally been strong among neighboring communities. Good spirit usually prevails, but occasionally the rivalry gets heated, as can be seen in accounts which appeared in the Geddes and Armour newspapers after a baseball game in 1902. The *Armour Chronicle-Tribune,* said,

> The Geddes umpire made some of the rottenest decisions ever given out on a base ball diamond. . . .The members of the Geddes ball team are gentlemen and conducted themselves as such, but their landlord manager, umpire and and number of others in that little burg might be pretty favorably compared to a well organized gang of horse thieves. Their conduct throughout was most disgraceful, and we are thankful our boys reached home alive, though the escape was miraculous. After all, there is but one redeeming feature about the visit to our neighboring town, it enables one to put a true value on civilization after a couple of days' association with the slums and unprincipled classes in the Charles Mix metropolis. [124]

The *Geddes Record,* responded:

> . . .when a team comes to play us and are accompanied by an aggregation many of whom are void of all honor and principle, and who would stoop so low as to offer a few of our boys a bribe -$40 each - to throw them the game that they might win their bets, and we are informed they did this, wide as is the range of the English language, we fail to find in it fit words to excoriate them. [125]

GETTYSBURG, 1510

White men saw a huge rock on a hillside near the Missouri River, and Native Americans told them it was a Sacred Rock.

Originally found 15 miles west in a location later put under water by the the Oahe Dam, the Medicine Rock was moved to the northeastern side of Gettysburg where it can be seen today. The boulder has footprint like indentations of enormous size and impressions of animal tracks and a human hand. Native Americans placed gifts and offerings and hung medicinal herbs from poles above the rock to absorb additional powers, believing the prints were made by the Great Spirit. Skeptics and scientists speculate that the impressions may have been done by a jokester or medicine man who wanted to further impress followers, but the origin of the prints remains a mystery.

Named for the site of the famous Civil War Battle which was fought July 1 - 3, 1863, Gettysburg has celebrated the Fourth of July in recent years with related events, including a reading of the Gettysburg Address on the courthouse steps and encampments reinacting the battle of Gettysburg. A buffalo barbecue, military ball and fireworks provide the finale.

GOODWIN, 126

The little town was named Goodwin to honor a railway laborer who lost his life while working on construction. Three hotels provided lodging in the lively town in 1888. People came from as far as 50 miles away by ox team to bring their grain and buy supplies. Many such travelers stayed at the Central House, a hotel of ten rooms, where for 25 cents you could get a good meal and for 50 cents you could get a room for the night, sometimes shared with a stranger.[126]

Life is low key in Goodwin. In 1994, an election was held for town trustee, the first time in 41 years. Lack of competition for the positions results in appointments to the three member town board which rarely has formal meetings. Business usually consists of a discussion of drainage related issues and is most often taken care of during dinner or at an informal meeting.[127]

GREEN GRASS

Many years ago, a beautiful young woman carrying a pipe came to a gathering of Native American people of the Plains and addressed the group after being welcomed by the chief. She spoke to the women and had words for the children after which she addressed the men and lastly, the chief:

> "My older brother: You have been chosen by these people to receive this pipe in the name of the whole Sioux tribe. Wakan'tanka is pleased and glad this day because you have done what it is required and expected that every good leader should do. By this pipe the tribe shall live. It is your duty to see that this pipe is respected and reverenced. I am proud to be called a sister. May Wakan'tanka look down on us and take pity on us and provide us with what we need. Now we shall smoke the pipe."
>
> Then she took the buffalo chip which lay on the ground, lighted the pipe, and pointing to the sky with the stem of the pipe, she said, "I offer this to Wakan'tanka for all the good that comes from above." (Pointing to the earth), "I offer this to the earth, whence come all good gifts." (Pointing to the east, west, north, and south), "I offer this to the four winds, whence come all good things." Then she took a puff of the pipe, passed it to the chief, and said, "Now my dear brothers and sister, I have done the work for which I was sent here and now I will go, but I do not wish any escort. I only ask that the way be cleared for me."
>
> Then, rising, she started, leaving the pipe with the chief, who ordered that the people be quiet until their sister was out of sight. She came out of the tent on the left side, walking very slowly; as soon as she was outside the entrance, she turned into a white buffalo calf.[128]

A succession of 19 generations of Keepers of the Sacred Pipe have taken responsibility for the Sacred Calf Pipe. Arval Looking Horse of Green Grass holds a position of spiritual leadership as the present keeper of the pipe, and someday he will pass it to another as his grandmother did, guided by dreams and visions. Looking Horse said,

> The pipe is used for prayer in our way of life. We say we "pray with the Pipe." The Pipe is for all people, all races, as long as a person believes in it. Anyone can have a Pipe and keep it within their family. But only the Sioux can have ceremonies with the Sacred Calf Pipe.[129]

GREENWOOD

Lewis and Clark encountered Yanktons living on the Missouri River near the present site of Greenwood. In 1858, about 50 years later, the tribe ceded 12 million acres and received a 430,000 acre reservation and the promise of educational, health and annuity benefits. Greenwood became the agency headquarters of the Yankton (Ihanktonwan) Sioux.

The Rising Hail Colony established in 1938 was a novel experiment designed by a reservation superintendent to help the Yankton Sioux. The colony was a natural extension of the Yankton Sioux's strong tradition of communal caring and sharing. Eight or nine families, totaling 40 to 50 people, pooled their resources and borrowed money from the government to build structures for their communal farm of 1500 acres. The livestock, orchards and vegetable produce were shared by the group and brought a modest profit in the colony's ten year existence before it became a private operation in 1949.[130]

GREGORY, 1384

The local residents who usually cheer for the Gregory "Gorillas" cheered for an area resident when she claimed a $12.4 million dollar Lotto America Prize in 1991. Controversy developed as the whole story was told. The five dollar ticket was issued at a Gregory convenience store but was refused by a patron who wanted five one dollar tickets. The unwanted ticket was left beside the cash register. When a clerk came to work on the morning after the drawing and realized it was a big winner, she bought it for five dollars and claimed the prize. The store owners also claimed ownership, and after going to court, there was a settlement with enough millions to satisfy all.

GRENVILLE, 81

Grenville is a community founded by Poles who established a Catholic church there in 1885. The Polish were people of agricultural interests who loved the land, but they came later than other ethnic groups. Those of Polish heritage have preserved some of the old world traditions to add variety to the fabric of our lives and pierogies and Polish sausage to some menus. Perhaps because they are such a minority in the mix of South Dakotans, we don't hear Polish jokes, but the corresponding Ole and Lena jokes have become an industry.

GROTON, 1196

When the land was first broken, many farmers did very well with large flax yields. One good crop could pay for the land. The flax fiber was used in fabrics, and the seed was used for linseed oil and meal. In the late 1880's, linseed oil mills were hyped as the enterprise of the future, and in 1888, Groton had a mill which processed flax seed. The linseed oil mill had a short life, however, as the flax market went into decline. Today Groton is known as the Sunflower Capital because of the many sunflowers grown in the area.

GROVER

". . . And the band played on . . ." even as some of its members left to serve in World War I. The Grover Concert Band played as young men left their families to participate in The Great War. Women and children gathered to say good-bye on the balcony of the Lincoln Hotel while the band played at the bus depot.

HAMILL

Cattlemen in the Hamill area had their hands full in caring for their livestock in the blizzard of 1952. One Hammill rancher risked his life to walk out to save his cattle, thirty of whom he found standing in a creek with water up to their bellies and ice frozen around their tails and feet. They had gone out on the ice which cracked and allowed running water underneath to come to the surface.[131] The good cattleman works to protect his cattle from the threats of disease, predators and weather. Severe weather in both summer and winter can bring livestock warnings which put both cattle and cattlemen to the test. If you have a romantic image of the cowboy sitting contentedly around the glowing campfire and singing songs, remember there is more to the picture, including a lot of hard work.

**Joys of a Cowpuncher in Winter
by "Hard Boiled Bill"**

The snow is deep; the weather is cold
The youngest dogie looks twenty years old.
We have four half fed cayuses to haul in feed
And about sixteen more is what we need.
Two loads of straw and two loads of hay
Is hardly enough to feed one day.
Two trips a day in a five mile haul
With horses so poor they can hardly crawl.
When a load of hay come down the hill
All hell can't keep the cattle still.

A hungry cow is the worst there is
Or us cowpunchers don't know our biz
Some poor honyocker may think cowpunching sweet
But I'd like to see them keep 300 cows on their feet.
And 200 yearlings as thin as a rail
Every morning we have to lift some up by the tail.
It's tail up a calf and tail up a cow
We have done it so much we know just how.
You get right behind, put her tail around your neck.
And straighten your spine.   (What the heck! ed.)

Seventy-five Years of Progress,
Mc Laughlin Golden Jubilee: 1909-1984, p. 33.

HAMMER

When the railroad came through in 1913, the railroad camp was set up near the site of the present town. The mules used in grading for the railroad could be heard braying every night at six o'clock, protesting their long working hours. Can't say we blame them! Iver Hammer owned the railroad siding property used for loading grain cars, and he also owned the hardware store early in the town's history. Yes, there was a Hammer at the hardware store.

HARRISBURG, 727

A Harrisburg family has been living in a home with a history of bizarre experiences: apparitions, strange moving of household objects, and more. In an attempt to understand the unusual phenomena, also experienced by previous residents, the residents sought the help of a psychic medium. The clairvoyant determined that four ghosts were present, including the spirit of a young pioneer girl, a little boy who had been abused and killed, a matronly lady in her 60's, and an adult male who was creating most of the disturbances. Fortunately, the four spirits were persuaded by the medium to leave the house. The psychic medium explained that these poor souls sometimes do not know they are dead and are actually seeking the light, and with guidance they move in the direction of God's light. For some reason, the house, a former parsonage, is said to have an energy that attracts troubled, disembodied souls. The Howes of Harrisburg are hoping that no more ghosts come to their home. They prefer to have the house to themselves.[132]

HARRISON

Long before the Wright brothers made their first successful flight in 1903, Harrison area people took an interest in the project of their neighbor Ringert Jongewaard who was convinced that it was possible to fly. A man ahead of his time, Jongeward went to Washington in 1886 to obtain a patent for a flying machine which somewhat resembled a helicopter. The machine had one problem; it didn't fly.[133]

Another area resident, Sail Versteeg, was also interested in taking to the air, and he did so in a balloon. Balloon ascensions were popular attractions, and in the 1890's, Versteeg performed death defying feats as he did aerial acrobatics and parachute jumps from hot air balloons. Mr. Vander Ploeg, the church bell ringer, rang the bell one August afternoon before the turn of the century. A crowd gathered on the north edge of town, and a band played as the balloon was inflated. The early balloons had no burner attached and were filled by building a pit fire and using a flue to direct the hot air into the balloon held down by ropes. The balloonist wore a harness, allowing him to detach from the balloon to descend with a parachute. At about two o'clock, Sail was in his harness and yelled, "Let her go!" He rose to a height of 3000 feet while the crowd below "oohed and aahed." Sail landed on the prairie about a mile north of town. After some close calls, he promised his wife not to do any more balloon ascensions.[134]

HARROLD, 167

A woman looking for a husband might want to go to Harrold where an estimated 30 or 40 area bachelors are available. "The marriage market is in depression," and it is attributed to the fact that the young women of the area go off to college and get jobs in the larger cities.[135] Finding partners for the bachelors could provide a boost for the school population also. In 1993, Harrold had the smallest public high school in the state with 25 students. Schools with an enrollment of fewer than 35 struggle because they lose a portion of state aid, but these communities work tenaciously to keep their schools which are the focus of loyalties, memories and the future.

HARTFORD, 1262

While men of Hartford were participating in the war on a nother continent, the women of Hartford Methodist Church organ-ized the "World's Only Women's Husking Contest" on Thursday, October 2, 1941. Festivities began with a parade at 11 a.m. followed by a chicken dinner at noon. In the field, the huskers were accompanied by a wagon with a backboard into which ears of corn were tossed as the pickers moved down the rows, stripping the ears from the stalks of corn. Fifteen competitors participated, and the champion picked and husked six bushels of corn in a half-hour. One account stated, "The event is reputed to be the only one of its kind in the country, and was managed entirely by the women from the firing of the starting gun to the picking of the last ear. It is believed that this event will soon become a state wide affair and. . . national event. The fact that it originated at Hartford makes it a more prominent affair to citizens here. We look for great possibilities in the very near future."[136]

HAYES

Shucks! Hayes is a revised and tame version of the original town which was located a half-mile south. It would have been fun to see it in its prime when it was a rootin' tootin' place with general store, saloon, dance hall and hitching posts.

From 1877 to 1886, the Plum Creek Stage Station of the Pierre Deadwood Trail was located southwest of Hayes, one of the first stops out of Ft. Pierre for those eager to get to the gold. Beasts of burden pulled millions of tons of freight over that stage route. If conditions were good, horses could pull the stage coach from Ft. Pierre to Deadwood in 48 hours. Plodding oxen pulling the belongings of settlers and seekers of fortune took considerably longer.

HAYTI, 372

Fuel on the prairies was scarce when settlers came to the Hayti area in 1880. Anything disposable that burned provided fuel, including buffalo and cow chips, sometimes called "grass-olene." The pioneers also burned twisted hay for cooking purposes in a special drum placed over the open fire-box of a cook-stove. Such a fire could last an hour or two. Families spent evenings together twisting and tying the prairie grasses into "cats." Pioneers were talking about a name for their new town while tying hay at a gathering and came up with "Hay-tie."

Hayti is home to the Fall Farkleberry Festival held in July. The farkleberry came to the area as a figment of the imagination of native son, Gordon Hanson, a teller of tall tales with a sense of humor. The farkleberry shrub actually grows in the South as a leather leafed evergreen producing large white flowers and a hard black berry, sometimes called a sparkleberry.

HECLA, 398

Although named after the Icelandic volcano, there is no volcanic action in Hecla. Perhaps the most excitement the town has ever known occurred on a winter day early in 1931 when quadruplets Jay, Jimmie, Jean and Joan were born to the Schense family. The national publicity they were given quieted after the birth of the Dionne quintuplets in Ontario in 1934. The Schense father was a poor tenant farmer who took the family on an exhibition tour of county and state fairs when the quadruplets were about a year old, making scarcely enough money to pay expenses. The mother died when the quads were two years old, but happier days followed when, a year later, Mr. Schense married the housekeeper who was well acquainted with the busy household.

HE DOG

The community and school took the name of Chief He Dog (Sunka Bloka), a trusted friend of Crazy Horse. A 1900 photograph of He Dog wearing a Grant peace medal suggests that he was one of the delegation of Oglala Sioux who went with Spotted Tail and Red Cloud to Washington to meet with President Grant in May of 1870. Wearing their finest beaded shirts and leggings, the Native American delegation met with Washington officials to ask for protection of their treaty rights. President and Mrs. Grant invited these Oglalas to the White House along with members of the cabinet and diplomatic corps. The evening was long and awkward for all. Foreign guests were especially interested in the Native Americans, but conversation faltered. When the British ambassador failed to make himself understood, the Russian ambassador tried French without success. The President attempted to ease the tension and silence by escorting the guests into the dining room, but the Native American delegation declined the strawberries and cream. They excused themselves, gravely shook hands with the President and departed.[137]

A photo of He Dog at the age of 82 shows the venerable chief in full headdress, proudly wearing the Grant medal over the beadwork on his chest. Each President from George Washington to Benjamin Harrison had specially minted medals presented to Native American leaders as tokens of friendship and honor.[138]

HENRY, 215

Pheasants of the area have provided tasty meals on many family tables. An enterprising advertising man and his family capitalized on the pheasant hunting, advertising the Red Rooster Hunting Camp in the *Dakota Farmer* in 1946. The hunting attracted leaders of large corporations, entertainers and people from across the country to enjoy the hospitality of the Eck family on their farm north of Henry.

HERMOSA, 242

After discovering some of the wonders of South Dakota while filming "Dances With Wolves," Kevin Costner returned to the state to film portions of another movie about the Old West. Costner and a production crew filmed segments of "Wyatt Earp" at the Triple 7 ranch south of Hermosa. In the film, Costner portrays the lawman and gunman Wyatt Earp.

HERREID, 488

The town was founded in 1901 and named for South Dakota's fourth governor, Charles Nelson Herreid, who took office in that same year. Herreid first came to Dakota Territory from Wisconsin as an attorney to do work for a client in 1884, looking into land titles and chattel mortgages. After seeing the opportunities in Dakota Territory, he closed his Wisconsin law office and moved to what is now Leola, South Dakota, where he built a law practice. Herreid became president of the Bank of Leola and a partner in the newspaper. Active in politics, he was elected lieutenant governor in 1892. About that time, the Herreid family moved to the boom town of Eureka. When Herreid was elected governor in 1901, the family moved to Pierre, the first gubernatorial family to take residence in in the state capital. Gov. Herreid said in 1905 as he was leaving office, "South Dakota needs a new statehouse, fireproof, commodious and in harmony with its progress and prosperity."[139]

HERRICK, 139

Black settler, Oscar Micheaux, described this community in his book, *The Conquest: The Story of a Negro Pioneer.* He wrote, "After driving about fifteen miles we came to the town, as they called it, but I would have said village of Hedrick - a collection of frame shacks with one or two houses, many roughly constructed sod buildings, the long brown grass hanging from between the sod, giving it a frizzled appearance. Here we listened to a few boosters and mountebanks whose rustic eloquence was no doubt intended to give the unwary the impression that they were on the site of the coming metropolis of the west."[140]

HETLAND, 53

A settler from Hetland, Norway, chose the name for his new community. The Phelps family came from Minnesota in the spring of 1880 and made a temporary home in a dugout while putting their time and energy into working the land that summer. An unmarried brother, Willis Atwater, also came to the area to file a homestead claim and moved in with the family. A mid-October blizzard was the first of a series of severe winter storms of 1880-1881. May Wheeler came from Wisconsin on the last train to make it through the snow which accumulated to 12 feet, and she took shelter with the Phelpses also. The dugout was completely buried in snow, and when the supply of kerosene was exhausted, a saucer full of grease with a rag wick provided light. Willis and May had lots of time to get well acquainted, and as you may have guessed, romance developed during that long winter. The first spring thaw came on April 17, and sudden warm weather rapidly melted the snow. The settlers looked with hope to the future, and none more than Willis Atwater and May Wheeler who married and eventually built a large and prosperous farm.[141]

HIGHMORE, 835

Tensions were strong at the time of World War I, and German allies were suspected of grain elevator arson. In 1917, local elevators placed guards on duty to prevent such activity. Ten men from Highmore were drafted that year, and three of the town's men gave their lives in the war. Those at home demonstrated their patriotism by buying Liberty Loan bonds. Names of those who didn't purchase bonds in the expected amount were published in the newspaper. A tank came to Highmore on a railroad car as part of a nationwide promotion for the sale of Liberty Bonds. Two cocky, young drivers attempted to display the tank's abilities to "traverse any terrain and surmount any obstacle." They drove the tank into an old cellar hole at Second Street and Iowa Avenue in Highmore, but, to their chagrin, they couldn't get it out. It took a well-drilling rig with a block and tackle and a powerful team of horses to get the tank out of the hole.[142]

HILL CITY, 650

Hill City, the center of "The Hills," has also been at the center of controversies. In 1887, the Harney Peak Tin Mining Company, a fraudulent British operation, circulated a prospectus in England to sell stock in Dakota tin mines. People didn't buy the stock, and promoters tried again the next year as the Harney Peak Consolidated Tin Company, assembling an impressive board to convince stockholders. Management employed 400 men and constructed a group of buildings in Hill City, some of which remain. Less than five years later, however, the mine was closed and the whole scheme collapsed.

The most recent controversy in Hill City centers on a ten ton Tyrannosaurus rex fossil named Sue, the largest and most complete of its kind. Workers of The Black Hills Institute of Geological Research in Hill City found the prized fossil in 1990, but the U.S. government claimed it was taken illegally from federal trust land on the Cheyenne River Indian Reservation. Institute workers had paid a Native American rancher $5000 for the right to look for fossils, not realizing the land was held in trust. In 1992, Federal agents seized the fossil from the institute; it remains in federal hands but is not yet a dead issue.

HISEGA

If you think this sounds like an interesting Native American name, you will be disappointed. Six young women were the first to use the campground on the townsite in 1908, and the name, Hisega, is taken from the first letter of each of their names: Helen, Ida, Sadie, Ethel, Grace and Ada.[143]

HITCHCOCK, 95

Early Spink County settler, Jacob G. Spencer, wrote to a relative in Canada:

> January 14, 1895. If we have poor crops and but little money, we have good meetings. We had a great revival in our schoolhouse and between thirty and forty were converted. Our little Sunday School has grown to be a large one. Besides, we have a thriving Christian Endeavor Society for the young people. In addition to that, a large prayer meeting once a week, and Methodist and Baptist meetings alternately every Sunday. Besides we frequently attend other meetings four or five miles out of our neighborhood.[144]

Spink County chronicler, Dana Harlow, told of a Methodist camp meeting near Hitchcock where "many found Jesus Christ as their personal Savior, and became changed men and women. They were really blessed and found peace and contentment under hardships and trials, cold of winter with no coal, heat and drought, flies, and after rain, mosquitoes."[145]

The circuit riders, who traveled on horseback across the prairie to minister to the early settlers, endured perils and hardships as they fostered the faith which provided an anchor in the storms of life. When the community formed, Methodists in Hitchcock met in the depot, a butcher shop and the Workman Hall before building a church. The elderly Reverend Phillips came to Hitchcock in 1902 and also served the communities of Redfield, Broadland and Tulare. Harlow described Sunday activity of the old parson with the long white beard, "After the Hitchcock service in winter, he would eat a hasty lunch such as a bowl of oatmeal, which he kept hot on the back of the hard coal burner, then hitch his horse to the cutter, wrap up in a fur robe and drive the ten miles to Broadland in all kinds of weather, and over all kinds of roads. The Hitchcock people presented him with a fur-lined coat and mittens which were much appreciated on these long cold rides."[146]

HOLABIRD

The railroad superintendent married Louise Holabird and named the town in honor of her family. The future of Holabird seemed promising when Governor Ordway and the land company of the railroad actively promoted its selection for the county seat. Nevertheless, Highmore won the election over Holabird, referred to as "Gumbo Holler." Holabird was larger than Highmore at one time and had the first school building and a large two-story structure used for church services, lyceums and other other activities. The lyceum programs offered music, poetry, lectures, debates and recitations for the enrichment and entertainment of Holabird and the surrounding area.[147] Airplane inventor Wilbur A. Wright taught school in Holabird in 1893, ten years before the historic flight at Kitty Hawk, North Carolina.[148]

HOLMQUIST

The Holmquists, Johnsons and Jensens had a lot in common. The little town has three large white houses that are identical and certainly were very fine in the 1890's. They decided that if you have a good plan, you might as well stay with it.

HOSMER, 310

There are oodles of noodles at the Hosmer Noodle Company which makes flour and egg noodles from an old German recipe. The business had its start in 1987 when the Feyereisens took 100 pounds of their noodles to Mobridge for a "Capital for a Day" event. The noodles sold quickly with orders for more, and the family business has been going ever since. The operation is housed in a downtown building where four workers share good camaraderie as they keep rolling out noodles which are distributed in South Dakota and North Dakota. The Hosmer Noodle Company produces 28 flavors of noodles, including chocolate and cinnamon noodles used in desserts. Vegetable flavors include beet, carrot, garlic, spinach and tomato, in addition to cheddar, taco and chili flavors. The less adventuresome consumer might prefer the regular, beef or chicken flavors. The Hosmer Noodle Factory prepares wrapped and ribboned Christmas baskets of noodles for holiday gift giving.[149]

HOT SPRINGS, 4325

Many Columbian and wooly mammoths of over 25,000 years ago died in a slippery-sided sinkhole which has the greatest concentration of such fossils in North America. This site in Hot Springs draws scientists from around the world. Less than 15 percent of the site has been explored, but parts of over 40 mammoths have been found, and scientists think that as many as 100 mammoths may have died at the site. One can see the exposed fossils in place and up close. Scientists speculate that the mammoths and other animals got stuck while drinking and starved or drowned.

HOUGHTON

Native Americans called the lake Tehanchicahah, but early settlers who enjoyed picnics there called it Sand Lake. When Teddy Roosevelt came by presidential train to hunt ducks, a special siding was built in Houghton to accommodate his train. Years later, duck stamps provided money to purchase land for the Sand Lake National Wildlife Refuge to preserve wetland habitat for waterfowl. More than 100 species of birds nest there, and others, including 300,000 snow geese, stop on their migratory flights.[150]

HOVEN, 522

Hoven is the home of the Cathedral on the Prairie, the pride of the area. The hard-working German people who came in 1883 built a small church named for St. Bernard in 1886, but it burned to the ground a few years later. The parishioners quickly built a modest replacement structure. By 1910, Hoven was prospering and had five grain elevators, three general stores and other business establishments. German speaking Father Helmbrecht came to be pastor in 1908 and witnessed much change in Hoven during the years he served there until 1955. As the parish grew, the faithful people of Hoven dreamed of a church building that was a fitting expression of their faith. The Cathedral of the Prairie was completed and dedicated to St. Anthony in May of 1923. The structure seats over 1000 people and was filled to capacity while others stood outside on the day of dedication. The bishop confirmed 170 people that afternoon, a high point in the history of Hoven.[151]

HOWARD, 1156

Establishment of a county seat was of great consequence to a community, and the people of Howard did everything they could think of to insure that their town would be the seat of Miner County business. Vilas, three miles to the west, was expected to have the county offices, but Howard won a questionable election. Votes were bought with cigars, sweets and beverages, and more people voted than lived in the county. One man was said to have voted four times, altering his appearance with changes of clothing and, finally, a shave.[152]

HOWES

David Beautiful Bald Eagle lives on a ranch east of Howes, on the same reservation where he was born in a tepee 75 years ago. Although Bald Eagle doesn't like towns and cities, he has seen much of the world as an invited guest of countries in Europe and Asia. His wife is a former Belgian actress whom he met in 1958 while on tour with a wild west show. As goodwill ambassador of the Cheyenne River Tribe, Bald Eagle has enjoyed sharing the culture and history of his tribe with others, and he dreams of developing his home on Bull Creek into a learning center where Native American children can learn more about their Lakota heritage.[153]

Prairie Skyscraper

HUB CITY

A city it isn't! The Dalesburg Lutheran Church located at the crossroads that mark this community is named for the Swedish province of Dalarna. Swedes inhabit this area and enthusiastically celebrate Midsommar in June. The Dalesburg Lutheran Church is the place to be for a wonderful Scandinavian Show and Taste during Midsommar festivities. Bring any home-sick Swedes for some real Swedish meatballs, knakebrod, and a truly Swedish smorgasbord.

HUDSON, 332

There aren't many places where a bank robber could bicycle away from the site of the crime without immediately getting caught, but it happened in Hudson in 1993. The gentlemanly robber asked the arriving bank president and another employee to open the vault. They did as told, and the robber took the stash of cash, locked the two bank employees in the vault and bicycled away. He was not caught.

HUMBOLDT, 468

This town is proud of U.S. Senator Larry Pressler who grew up on a farm in the community. As a youth, Pressler helped on the family farm, participated in 4-H and belonged to St. Ann's Parish. He graduated from the University of South Dakota, became a Rhodes Scholar, and then went on to law school. Senator Pressler still remembers how to drive a tractor and is happy to demonstrate that ability in local parades when he is in town. Then, he cleans and polishes his boots and goes back to Washington, better able to deal with clutch situations there.

HURLEY, 372

A railroad ad of 1884 touted Hurley as "one of the most promising towns in central Dakota" It extolled the virtues of the town at length and advertised lots priced at $100 to $250 and the best farming lands from $5 to $15 an acre. Town promoters may have been dreamers or schemers when they indicated that Hurley would surely become the county seat. The county courthouse did not come to Hurley, but the Climax Roller Mill came in 1894.[154] Today, Hurley is a quiet community except when street dances and sports events liven the town. Their teams gave them reason to cheer in 1993 when they captured three state "B" championships.

HURON, 12,448

Ernest Sutton was an adventurous fellow who lived in Huron in the 1880's when he worked for the *Huronite* and the *Dakota Farmer*. Sutton wrote of Huron in his autobiography published in 1948:

> Originally Huron was spoken of as "rag" town because so many lived in tents, but when I came most construction was wood. As was the case in many railroad towns, two factions were still fighting over the question of where the business section should be. One wanted to develop toward the south while the other favored a section nearer the depot. For several weeks after I came the fire bell would clang every night calling the volunteer fire department with its two-wheeled hose cart, who, after carrying to safety such furnishings as could be easily moved, stood around watching until the fire burned itself out. . .
>
> Huron was a wild western town such as Deadwood or Dodge City, but there were a few fatalities among the transient gamblers and railroad workers. Citizens attending to their own affairs were seldom in trouble, although differences were not settled by lawsuits.
>
> Gambling joints and saloons ran wide open the same as other lines of business, but they never put on floor shows or employed female entertainers. Occasionally some dizzy blonde dealt faro simply as an advertisement for the place, but this was generally considered unethical. Today it might be considered against union rules because it interfered with the "working" girls' rights to give female entertainment.
>
> "Working" girls did most of their entertaining in some house run by a madame, usually spoken of by a shorter name but advertised as "The Bird Cage," "Lilly's Place" or just plain Madame So and So's. . . .[155]

IDEAL

The name says it all.

IGLOO

Concrete igloos remain as reminders of the Black Hills Ordnance (Army) Depot in operation from 1942 to 1967. The Army built 802 bunker style 25 by 80-foot igloos for the storage and testing of weapons. In 1967, the government sold much of the depot to private owners who use it mainly for livestock grazing. A population count of seven in 1994 is a sharp contrast to the several thousand people who lived and worked there when the depot was in operation. The town had an Olympic size swimming pool, theater and school. Although closed for over 25 years, surveyors found remnants of conventional weapons and a practice chemical rocket in 1992. The United States Corps of Engineers is locating metal with infrared cameras and working to remove remnants of weapons from the area.[156]

INTERIOR, 67

Interior is an old Badlands town located near Sheep Mountain and "Hell's Ten Thousand Acres." The Badlands were given the name "Mako situ" (which translates "lands bad") by the Native Americans, and early French explorers used the terms "mauvais terres" meaning bad lands. General George Custer described the area as, "a part of hell with the fires burnt out."[157] The Badlands offer a unique panorama, and the terrain has been likened to that of the moon. The area is rich in prehistoric fossils and home to a variety of wildlife today.

Doc Reynolds, who lived in the area, wrote,

> I think one of the best rodeos I saw in my life was at Interior, South Dakota, the summer of 1920. Jake Herman was the clown and Pete Knight was one of the bronc riders that was there, and he wound up to be the world's champion bronc rider at one time. They had a carnival there at the Interior rodeo. One concession was supposed to be a wild man. He wasn't supposed to eat anything but raw meat. They gave him a live chicken down in the pit and he bit it on the neck and sucked the blood out of it and made a lot of growling noises.

A fellow that lived over there on Medicine Root Creek by the name of Guy Bradford, a big tall fella about 6' 2'', had a few drinks in him. He went up there and was looking down in the pit at the wild man. The man told him to get back, that he's a wild man and he'd bite. Old Bradford said, "Well, that's my job, taming wild men," and he jumped down into that pit, got ahold of that man and boosted him out. He turned out to be a kind of a consumptive looking little. . .fella that they had put in there.[158]

IONA

The Lewis and Clark expedition was the idea of President Jefferson who gave the explorers instructions:

> The object of your mission is to explore the Missouri river, and such principal streams of it, as, by its course and communication with the water of the Pacific ocean. . .may offer . . .water-communication across the continent, for the purposes of commerce. . . .Your observations are to be taken with great pains and accuracy; to be entered distinctly and intelligibly for others as well as yourself.[159]

Diaries and journals detailed events of the two year exploration. A September 11, 1804, entry recorded a happy reunion which occurred near Iona. George Shannon rejoined the other members of the Lewis and Clark expedition after he was lost for 16 days. Shannon left camp to look for two stray horses and mistook tracks for those of his party, wrongly concluding that the expedition was ahead of him. He ran out of ammunition after four days and subsisted for 12 days on some grapes and one rabbit which he managed to kill by using a piece of stick. Weak and near starvation, he hoped to catch a trading boat on the river when, happily, the other members of his party came along. George Shannon was 17 years-old at the time but a respectable woodsman and the best educated of the enlisted men.

At the conclusion of the expedition, William Clark sent Shannon to Philadelphia to assist Nicholas Biddle in writing the history of the expedition from the bundles of rough notes, diaries and journals of the party. George Shannon provided clarification and explanation for Biddle who published the *History of the Expedition under the Command of Captains Lewis and Clark in 1814.*

IPSWICH, 965

Some good ideas have come from Ipswich including a library begun when each member of the Ladies Library Association donated one book in 1886. Ipswich was also home to the Yellowstone Trail organization which promoted Highway 12 for transcontinental travel from Plymouth Rock to Puget Sound in the early days of automobile travel. Completion of the coast-to-coast highway was commemorated with a Memorial Arch over the highway in Ipswich. The arch, now in the city park, honored the vision of Joseph W. Parmley and the work of others involved in the 1912 transcontinental highway, the Yellowstone Trail.

IRENE, 464

The little railroad town established in 1893 got off to a shaky start due to a bad drought in 1894 and a financial depression in the years 1893 to 1896. Over the years, however, many folks found a good life in the "village in the valley." Residents celebrated the town's centennial July 2 - 4, 1993, and Main Street was buzzing with activity. Since it's a three-county town, folks from Yankton, Turner and Clay Counties helped celebrate, and some traffic engineering was required to get 175 centennial parade entries through the town.

A focus of admiration during the centennial was the new Main Street Veterans Memorial honoring all area people who have served their country. The grateful and patriotic community erected the memorial of five large granite blocks on which are engraved almost 800 names of Irene veterans from the Civil War to the present.[160]

IROQUOIS, 328

In 1874, Michael Waldner led a group of German-Russians from Russia to Dakota Territory. Some of the group chose to live individually and affiliated with the Mennonite church;

others lived together as the Hutterite colony at Bon Homme. The Hutterites followed the teachings of Jacob Hutter, a clergyman who organized the group in 1529 and later was burned for his beliefs. At that time, as today, they held strong biblical beliefs and chose to share life and work, living as an extended family according to Acts 2: 44-45: "And all that believed were together, and had all things in common; and sold their possessions and goods, and parted them to all *men,* as every man had need." From 1878 to 1913, the number of colonies in South Dakota grew rapidly. Their conscientious objection to war and strong German background caused all but the original colony to flee to Canada during World War I.

After the war, many returned, and their growth continued. South Dakota now is home to more than 30 colonies, one of which is the Pearl Creek Colony near Iroquois. This daughter colony of the Jamesville colony was established in 1948. When a colony population reaches 100 to 150 people, a daughter colony is formed. Each colony is independent of the others, politically and economically. The males elect colony officers and also cast lots to select farm and business managers, the minister, the German teacher and other positions of responsibility. As spiritual leader, the pastor commands great respect. The Hutterites live in a closely knit society as they seek to combat the sinfulness of the world, the "outside" as they call it. Male members must make public confession of their relationship to God each year. Gemeindeordnung (Community Observances) dictate behaviour and dress. Women wear dark clothing with long skirts and cover their heads. The men wear dark pants and white shirts, suspenders and black hats. Families have modest living quarters without kitchens, since meals are shared. Families are large, and, with rare exception, children are educated in a public school at the colony, through the eighth grade. At the age of 15, Hutterite children are treated as adults and usually end their formal education. They then go to work on the farm and eat in the same dining room as the adults. One observer of South Dakota Hutterite life said, "I have been impressed by the wealth of spiritual and emotional power which resides in the community way of life."[161]

ISABEL, 319

Madonna Wortman Alley attended the Severns School northeast of Isabel as a student and returned as the teacher in 1943. Upon completing a year's study at Northern State Teachers' College, Madonna Wortman signed a nine month contract to teach for $100 per month. She married Maurice Alley after her first year of teaching, and they lived in the one-room teacherage for two years until their children were born. Said Mrs. Alley, "I think attending and teaching a country school is one of the greatest treasures for anyone having had the experience." On cold days they did warm up exercises by marching around the room and clapping hands to warm cold feet and hands. At recess, teacher and students put food on the coal heater for a hot lunch.

> We would bake our potatoes in the ashes. This was before aluminum foil so they were not wrapped. I don't think any baked potato ever tasted as good as those. Soups were also heated in a pan on top of the heater.
>
> There was no playground equipment so our favorite games were softball, pump-pump-pull away, New Orleans or, in the winter time, Fox and Goose.
>
> On Friday afternoons we would have art (everyone looked forward to that) or Young Citizen's League meetings. . . Committees would be appointed to help out with the chores such as hauling in the coal, sweeping, wiping boards, dusting erasers and washing off the desks. . .
>
> One highlight of the year was a hike in the spring. It was like a skip day that they now have in high school. We would skip a couple classes and hike down to the Firesteel Creek, watching and finding treasures of nature.
>
> At Chrismas time there was always the Christmas program, Santa Claus, and a box social. The children always came dressed in their finest for their performances in the program. Santa would come, bring sacks of goodies and help pass out the gifts exchanged among the students. The girls and moms would bring a lunch packed in a decorated box to be auctioned off. It was a gala event.[162]

JAVA, 161

It is tempting to believe the story that such good coffee was served at a small shack in the area that it was called "Coffee Town" by railway workers laying track. Officials of the Milwaukee railroad gave the town its name, and perhaps the Coffee Town story is true. Stop by and have a cup, and see if it's still as good as they said.

"Tough times don't last, but tough people do," is an idea well demonstrated by the life of pioneer woman Christine Kinz Boehler. In 1882, she courageously decided to make a fresh start in unsettled country with her two young children after the death of her husband. She sold her home in Yankton for $100 and made arrangements to travel northward to Campbell County with five other families, since she didn't have enough money to buy a team of oxen. It was a difficult 21 day trip from Yankton to her claim, eight miles north of Java. A late spring snow delayed travel for a couple of days, and the trail westward from Aberdeen had to be broken. When they arrived at their destination on May 29, 1882, it rained for two weeks, making it difficult to burn the grass which was their only source of fuel. The men in the party immediately broke the sod so they could plant crops and have "Dakota bricks" for their sod houses. Christine and her sister successfully dug a well and worked hard that summer, only to lose their crops to frost. With 50 pounds of wheat flour and 100 pounds of corn meal and milk from their cow to get them through the winter, they lived on a monotonous diet of milk and corn meal mush with little variation. Old gunny sacks provided covering for the feet of the children. A biographical sketch described the experience of Christine Kinz Bohler: "What trying times for poor Christine who often wept bitterly because of loneliness, homesickness and panic, but who never faltered and who never forgot that God was with her. Such faith, such courage, such strength!"[163]

JEFFERSON, 527

The story of the Grasshopper Cross located outside of town goes back to 1874. That year brought high hopes when crop yields appeared exceptional, but on a Sunday in July, people coming home from church saw a dark cloud. According to an eyewitness account, "The sky became dark. . . .Hoppers began falling on the roof and against the windows. It sounded like a continuous hailstorm. In one hour the field had been stripped. . . .In the garden everthing was taken. Onions and turnips were eaten out of the ground."[164] Some animals became crazed by the omnipresent insects. After about three days, the grasshoppers rose with the wind and left, leaving bitter reminders, even in the flavor of the meat of turkeys which had eaten the grasshoppers. The following year brought less hope and more grasshoppers, leaving settlers discouraged, disheartened and, in some cases, destitute. In May 1876, Father Boucher, a white haired man of faith, organized and led a procession around the fields that were devastated the previous two years. Many came to make the pilgrimage on that warm and muddy day in May. The procession left the church at 9 a.m., after the morning service, and was more than a mile in length. Father Boucher and his long line of followers prayed and sang as they walked, first to one cross set up in a field and then to another site where a cross had been erected. At sunset, the solemn group went back to the third cross at the church. In the year of the pilgrimage, grasshoppers were seen in the air above Jefferson, but they did not descend. *The Centennial History of Jefferson* says, "The people of the Jefferson area have said little about the power of the crosses, but among themselves they regard it as a tradition, and have come to look upon it as a miracle." The procession has been carried on in many of the years following as members of the community come together in thankfulness to pray for God's blessing on the crops.[165]

JUNIUS

It is hard to imagine reports of Junius in the *New York World* as a jumping land-boom site at the turn of the century. The booming town rocked on Saturday night, and the dances there were the place to be. Junius was nicknamed "Hollywood" because of all of the entertainment available.

KADOKA, 736

Kadoka, a Sioux word meaning "Hole in the Wall," was home to the movie crew for "Thunderheart" filmed in the area in 1991. Otherwise, it's a slow-paced western town, except when they have the World Outhouse Races, an event sanctioned by the World Outhouse Racing Association. Outhouses of certain specifications are pushed up and down Kadoka's main street, and pushers enter and exit the outhouse at designated exchange zones. (As outhouse rules go, what they do inside is their business.) Teams consist of two men and two women in this spiffy-biffy competition.

KELDRON

If you're looking for Hope, you'll find it about 13 miles south of Keldron. Kathleen Norris has put this special place of Hope on the map, having described it well in her book *Dakota: A Spiritual Geography.* Hope Presbyterian Church has 25 members and meets in an "an unassuming frame building that stands in a pasture at the edge of a coulee where ash trees and berry bushes flourish; choke cherry, snowberry, buffalo berry. The place doesn't look like much, even when most of the membership has arrived on Sunday morning, yet it's one of the most successful churches I know."[166] They sing the old hymns of the church accompanied by a honky-tonk style piano. If you need indoor plumbing or an organ, you will not like it. If, however, you appreciate warmth and friendliness with a flavor of ecumenicism, you will feel at home in this small, caring community which gathers for worship each week, sometimes with a pastor and sometimes with a lay preacher. Don't underestimate this group of farmers and ranchers who appear to be quaint, country folk. Most of them have college degrees, and they are thinking people with a global view who know and care about what is going on in the world. While they wholesomely affirm life, these are people who truly know that "All flesh is grass," but there is hope.

KENEL

Short-lived Fort Manuel was located between the present towns of Kenel and Wakpala on the bluffs of the Missouri River from August 8, 1812, to March 5, 1813. The fort was named for its founder, Manuel Lisa, who heard reports of Lewis and Clark as a trader in Saint Louis and planned the establishment of fur-trading posts farther up the Missouri. Fort Manuel had a blacksmith shop, warehouse, stockade and other buildings to which bands of Native Americans came to trade. Some Indians lived within the fort, one census count showing 65. Manuel's clerk, John Luttig, kept a journal that documented life at the fort, and on December 20, 1812, he wrote, "This evening the wife of Charbonneau, a Snake Squaw, died of a putrid fever. She was a good [sic] and the best woman in the fort, aged about 25 years. She left a fine infant girl."[167] Many think this was Sacajawea who, with her husband, assisted the Lewis and Clark expedition. Native Americans sympathetic with the British in the War of 1812 destroyed Fort Manuel (probably on March 5, 1813, the date of the last entry in Luttig's journal). Manuel Lisa then moved down the river with what he could salvage and traded at the Big Bend in the Missouri River.

KENNEBEC, 284

Someone lost a lot of money in Kennebec in late 1993! Honest finders in Lyman County turned the money in to the sheriff who waited to see if anyone would report money missing before making a public announcement. After publishing news that a large but unspecified amount was found, seven people indicated they had lost amounts from $7000 to $28,000, but only one story was a plausible match. If the money is not determined to be criminally linked, it will be returned to the finder. If the money is linked to criminal activity, it goes to the county coffers.

KEYAPAHA

It must have been a "Snow Goose!" An area resident's goose was missing for two weeks after a major snow storm. The farmer found it at the bottom of a deep hole in the snow where the plucky goose was alive but light as a feather, since it had no food after the storm. Her down coat served her well![168]

KEYSTONE, 232

Keystone is a tourist town which is greatly indebted to Gutzon Borglum who chose the nearby mountain for his monumental sculpture. An historical marker in Keystone tells the story:

GUTZON BORGLUM
John Gutzon de la Mothe Borglum
Born March 25, 1867 - Died March 6, 1941

His birthplace was Idaho. California first taught him art. Then France, who first gave him fame. England welcomed him. America called him home. His genius for the exquisite as for the colossal gave permanence on canvas, in bronze, in marble, to moods of beauty or passion, to figures of legend and history . . . At last he carved a mountain for a monument. . . .

The first actual carving was begun in 1927. The Washington head was dedicated in 1931, representing the founding of our government; the Jefferson in 1936 for the man who made our first great expansion west with the Louisiana Purchase; Lincoln in 1937 for his preservation of the Union; the final head, Roosevelt, in 1939, for the completion of the Panama Canal.

Borglum said, "I want somewhere in America a memory of the great things we accomplished as a nation, placed so high it won't pay to pull it down for lesser purposes."

The project was nearly completed in 1941 when Borglum died. Mount Rushmore was completed by his son Lincoln with the final drilling done October 31, 1941.[169]

KIMBALL, 743

The saloon keepers of the town had reason to worry when Carrie Nation, the temperance crusader, came to town. They put up a sign that said, "All Nations Welcome But Carrie." After Carrie Nation's first husband, a physician, died of alcoholism, she married a minister-lawyer in 1877 and was living in Kansas when she received a divine calling to destroy saloons. At first she delivered lectures and prayers, but then she took to using a hatchet to ruin saloons, resulting in 30 arrests. The sale of souvenir hatchets and lecture proceeds paid for her bail. One of her last tours was in South Dakota. A March 20, 1910 article described her:

> Mrs. Nation is a unique character. An old lady of 60 odd years, who has seen considerable of the hard side of life, been identified with the prohibition movement for years, growing more fanatical as each year rolls by, possessing a sharp tongue that knows how to say cutting things and isn't afraid of man or the devil. She is a drawing card at nearly every point where she is billed to lecture. . . .She says there is but one way to get rid of any evil, viz: to strike at and remove the cause; that absolute prohibition both of the manufacture and the sale of intoxicating liquors was the only solution of the saloon problem, and this can be accomplished only through the prohibition party.[170]

In her stop at Kimball, Carrie Nation gave one of her smashing lectures and had wooden hatchets available at the door but didn't engage in her "hatchet-ations" in the saloons.

KRANZBURG, 132

Fire was a constant dread in the lives of the prairie communities with vulnerable frame buildings. Whether sparked by a passing train or caused by an unquenched campfire ember, lightning or of unknown origin, fire represented a real threat to communities. Kranzburg endured much loss to fire over the years as it claimed a store, the Pioneer Cheese Factory, Spanish Villa, Holy Rosary School, Gillis' Playhouse and Heckathorn's place. But the Gump General Store endured, and Ludwig and son Louie presided there from 1904 to 1929. Louie Gump sported a handlebar moustache, black hat, pistol and red neckerchief. After the Spanish Villa burned in 1936, the town liquor business was moved to the Gump Store, then run by Mr. Kranz. Fire was not

Little Church on the Prairie

the only threat to Kranzburg, of which a Codington County historian wrote, "They faced the 'dry years', the 'black diptheria', 'Spanish influence', the 'crash', the 'depression' and are still a thriving community." [171]

KYLE

Nanwica Kciji, better known as Tim Giago, who is the publisher of *Lakota Times,* has fond memories of life in Kyle. He has written about life "around my home village of Pejuta Haka (Medicine Root), called Kyle by the Bureau of Indian Affairs." He reflected on the economy of Native American life in former times when, ". . .Lakota women made chokecherry jelly, plum preserves and canned vegetables from their garden." He recalled a day in 1939 when lightning struck and killed two cows:

> My dad and my Uncle Tom Vocu took out their knives and started to skin the two cows. . .
>
> After the butchering had progressed, Mr. Red Blanket placed his tub near one cow, and my dad and uncle put the intestines into it. I remember they filled the tub. Later I learned this was used to make a favorite Lakota (Sioux) meal called taniga. The tripe was boiled with timpsilas, a native turnip, or other vegetables and made into a soup.
>
> After Mr. Red Blanket loaded the tub on his wagon, he pulled away, and another Lakota family drove up in a Model-T pickup and unloaded its tub. And that's the way it was back then . . . everybody pulled together to get the job done and the meat was shared with the needy in the community. [172]

LADNER

Tucked away in the far northwest corner of the state are Cave Hills which contain a wealth of resources, history and geologic interest. Native Americans left pictures on the rocks. President Teddy Roosevelt was familiar with the area and established the Custer National Forest preserve in 1904. The land has uranium deposits which were mined in the 1950's and oil which is pumped today. Scenic Harding County is the most sparsely populated county of the state, with more square miles than people. If you want to get away from it all, Ladner is the place to go.

LAKE ANDES, 846

Native Americans came to the nearby lake to hunt and fish. The lake was first called Handy's Lake for an early fur trapper and later became Lake Andes, from which the town took its name. Andes is explained as a corruption of Handy in some sources, but Edward Andes was a surveyor for the American Fur Company.

The Lake Andes National Wildlife Refuge was established in 1936 with the purchase of 365 acres of land which was augmented by subsequent land purchases. Today, the Lake Andes complex consists of the Lake Andes National Wildlife Refuge, a waterfowl production refuge; the Karl E. Mundt National Wildlife Refuge, a sanctuary for a wintering bald eagle flock; and the Lake Andes Wetland Management District for preservation and management of 20,000 acres of waterfowl habitat in a 20 county area.

LAKE CITY, 43

Native Americans say a flour sack containing gold coins was buried between two straight willows at the east end of Long Lake. On his deathbed, Gray Foot told his sons about the treasure he had buried after some Santees took gold payroll coins from the agency at Marin, Minnesota, in 1862. When the War Department gave notice that possession of gold would constitute evidence of murder, Gray Foot buried the coins which have never been found.

Fort Sisseton was built in response to hostilities in 1862 that grew out of the frustration of Native Americans because of encroachment by settlers. The unrest of the Minnesota Santee Sioux spread into Dakota Territory, whereupon the United States government established a string of military posts to keep order. The soldiers at Fort Sisseton, built in 1864, never participated in a major battle but spent their time in keeping peace, patroling, performing daily tasks, and building the fort's stone and brick structures. In the 1880's, Fort Sisseton's military balls were the height of social activity. The fort, which can be visited today, was closed as a military post when the territory became a state in 1889.

LAKE NORDEN, 427

Baseball has long been a favorite pastime in the small towns of South Dakota; the game was played in fields and pastures when there wasn't an actual diamond. Today, as in yesteryear, youngsters learn to keep an eye on the ball at an early age and are eager to step to the plate and swing for all they're worth. Many pleasant afternoons and evenings have been spent at South Dakota ball games. Lake Norden is the site of the South Dakota Amateur Baseball Hall of Fame and has a fine ball park which Mel Antonen, a sportwriter for *U.S.A. Today,* remembers warmly:

> At Lake Norden's Memorial Park the infield grass is weedless and smooth. The base lines are cut into neat, straight lines. The foul poles are painted. The lights are the county's brightest. The popcorn is fresh and not sold in bags. There's an electric scoreboard in the outfield.
>
> A well-tagged home run to left field soars through the twilight and lands four or five rows deep in a cornfield. There is a grove of trees beyond center field and a red-brick nursing home behind the right-field fence.
>
> No batter has ever hit the nursing home on the fly, but the speculation always comes as players stand around during batting practice: Could it happen if Burt Tulson, a local carpenter known for his line-drive power, got hold of the right pitch?[173]

LAKE PRESTON, 663

The great pathfinder John C. Fremont passed through this area, surveyed the nearby lake and named it for his South Carolina senator. The first settlers found incredible flocks of waterfowl. In 1885, two hunters claimed to have brought down 49 birds with two shots, and some think this is entirely possible if every pellet of a possible ten-gauge claimed a bird in a huge flock.[174] With its strategic location close to a group of lakes, it is appropriate that Lake Preston should be the site of a spring wildlife festival emphasizing waterfowl.

LANE, 71

The *Alpena Journal* of July 19, 1907, reported: "Lane is a dry town since July 1st and the citizens thereof are learning that there is one thing more terrible than drink, and that is thirst."[175]

LANGFORD, 298

Old settlers were still around to help celebrate the 50th anniversary of Langford in 1936, and the June 12, 1936, *Bugle* provided this account:

> More than two thousand people lined our streets Thursday, June 11th for the parade which featured the opening day of the big event commemorating Langford's fiftieth birthday. . . . Popular airs by the Webster band, the banquet at the Methodist church at 12:00 o'clock noon for the pioneers, speaking, a ballgame between Claremont and Langford, free street acts, doll buggy parade and the bowery dance made up the first day's program, with the Art B. Thomas attractions thrown in for good measure on both days.[176]

LA PLANT

In the heart of the Cheyenne River Reservation, La Plant has long been a trading post for Indians, cowboys and ranchers. In this country, it is easy to imagine Native Americans pursuing herds of bison before the days when big cattle outfits ran their large herds on the open range. The cattle kingdom began in Texas before the Civil War and expanded northward into the grasslands of the plains region to cover an area of twelve states by 1876. The Homestead Act of 1862 promised 160 acres of land to homesteaders who would live on the land for five years, and wagon trains began rolling westward. Barbed wire, invented in 1873, made it possible to keep livestock within a confined area. The scene changed further as railroad interests promoted traffic in the Great Plains and advertised even as far away as Europe the wonderful opportunities in South Dakota. The open range closed, and the life of the cowboy changed forever.

LEAD, 3632

Lead, pronounced "Leed," was a mining camp which has endured. The name Lead City came from the lead mines containing rich veins of gold. That precious metal lured many miners and prospectors who camped in the area in 1876, and the town sprang into being. The Homestake operation staked a claim that year and began the removal of 48 million tons of rock, 15 percent of which was ore, giving rise to what was known as "The Open Cut." As the cut expanded, the very center of the city was torn out and relocated. Today, the Homestake operation continues with underground mining. For over a hundred years, miners have sought a rich but elusive deposit. In the 1990's, the Homestake Company invested $23 million dollars in an exploration tunnel known as the North Drift, hoping to hit the jackpot, but it hasn't "panned out."

LEBANON, 115

The country of Lebanon sent two cedars to each town with that name in the United States. The mayor of Lebanon, South Dakota, planted them in his yard with hopes that they would grow like a Cedar of Lebanon should. According to Psalm 92:12, "The righteous shall flourish like the palm tree: he shall grow like a cedar in Lebanon."

LEE'S CORNER

Intriguing glimpses of life in the fourteenth century have come from an area designated as a National Historic Landmark. The so-called Crow Creek massacre took place south of Lee's Corner on the Crow Creek Reservation. Archeologists learned that Native Americans living in earth lodges made pottery, hunted bison and grew crops of corn, squash and beans along the Missouri River. This site is unique because extensive fortifications and a long deep protective ditch and palisade surrounded the landward side of the village. Most remarkable, however, were the immense bone piles in which archeologists found 489 bodies which showed evidence of scalping and mutilation, an indication of a large battle fought there. The story of what happened to the people who lived in the fortified village 500 years ago will probably remain a mystery.

LEMMON, 1614

The illustrious G. E. Lemmon was one of South Dakota's first cowboys inaugurated into the National Cowboy Hall of Fame established in 1958. Ed Lemmon handled a record number cattle, estimated at over a million, in his lifetime from 1857 to 1946. G. E. (Ed) Lemmon owned the land where the town developed in 1907 and secured a fine home site for himself. He helped sponsor a 1908 three day jamboree that brought 5000 people to the town to celebrate the Fourth of July. In his later years, Ed Lemmon settled into the town named for him and counted his blessings as he reflected, "And now as I slowly mount the last, dim, distant mesa that marks the end of life's road, I have many of its rewards to enjoy. . .I have a fine little town on the Milwaukee Railroad, named after me."[177]

Although this town of less than two thousand may seem like an unlikely home for a pair of writers from New York City. Kathleen Norris and David Dwyer made that move in 1974, planning to stay only a few years. They moved into the home that had been Norris' grandparents and remained there, coming to an appreciation of the people and the prairie country with its buttes and grasses. Norris is somewhat surprised, but surely pleased by the interest in her book, *Dakota: A Spiritual Geography*, which describes a soulful journey in and around Lemmon.

LENNOX, 1767

On Thursday evenings in summer, a unique drive-in takes place as a semi-circle of cars forms around the Lennox band shell. While some of the audience line up their lawn chairs in front of the cars, others listen from their vehicles and register applause by honking horns, a tradition of long standing. The Lennox Municipal Band has been playing marches for over 100 years. Youngsters blend with oldsters to make music; a junior high drummer and an 83 year-old tuba player play in

Oh, the little old band in the little old town
And the silvery notes which come echoing down,
Which drift in a cadence of song all aglo
With memories sweet of the dim long ago.
The blare and the toot and the rattle and thrum,
And the resonant roll of the snappy drum;
Once more, as in hours of boyhood I stand,
With my feet keeping time to the little old band.
Oh, the little old band, what a welcome sight,
When they played on the square every Saturday night;
When lovers drove in from the country to hear
Those melodies echoing seetly and clear.
How soft was the music, how coaxingly sweet,
As you stood keeping time to the notes with your feet.
The little Main Street seemed a quaint fairyland
As you listened spellbound to the little old band.

Excerpted from the *Brown County News 75th Anniversary*
edition, p. 16

the band. Most of the thirty members come from other communities to make music which is greatly appreciated by local residents on summer nights in Lennox.[178]

LEOLA, 521

Leola has more rhubarb plants than people, 521 people and 942 rhubarb plants at last count. They do some wondrous things with that plant, the tastiest of which is the rhubarb kuchen that is served at their June Rhubarb festivals. In Leola, rhubarb is even used to make catsup.

LESTERVILLE, 168

The sturdy, hard-working people of German and German-Russian origin comprise approximately one-fourth of the state's population. Passions ran deep at the start of World War I, and it was a difficult time for some settlers of German origin who went extra lengths to prove they were loyal Americans. Menus omitted German dishes, and libraries put away German books. Place names related to Germany were renamed, and hamburger was called "victory steak." The use of the German language was banned in public gatherings, and those who used it in private were suspect. Feelings were so strong that Lesterville merchant C. F. Carlson was tarred and feathered on April 10, 1918, for continuing to do business with German people living in the area.

LETCHER, 164

Winter is a big part of life in South Dakota, enjoyed by many and endured by others. Farms rimmed in snow on sunshiny days of winter when the air is fresh and crisp are etched in the memories of many South Dakotans. Deb McIntyre, who grew up in Letcher and now lives in Sioux Falls, truly loves winter and said, "I love snow. I love sliding around. I love shoveling even, and building forts and making angels. I like the big flakes. I like the little ice drop things, too, even though they're slippery." McIntyre has fond memories of driving in the Letcher area with friends in her Ford Falcon and "drift bouncing" as they would go "in and out of ditches. It was like riding the waves."[179]

LILY, 26

The two dozen residents of Lily were saddened by the recent closing of the Lily Lutheran Church, the last of the town's three churches. There were fond reminiscences of baseball games in the pasture behind the parsonage and 4th of July fireworks put on by the Lutheran Brotherhood in years past. Members recalled kids smudged with coal dust after a Sunday School class in the furnace room and lutefisk and lefse banquets. The old church has been turned over to the Buffalo Plains Historical Society but will still be used for weddings and funerals.[180]

LITTLE EAGLE

A white woman whom the Native Americans fondly called Winona, meaning Princess, made her home among them at Little Eagle. Mary Collins came as a missionary in 1875 and lived among the Native Americans at Little Eagle for 25 years. Her log cabin home was used as school and church, and the Native American people often came to seek her advice and help. After ministering to the Indians for over 20 years, she was ordained. Rev. Miss Collins had great understanding and sympathy for the Native American people among whom she lived and worked. She wrote, "I so long to see the Indians of our land saved, treated as we should treat our own, with patience and love and every consideration. . ."[181]

LONE TREE

A well-known intersection between Colman and Egan is named for a tree which no longer exists. Lone Tree took its name from a cottonwood tree which Mrs. George Cameron planted in a hole left by a surveyor's stake in 1881. The tree became a familiar landmark which provided direction for a teacher and her 12 students seeking shelter in a blizzard in the late 1800's. The cottonwood was the subject of much debate when a highway came through, and its future was threatened. The massive tree was left standing as the highway was built around it, but disease necessitated removal of the lone tree in the 1950's.

LOWER BRULE

Lower Brule is at the southern end of a big bend in the Missouri River noted by all the early explorers of the area. River travelers often walked four miles across the narrow neck of land while their boat traveled the 25 mile loop. John James Audubon was pleased to do this on a steamboat trip up the Missouri River in 1843 because it provided an opportunity to observe the mammals and birds of the area. Three men from the boat were assigned to carry provisions and assist as guides and hunters for the overnight on land. From a hill, the party watched the progress of the boat and heard men cutting wood for the engines. On Saturday, May 27, 1843, they camped on the neck of land enclosed by the Big Bend, and Audubon wrote:

> At half-past three this morning my ears were saluted by the delightful song of the Red Thrush, who kept on with his strains until we were all up. . . No Wolves had disturbed our slumbers, and we now started in search of quadupeds, birds, and adventures. We found several plants all new to me, and which are now in press. All the ravines which we inspected were well covered by cedars of the red variety, and whilst ascending several of the hills we found them in many parts partially gliding down as if by the sudden effects of very heavy rain. We saw two very beautiful Avocets (Recurvirostra americana) feeding opposite our camp; we saw also a Hawk nearly resembling what is called Cooper's Hawk, but having a white rump. Bell joined the hunters and saw some thousands of Buffalo; and finding a very large bull within some thirty yards of them, they put in his body three large balls. . . .Our boat made its appearance at two o'clock; we had observed from the hill-tops that it had been aground twice.[182]

Audubon completed his acclaimed portfolio of birds and had begun studying and painting mammals by the time of his Missouri River travels. As a 58 year-old man, Audubon complained that he could "no longer draw twelve or fourteen hours without a pause or thought of weariness," but his eyesight was keen and his enthusiasm unfailing. He traveled up the Missouri to Fort Union in present North Dakota (close to the Montana border) and began the return trip to St. Louis on August 16, laden with specimens, journals and drawings. He promised his wife he would return home to New York before winter. Audubon worked on the mammalian project until his health failed. His sons, Victor and John, who were also artists, completed the work and published *The Viviparous Quadrupeds of North America*. John James Audubon died in 1851 at the age of 66.

The Missouri River journals, along with other journals of Audubon, were lost after his return to New York in November of 1843. More than 50 years later, two of Audubon's granddaughters found them in the back of an old secretary in 1896. Granddaughter Maria R. Audubon published the material in *Audubon and His Journals* in 1897.

LUDLOW

Gen. George Custer named nearby Ludlow Cave for his engineering officer when they were in the area in 1874, and the community took that name, too. Archeologists studying the cave had a particular interest in connections between Indians of the Great Plains and Rocky Mountains. Native American petroglyphs, old burial scaffolds, eagle-catching pits and teepee rings can be found in the area. Across the valley from Ludlow Cave, settlers found initials dated July 11, 1874, etched into the stone and added their initials to those of Custer's soldiers.

LYONS

There is no lyin' about the lion in a Lyons home. More than 50 mounted animals, including the mountain lion, were donated to the North American collection of the Delbridge museum at the Great Plains Zoo in 1993. Hunting became a passion of Vernell Johnson, a local auctioneer, who assembled a showcase of big and small game animals hunted in various parts of the world.[183]

MADISON, 6257

For 40 years after 1890, Madison was home to summer Chautauqua conferences which grew out of the summer assembly begun at Lake Chautauqua, New York, for the instruction of Sunday School teachers. Through books and lectures, the early

At the old depot: Conductor Paul Redfield

adult education program provided study in many subjects. In the 1890's, the Lake Madison Assembly offered classes in languages, English, political economy, pedagogy, geology, drawing, physical culture, botany, vocal drill, elocution, shorthand and typewriting.[184] The program attracted people who came by horse and stayed in 200 tents on the grounds. The Chautauqua association bought 60 acres of land, and as the popularity grew, facilities were built, including an auditorium for 2500, a Grand Hotel and a dance hall. Cabins were built in the area which developed as a summer resort on Lake Madison. The Chautauqua programs brought notable speakers including Booker T. Washington, William Jennings Bryan, Eugene Debs, William Howard Taft and Billy Sunday. There were such attractions as Opal Mae, "the world's greatest Child Elocutionist in Humorous and Pathetic Selections, also strong sacred numbers." The Fourth of July brought thousands (3000 - 10,000) of people to the Chautauqua grounds which provided "an opportunity for culture that no right-minded person should miss!!."[185] The Chautauqua series in Madison was offered for 42 consecutive summers, the last taking place in 1932 when other forms of summer entertainment replaced the summer gathering.

MANCHESTER

Harvey Dunn, the noted painter, illustrator and teacher, was born on a homestead in the Manchester area in 1884. He left the state to study at the Art Institute in Chicago and then opened a studio on the east coast. After visits to South Dakota each summer, the artist returned to his studio where he put his memories on canvas. Harvey Dunn said, "My search for other horizons led me around to my first," and his best known paintings are those which captured early South Dakota life. In 1950, Dunn donated to his home state a collection which is housed in the South Dakota Art Museum on the campus of South Dakota State University.

MANSFIELD

Lawrence Welk was playing with a small band at the time he dated a Mansfield woman. On a visit to the town, he asked to rent the Mansfield hall for a dance and was told he could rent the building if he provided the coal to heat it. Welk found a sack of coal at the coal yard, and the deal was done.[186]

Of dances in early Mansfield, a local resident recalled:

> It is no wonder people were so lively at the dances in the hall. You had to move to keep warm. The old coal stove in the northeast corner would be fired so hot, it blistered the wall behind it, but that was the only warm place. . . .The old theater seats completely circled the outside walls. They'd be filled with small children and older people watching the fun but dancing once in a while. When the youngsters got too sleepy they'd just curl up and nap in the seats.[187]

The Eva Novak Dancers came by railroad car with their own band and provided "dime a dance" entertainment. A fellow needed a pocket full of dimes if he wanted to do much dancing because the music stopped after just a swing around the hall, and then another dime was needed. The women were closely chaperoned and prohibited from dating the customers; so Mansfield men were discouraged from high hopes.[188]

MARION, 831

At last report, Doc Reding is still practicing medicine in Marion. He graduated from the high school there in 1928 and returned to set up a practice in Marion over 50 years ago. He remembers his patients with birthday cards and greetings because in his more than eighty years of living, patients have become friends. Dr. Reding still makes occasional house calls and schedules nursing home visits for Wednesday afternoon. Otherwise, he's in the office each day and Saturday mornings, too. His practice may pick up if word gets out that office calls are only $16.

MARTIN, 1151

Bravo for the people of Martin in their attempt to promote understanding through a group called UNITE, Understanding Neighbors in True Equality. Sometimes the Native American and whites in the community have had difficulties getting along. Said a Sicangu Lakota woman, Barb Sokolow, "I grew up very prejudiced, hating white people. I grieved over what our people have lost, how we handle things now, the loss of our land and buffalo. They took them. It's hard to get over growing up with that." A white resident spoke similarly of the prejudice with which he grew up. Jesse Gloe said, "I was as racist as anyone growing up in eastern South Dakota." As a Marine stationed in Egypt and Ecuador, he gained a perspective on being different from the dominant society. Now a Highway Patrol Officer based in Martin, Gloe is working with Sokolow as part of UNITE. The group seeks to promote understanding by bringing "Martin people together in a unity walk and picnic, special holiday programs, essay writing in the schools and support for the Indian center. A writers group is collecting interviews with people whose families have lived in the area for many generations." Breaking down barriers is a process of understanding taking place in Martin.[189]

MARTY

The donation of $1100 by a New York seamstress for land and a chapel on the Yankton Indian Reservation resulted in the St. Paul Indian Mission in 1913. Marty was chosen as the name of the community to honor the first Bishop of South Dakota, Abbot Martin Marty. The mission operated a boarding school, a vocational school, an orphanage and had the only community of Indian nuns in the United States. Printing became an important activity as the Marty mission published *The Catholic Indian Herald* and *The Little Bronze Angel.* In 1942, the Native Americans consecrated a new church, the result of their labor in making the bricks, cutting the stones, and doing the construction and decoration.[190] Sister Madeleine LeCompte was present on the day of dedication and today serves at St. Paul's. Four of the seven nuns assigned to the parish are Native Americans who help to minister to 130 families. Realizing the importance of self-determination, Benedictines gave responsibility for the school to tribal leaders in 1975.

MARVIN, 38

When the post office was established in 1882, Marvin was the name suggested by a local punster. He saw a Marvin safe in the railroad office and suggested that Marvin was a "good, safe name."[191]

Blue Cloud Abbey is a beautiful Benedictine monastary built in 1950 and named for Chief Blue Cloud, a convert of Father De Smet who brought the Gospel to the Native Americans. The abbey provides a serene place for retreat, and participation in evening vespers with the Benedictine community there is a meaningful experience. Visitors are welcome at the American Indian Culture Research Center on the grounds where Native American dress and relics, pictures and memorabilia are on display. Many of the pieces were gifts to Father Stan Maudlin, a great promoter of racial reconciliation and respect for cultural differences.

MAURINE

This little town in ranch country provided warm memories of Christmases past:

> Christmas Day dinners were home-raised turkey or beef. Vegetables from summer gardens, chokecherry and buffalo berry jam and Christmas cookies and cakes were part of my mother's menu. Fudge and divinity were home-made, too.
>
> Rural school Christmas programs included recitations and Santa Claus. All the kids tried to determine his identity by voice; few were fooled. Treats were sacks of Christmas candy from the Maurine, S.D., store. A neighbor who has a beautiful voice sang Silent Night at Red Top School programs. . . .
>
> It was fun during Christmas vacations to help one of my uncles with chores at this place.
>
> Sleeping in the sheep wagon and listening to yuletide songs on KFYR out of Bismarck and WNAX of Yankton enhanced the visit.[192]

McINTOSH, 302

After much debate and political maneuvering, two states were formed from Dakota Territory in 1889, adding four Republican senators rather than two. South Dakota Senator Pettigrew urged the Federal government to place markers along the boundary between South and North Dakotas, and 720 granite markers, weighing 800 pounds each, were installed along the border at a cost of $25,000. "S.D." and "N.D." were chiseled on opposite sides of the ten inch square markers, and the mileage from the easternmost boundaries was indicated on a third side. Many of the markers remain in place along the boundary which passes a mile north of McIntosh.[193]

John Gunther observed in 1947, "Nothing is more remarkable than the differences between the Dakotas. . . .North Dakota is probably the most radical state in the union, and South Dakota is one of the most conservative."[194] The skyscraper style statehouse in Bismarck and the stately capitol in Pierre, a modified Montana capitol design, reflect the differences. Although similar in population, geography and having an agricultural based economy, South Dakota has gold, timber, a diversified industry and more tourism than its neighbor to the north. North Dakotans grow wheat, whereas most South Dakota farmers and ranchers raise livestock. Loyalties prevail, and South Dakotans in McIntosh and elsewhere are glad, for whatever their reasons, to be "south of the border."

McLAUGHLIN, 780

Major James McLaughlin, for whom the town was named, was an Indian agent assigned to the Standing Rock Reservation in Dakota Territory in 1881. The agent served under twelve Presidents and "conducted more treaties with the Indians than any other official in the history of the country."[195] McLaughlin and his wife, who was one-quarter Sioux, understood and appreciated Native American culture, and he wrote a book entitled, *My Friend, the Indian,* first published in 1910. When he died in 1923, James Mc Laughlin's funeral was held outdoors so his many friends in the West could pay tribute.

MEADOW

Madge Pickler, the daughter of the state's first Congressman, was a colorful woman who grew up in the family mansion in Faulkton. After study in St. Louis, she taught "expression" and dramatic reading at Redfield College and Fort Worth University. Madge was the subject of a New York newspaper article which told of her summer work as a superintendent of a Colorado mine. She put on a miner's outfit and descended with her candle to supervise her work force, spending the day underground. At the end of the day's work, she serenaded the crew on her guitar and sang songs learned in her family home. Nathaniel Hoy persuaded Madge to be his wife, and in 1908 they homesteaded near Meadow and established the first newspaper in the area.

MECKLING

The saying goes: "Make hay while the sun shines!" But the National Hay Association's convention in Meckling in 1993 was held in the rain. It didn't stop over a thousand people from coming together to do business and look at vintage equipment and the dream machines of today's haymakers. Hay bales were rolled in competition, and since it was too wet to work outside anyway, convention-goers enjoyed good food and fellowship inside.

MELLETTE, 184

One of the most colorful people in Mellette's history was Charles Morgan Howe, a Vermont native, who sailed around the world in his ship, "The Tropic Bird." Upon his return, he sold the ship, married a wealthy and socially prominent Vermont woman and moved westward. He became a Mellette businessman and also had farming interests, eventually holding many acres in the area. In about 1883, Howe and his wife built a unique round house which became a Mellette landmark. The idea of the rounded lines came from elevator design which held up to internal pressure and external forces of winds whipping across the prairie. Charles and Mary Jane Bickford Howe had a large collection of books, of which a thousand volumes were given to the Mellette Public Library.[196]

MENNO, 768

The early settlers of Menno were German-Russians who left Russia because of oppression. Happy to be free, they chose the name Freeman. However, Menno got the name that Freeman was supposed to have, because railroad employees put up the wrong signs at the two locations. Menno is taken from the name of Menno Simons, the early leader of the Mennonites who was influenced by the Anabaptist movement that came out of the Protestant Reformation.

MIDLAND, 233

One can step into the past in an old hotel in Midland which retains the feel of yesteryear. Besides rooms, the Stroppel Hotel offers mineral baths to preserve health and provide relief for ailments. Geothermal water, which comes out of the ground at 119°F, is cooled before going into the four-foot deep baths. The hotel enjoyed a heydey in the 1940's when Midland was on the major east-west route, and many thousands of people came for health baths. A brochure stated, "For the preserving of general health, we do not believe there is a better place in the world nor a more valuable mineral water." Twenty-one baths and sweats over a three-week period were recommended for best results. Business declined as tourists traveled on I-90, 13 miles south of Midland, and today the owner has time to relax at the Stroppel spa in the quiet ranch town of the Bad River Valley.[197]

Snakes alive! - and at the school! When one of the fourteen students at the Kirley Road School reached for her shoes in the cloakroom on an autumn day in 1993, she faced a rattler. Some of the older students bravely dealt with the snake which was probably seeking a warm place as the weather turned colder. When four more rattlesnakes were found in the schoolyard, almost everyone was rattled. School was cancelled for a day-and-a-half while cautious workers removed 30 rattlesnakes, bull snakes and their eggs from a sidewalk burrow, using a backhoe. Science projects developed from the experience, and all fourteen students at Kirley School learned about herpetology.

MILBANK 3879

Stone quarried in the area by six companies has been used for monuments and buildings throughout the United States and elsewhere. Milbank's beautiful reddish brown stone, known as Dakota mahogany, was used in the American embassy in Saudi Arabia. A massive formation of granite, stretching from Big Stone, South Dakota, eastward into Minnesota, contains some of the oldest known rocks on earth dated at 4.2 billion years. (You have to go to the moon to find rocks older than that.) A mountain range developed about four billion years ago when two large granite plates collided to form the Canadian Shield. The only remnants that can be seen today are the granite roots of that ancient mountain range in the area of Milbank and Big Stone City. Milbank granite is indeed a "Rock of Ages."[198]

MILLBORO

Have you heard about the laundry out on the line for two-and-a-half months? On a mild January day in 1952, a Millboro woman hung her laundry outdoors. A storm blew in quickly and with fury, leaving the laundry buried in a drift of snow. An eighteen-foot drift filled the space between two houses in Millboro. Some folks walked on top of the snow to tie ribbons in the tree tops to serve as a summer reminder of the height of the snowdrifts. The laundry hung to dry on January 21 was not seen again until April 9 when the tops of two of the sheets could be seen.[199]

MILLER, 1678

The women of Miller decided to take matters into their own hands to control the behavior of certain loose women in the early years of the town. The following was reported in a *Huronite* article of the time:

> For some time past the women of our little city have been considering the question of eliminating certain females from the public dances. While no names were mentioned, at a meeting held at the home of one of our prominent citizens, three well known female residents were singled out to be the victims. It was unanimously agreed that should any one of them be brought to the dance to be given Tuesday evening, the escort should be refused the privilege of dancing with other women there. Evidently through some misunderstanding one of our very best citizens escorted one of these women from the post office to the dance. He insisted it was only done as a courtesy done by others in the past, but the women didn't take it in this light. Even his own wife refused to have him for a partner. This started a row that broke up the evening's entertainment and so far as your correspondent can learn the situation is worse than it was before.[200]

MILLTOWN

A swimmer on the James River came to Milltown in spring of 1993. Wayne Thompson, a 50 year-old fitness instructor from Oregon, swam 150 miles of the James River from Mitchell to Yankton in nine days. Thompson spent eight to ten hours a day in the water, even eating while in the water. The spring swim was a prelude to a planned 2000 mile swim in 1994 from Mitchell to New Orleans, the only route "that offers 2000 miles of navigable water without a dam." The feat should qualify for the *Guinness Book of World Records.* Thompson had swum the navigational length of the Missouri River from Yankton to New Orleans in 1977, but because he wore fins, he was not credited with a world record.[201]

MINA

A big story came out of the little community of Mina with the find of a massive head of an Imperial Mammoth that died in a bog. Elephants lived in this part of the world in both pre- and post-glacial times, and the specimen found near Mina was one of five species of elephants that lived in the area. The head can be seen today at the South Dakota School of Mines and Technology in Rapid City.[202]

MISSION, 730

Beat the drums with news of the Eagle Creek Drum Group, a talented group of young Native American musicians who began singing and playing as a family group. Joe White Buffalo, of the Antelope community near Mission, carried on a family tradition as he sang with his sons. Joe's father was a singer, and Joe's son Calvin is now lead singer of the group that picked up the songs by listening to relatives. The performing group expanded to ten members, most of whom are related and under 20 years old. They travel the powwow circuit and have played as far away as Arizona and Ohio, taking honors in competition. A powwow takes place somewhere in the state almost every summer weekend, and if you are lucky, you'll hear the Eagle Creek Drum Group perform.[203]

Ray's Snake Den in Mission sells an unusual $75 toilet seat of clear plastic with a rattlesnake embedded. Actor Jack Nicholson is reported to have one of the seats, and a strategically placed sign in Nicholson's bathroom asks, "Does it really matter?"[204]

MISSION HILL, 180

The venerable Vangen Norwegian Evangelical Church is the oldest Lutheran Church standing in South Dakota. The white wooden structure built in 1869 is surrounded by gravestones and is quiet today, used only for special services since 1918 when a brick structure replaced it. If the sexton happens to be around, you can see the interior of the old church with its beautifully painted altar and old Norwegian Bible. A third generation Norskie, Melford Severson will translate the passage from Matthew, "Kommer hid til mig, Alle, fom arbeide, og ere befverede og jeg vil give eder kvile," and dispense some theology and a Norwegian joke, too.

MISSION RIDGE

The Triple U Ranch is home to the largest private buffalo herd in the world. About 3500 buffalo graze on the 60,000 acre ranch which deer, antelope, bobcats, coyotes, rattlesnakes and grouse also call home. Today, the ranch is run by Kaye Ingle, but her father, Roy Houck, was the boss until his death at age 87. The producers of "Dances With Wolves" negotiated with Roy Houck ($1000 per day for four days of work with the buffalo in addition to a few hundred dollars in other fees) to use the ranch for filming portions of the movie. The awesome scenes of thousands of buffalo on the move were filmed on the ranch with the assistance of area ranchers and wranglers who used ten pick-up trucks and a helicopter to move 3000 buffalo into camera range.[205]

The isolated Orton country school has sometimes had only one student. Few teachers last more than a year because it is so lonely, but a former student now in college said, "I loved it. I thought I learned a lot." *Weekly Reader* featured a story about the unusual school when Levi Tibbs was the only student in the 1989-1990 school year. He finished eighth grade leaving his cousin, kindergartener Dianna Tibbs as the only student. The board keeps the school open at a cost of about $30,000 annually. Several generations of Tibbs have attended the school, and riding a horse to school, at least occasionally, is a tradition in the family that claims rodeo standout Casey Tibbs.[206]

MITCHELL, 13,798

A public-spirited resident of a century ago promoted the idea of a Corn Palace in Mitchell. The idea was not unique since other communities decorated buildings as part of harvest celebrations, although the decorations were not permanent. Townspeople raised $3700, and in 1892, erected the first Mitchell Corn Palace, an elaborate and beautifully decorated structure. The achievement was celebrated with an agricultural exhibition and a week of festivities under the heading "Corn Belt Exposition." The grand success yielded a $3000 profit. A souvenir booklet in 1893 stated,

> . . .so grand an affair lifts the minds above the humdrum duties of life and gives play to the higher faculties of the man. . . .Then the visitor leaves the workshop, the farm or the home, and receives a lasting benefit from the beautiful sights and fine music. . . .This beautiful Corn Palace and the magnificent display of corn from all the corn belt counties is the most undoubted proof of the absolute truthfulness of all that has ever been claimed for south east Dakota.[207]

In 1905, a permanent structure was built, and it was used until the present Corn Palace replaced it in 1937. Each year the exterior facade is redesigned and redecorated with several hundred bushels of native corn and about 4000 pounds of grain and grasses at a cost in excess of $35,000 annually. The designs by the artist chosen are sketched on roofing material with codes indicating colors and materials. All colors are natural, but at least ten different colors of corn are used in shades of red, maroon, yellow, green and blue. Oscar Howe, a Native American artist who was a student in Mitchell, designed the exterior panels from 1948 until 1971. His designs for six interior panels are still in use, although the materials are replaced about every ten years. The Corn Palace attracts 10,000 people a day in peak season in July and draws crowds for a week of festivities and big-name entertainment each fall.

MOBRIDGE, 3768

On a hilltop overlooking the Missouri River bridge and west of the river, a statue honors Sacajawea, the Native American woman who traveled with the Louis and Clark expedition. (The name has been given varied spellings because of transliteration from the Shoshone language in which the name means Bird Woman.)

Sacajawea, a Shoshone, was captured by another tribe when 12 or 13 years of age and later became the wife of Touissant Charbonneau, a fur trader on the Upper Missouri. Captain Meriwether Lewis hired Charbonneau as an interpreter for the Corps of North Western Discovery and wrote in his journal of the birth of Charbonneau and Sacajawea's child in the winter camp at Fort Mandan in present North Dakota. On February 11 of 1805, Lewis described the difficult labor and the administration of bits of snake rattler mixed in water to help speed the delivery which occurred ten minutes after Sacajawea took the potion. Charbonneau persuaded Lewis and Clark to allow Sacajawea and their infant son, Jean Baptist, to accompany the expedition when the party broke camp in the spring. After the explorers endured a severe storm in May of 1805, Captain Lewis wrote, "This Indian woman to whom I ascribe equal fortitude and resolution with any person on board, caught and preserved most of the light articles that were washed overboard." In June, Sacajawea became very ill and was given medical care by Lewis. He wrote, "I blead her which rendered her great service." Her condition was noted as "extreemely sick" and "Verry [sic] bad and will take no medison."[208] Fortunately, the Shoshone woman recovered. A touching scene occurred when Sacajawea was called to interpret between Chief Cameahwait and the captains. ". . .she recognized Cameahwait as her own brother. She flew to him and embraced him most fondly and brother and sister were moved to tears of joy."

Sacajawea was called Janey by members of the Lewis and Clark party who became very fond of her. A record of the expedition stated,

> One of the first acts of the captains when they met the Shoshonie was to buy a horse for Janey that she might make the way easier with her child.
>
> The most difficult portion of the journey was through the mountains in the Shoshonie country and Janey was the good

angel that softened for them all the rigors of the hard road. Any request she made of her people was gladly granted and in times of great destitution the Indians cheerfully divided with them their scanty fare. They guided them by the easiest paths, taught them the wild-craft that made life possible in the inhospitable region and finally conducted them to the waters of the Columbia.[209]

At Christmas, the men exchanged gifts, and Sacajawea gave Captain Clark "her most cherished ornament, a sheaf of the tails of the white weasel." On the return trip in the months that followed, Sacajawea provided guidance in travel from winter quarters on the Columbia River to the Continental Divide, directing the party through Bozeman Pass. When Captain Lewis was accidentally shot by one of his men, ". . .she repaid the care given to herself the previous summer during her illness, by tenderly nursing him, staying with him almost constantly until her home was reached on August 17th."[210]

Captain Clark became very fond of the child, whom he called "my boy Pomp" and offered to take him at the end of the expedition in 1806. Historian Doane Robinson wrote that before 1810, they (presumably the parents) "took the child to St. Louis where he was kept and educated by Captain Clark." Sacajawea died in 1812, and according to Robinson, Captain Clark took responsibility for her ten year-old son and a one year-old daughter.[211]

MONROE, 151

It might seem strange that Monroe has two Reformed churches, but the separate congregations go back to a time when one group worshipped in German and the other in Dutch. Although both worship in English today and share the same theology, the traditions of long standing make the two congregations a fact of life in Monroe.

Gert and Lester Griebel run the Main Street hardware and seed store. For many years, Gert tended the store, providing supplies for area farmers. In between customers, she sewed, did needlework and enjoyed visiting with family and friends who stopped to see her at the store. If the cafe next door was busy

Looking Sheepish

and needed help, she left her place of business to lend a hand at the cafe. Customers knew where to find her if help was needed; otherwise, they helped themselves to supplies, leaving payment or a note on the counter.

MONTROSE, 420

Summer of 1993 was the time of the great Midwest deluge when water did much damage in Montrose. Pride and self reliance made the residents reluctant to accept help, but Red Cross volunteers came from many states. The American Legion hall became a cafeteria where Red Cross workers served 700 meals on July 7, 1993. The grateful people of Montrose were appreciative of the help as they struggled to get back into their flood-damaged homes. Friendships were formed between residents and volunteers from all over the country who will be receiving Christmas greetings from friends in Montrose.

MOSHER

"2 Men Drag Each Other to Mosher," was the header in a report coming out of the Rosebud blizzard of 1952. In the severe winter storm, an Old Home Bread truck driver decided to leave his loaves in his stuck truck and walk ten miles to Mosher from Highway 18, a "fer piece" in good conditions. Then, he found Alva Sampson all wrapped up in a quilt in his stalled vehicle. The two men decided to face the storm together and set off afoot for Mosher in the worst of weather. They helped to keep each other going and made it to the Mosher store, a mighty fine place to be on that January day in 1952.[212]

MOUND CITY, 89

A country school teacher has fond memories of her days of teaching near Mound City. Erma Zoss wrote:

> The first school I taught was the Sherman School in Campbell County near Mound City, South Dakota. All ten of my pupils were of German descent and we struggled with the language; they were a very good bunch of "kids.". . . the one-room school in that little valley in Campbell County still holds the dearest memories for me. The road going by was no more

than a trail; the mail was delivered three times a week, but the patrons were so nice to the "all English teacher." And when I'd leave to go to my boarding place a mile and three-quarters away, it would sometimes be dusk, and the lights of Mound City would be twinkling in the distance. . . .

I have many happy recollections of my fifteen years of teaching in country schools of South Dakota. I remember:
- the first day of school, the ringing of the brass handbell each morning, noon, and recess.
- the uncomfortable shoes and stiff new overalls. The younger children sat barefoot in warm weather and put their shoes on again before they went home at night.
- how we sang songs and read stories for opening exercises which always ended with the flag salute, the Y.C.L. (Young Citizens League) song and pledge.
- the sore thumbs and fingers the boys received from playing marbles. Each marble was usually lovingly named, such as Aggie, Pee Wee, and Clayball.
- the trouble the boys had remembering that they could not bolt the classroom everytime a gopher ran across the school yard.
- Y.C.L. Day in the spring when we took a sack lunch and went to Woonsocket to present a chorus and plays and entertainment.
- how "hot lunches" meant potatoes roasted in the ashpan.
- how the students rode horseback to school or came in horse drawn shods.
- the bouquets of pasque flowers, dandelions, and cat tails; the vase was a tin vegetable can.[213]

MOUNT VERNON, 368

The headline in the *Mt. Vernon Gazette* of Thursday, April 4, 1889, read, "The Business Portion of Mt. Vernon Entirely Destroyed by Fire. One Hundred Families Destitute." It was indeed "A Day of Dire Disaster" for the little town. Prairie fires were a great danger to the settlers. When the residents saw smoke off to the northwest of Mt. Vernon, they attempted to make a fire break by putting down wet gunny sacks, but fierce winds reduced the effectiveness of their efforts. Water was scarce and had to be carried a long distance while the bucket brigade fought bravely. All of the business structures and most of the homes were destroyed along with four grain elevators and twenty freight cars. One person perished, and a hundred families were homeless. The people of Mitchell sent a special train with supplies for the people of Mt. Vernon, and the rebuilding began at once.

MUD BUTTE

Mud Butte is not a pretty name, but it was taken from the nearby butte that lacks vegetation and looks like a pile of mud. Says one area rancher, "Mud Butte is where the sheriff knows where we're at and doesn't come for us, and the Jehovah's Witnesses seldom come." [214]

A partial skeleton of a Tyrannosaurus was found near Mud Butte in 1981. The world's biggest meat eaters were about 16 feet tall and weighed seven tons.

MURDO, 679

Ranching has always been an important part of Murdo's history, its name taken from an early cattleman, Murdo McKenzie, who managed the Matador Cattle Company which ran thousands of head of cattle on the rangeland of South Dakota.

Winifred Angel Ziemann told of when the Milwaukee Railroad came to Murdo:

> We thought it was going to be a city about the size of Chicago, the way people talked. The town was mapped out and lots put up for sale. They sold for anything anyone bid for them. There was no place for anyone to eat. There was a number of very important railroad officials coming. Something had to be done. Our niece had homesteaded a half mile from town but had never lived there. We moved her shack to town, borrowed a stove, built some saw horses, laid some heavy planks across them for tables. We built a sort of shadeout over the tables from the shack. The grass was the floor carpet. Thus the first restaurant was opened.
>
> We cooked the food in the shack and carried it out. We fixed things as nice as we could. They ate and enjoyed the meal immensely. We wondered if we dared ask 50 cents apiece. When they had finished, they each handed us $1.00.

They said it was well worth it. We would never have thought of asking that much but they said it was worth that much to eat in a dining room with such lovely floors.[215]

MYSTIC

According to one source, "A Burlington railroad worker found a mistake on his map and noted it plain as could be: 'Mystic'."[216] (Some spelling is bad - but that bad?) Another explanation is based on Indians' regard for the area as a place of mystery. Whatever the explanation, many vacationers have enjoyed the mystique of Mystic. The McCahan Memorial Chapel, a pretty little log cabin church, has a bell from a railroad engine that ran the Rapid City, Black Hills and Western Railroad route to Mystic. A John Crane painting entitled "Snowy Sanctuary" beautifully portrays the little church in Mystic.

NEMO

Gen. George A. Custer and his expedition of 1874 passed through the area as they moved northward out of the Black Hills. Some Nemo residents researched and marked the trail so that part of it can be followed on foot today. It has been said that, "Custer led the way. Half the world followed."[217] Northwest of Nemo where Box Elder Creek joins Bogus Jim Creek, the Custer expedition camped on their northward return trip to Fort Abraham Lincoln and reportedly, "buried arms, ammunition, and some whiskey. However, no discovery of the reported cache ever verified the truth of the story."[218]

NEW EFFINGTON, 219

Effington was named for spunky Miss Effie Staufer who successfully homesteaded on her own in the area, despite the doubts of many. Effington became New Effington when it relocated to a townsite on the Fairmont and Veblen Railroad in 1913. Lots in the new townsite were sold at a public auction, and a fine Main Street location could be purchased for $300 to $500, corner lots bringing the higher prices. Entertainment was provided by an African-American male quartette from Minneapolis. Hard work followed the hoopla as they moved the whole town down the road about a mile and added some new buildings.[219]

NEWELL, 675

"The Russians Are Coming! The Russians Are Coming!" In December of 1993, four Russian generals of the Russian Strategic Rocket Forces high command came to visit dismantled missile silo sites to verify compliance with terms of the Strategic Arms Reduction Treaty. News crews came, too. Ed Bradley of "60 Minutes" documented the inspection by the Russian commander-in-chief and other military leaders of the removal of the 124th missile of the 44th Missile Squadron at site November 3 near Newell. The other part of the "60 Minutes" story took place in Russia where Bradley visited Russian missile sites with an American general.

NEW HOLLAND

New Holland is the center of a pocket of Dakota Dutch who settled in Douglas County. When carelessness with a clay pipe caused a prairie fire, infuriated Native Americans almost chased out the Dutch before they settled.

The *Harrison Globe* provided news of its Dutch sister communities and in June of 1921 reported, "The young people of the New Holland and Joubert communities held a big picnic at White Lake last Thursday and it was a big success. A big dinner was served after which cigarettes were passed. (Some of the girls indulged, too.) Bathing was one of the features of the day's sport and we here suggest the next time those 'going in' bring along their bathing suits. . ." [220]

NEW UNDERWOOD, 553

Walter Dale Miller, Governor of South Dakota from 1993 to 1994, is a rancher and businessman from New Underwood, comfortable in a broad brimmed hat and boots. The veteran legislator became a leader in the state capitol. He was lieutenant governor under Governor George Mickelson and assumed the office of governor after Mickelson's tragic death in an airplane crash in 1993. Miller took some of his governing philosophy from his ranching experience: "A rancher in my part of the state knows you must continually check your fences. If he fails to do that, he knows he will lose his business. We have to do the same thing with state government." [221]

NISLAND, 174

Green grow the gardens of Nisland and surrounding communities which have benefited from the Belle Fourche Irrigation Project, a project of the Federal government. Parts of the Belle Fourche Valley are irrigated during summer months with water from the Orman Dam built early in the century. The far sighted Government Reclamation Project transformed arid land into productive land which has yielded cucumbers, sugar beets, alfalfa and other crops.

NORRIS

A young woman, who first came to South Dakota in 1914 to visit her brothers on a two-week vacation from school in Iowa, provided some exceptional glimpses of life in and around Norris:

> To a rather reserved young girl, the change from the rather restricted conditions which are usually found in older communitities to the open-handed, outgoing attitude of those pioneers was positively fascinating. One forgot the hardships, inconveniences and lack of comforts. Any social affair was welcome so we had a "Bachelor quilting Party" during my first visit. All the neighbors came. The men brought needles along (some of their needles were almost as big as spikes), and they tied two comforters that evening. Of course a dance followed. I had never danced before. I had never ridden on horseback either, so that was the first thing I had to learn.[222]

NORTH SIOUX CITY, 2019

This southeastern border community is truly a Gateway city. The boxes resembling spotted cows contain the products shipped from the Gateway 2000 Corporation in North Sioux City. The young corporation has taken the personal computer market by storm. The Fortune 500 company began in 1985 and was selling over a billion dollars of computer products a year in the early 1990's.

NORTHVILLE, 105

One of baseball's all-time great players came from the Northville-Ashton area. Charley (Deacon) Phillippe pitched for

Ashton in the 1890's, and word of his pitching arm spread far and wide. He was selected by the Pittsburgh Pirates for a tryout, pitched for a few minor league games and then was went to big league in 1901. Pittsburgh relied heavily on Phillippe in the World Series in 1903 when they played the Boston Red Sox led by Cy Young. In the nine games, Phillippe won three games and lost the last two, which, unfortunately, were the final games of that World Series.

NUNDA, 45

Lutefisk, scorned by some, is a treat for many Norwegian Americans. Says Gene Anderson of Nunda, "It's great. When you're brought up on it, you acquire a taste for it. . .My dad used to have a sack of it they kept under my bed. Mice would eat on it. We'd eat on it. It was dried and heavily salted." Some doubt that mice would want to touch dried and salted cod which is soaked in lye and rinsed before it's cooked. You can think of lutefisk as a piece of cod that passeth understanding.[223]

OACOMA, 367

This Missouri River area contains one of the world's largest manganese deposits. The ore nodules appear as reddish-blue chunks on the land surface. The metal has applications in making alloys for hard steels. The local manganese supply has been of interest when politics have interrupted imports from Russia and the African Gold Coast, but it has not been actively mined because, although plentiful, it is of a low grade.

OELRICHS, 138

In the area east of Oelrichs, the Black Hills and Canadian trail was the main route for thousands of cattle run from Texas to the open Dakota range until about 1887. Herds of 3000 cattle were driven northward, and by 1884, between 700,000 and 800,000 head of cattle pastured on South Dakota's range. Oelrichs took its name from the president and general manager of the Anglo-American Cattle Company and became headquarters for their operation, the largest in the area at the time with 34,000 head of cattle. That's a lot of beef!

OGLALA, 394

The oldest known prehistoric site in South Dakota is near Oglala. Archeologists from Augustana College in Sioux Falls, South Dakota, determined that hunters killed and butchered a mammoth there more than 11,000 years ago. The find, discovered in 1981, was an archeologist's dream come true, missed by the Smithsonian years earlier when the scientists ignored Mr. Ferguson's report of interesting evidence on his property. On the Lange-Ferguson site, archeologists found a Clovis spearhead with its partial fluting and two other spearheads close to the remains of a mammoth and also bone tools used in butchering.

OKREEK

Okreek is an old trading post and issue station originally known as Oak Creek. The name Okreek was an accommodation to postal service preference for a one-word name. Chief Good Voice, a leader instrumental in building the first church and school, encouraged his people to work the land and care for their stock.

"Indian Ranch on the Rosebud" was the subject of a painting by Okreek artist Godfrey Broken Rope a century later. Broken Rope, a self-taught artist, beautifully captured on canvas many Rosebud landscapes. His work was part of a 1970 exhibition called "Contemporary Sioux Painting" which displayed the work of outstanding Sioux artists including Oscar Howe, Robert Penn, Arthur Amiotte and 17 others.[224]

OLDHAM, 189

"Oldham's burning!" became an unfortunately familiar cry in pre-World War I days. The community was devastated by fires in 1911, 1914, 1915 and 1917 and must have had some very experienced firefighters. It was said that, "Everyone turned out to pray and fight, alternately."[225] One building that, fortunately, didn't burn was the Socialist Hall built by the Socialist Party in 1912. When the Socialist movement became unpopular, the "ist" was removed, although you can still see the shadow of those letters on the building which was moved in 1970 to Prairie Village where it is used for plays, old time fiddler concerts, polka bands and other entertainment. In 1991, the Social(ist) Hall was renamed the Lawrence Welk Opera House in honor of the band leader who made his stage debut there in 1924.

OLIVET, 74

The pastor of the Methodist church in Olivet was reminded of the Galilean Hills as he looked at the banks of the James River; a pageant based on the miracles of Jesus came to mind. The area provided a natural ampitheater, and in 1977, the pageant, which became a tradition, was born. Farmers, homemakers, salesmen, teachers, students and others participate in the cast of 65. The audience provides their own seating, but they don't mind since there is no admission charge, although a free will offering is taken.

ONAKA, 52

If you like mountain oysters, you might want to visit Onaka.

> For the past several years Onaka has been putting on two or three mountain oyster fries every winter. These usually are held at Ralph's Bar with an assortment of other goodies for the less hardy souls. These little jewels are saved up all summer on the farms and ranches of our community. The farmers and cattlemen in our area were brought up to waste nothing and find a use for everything. I question the name mountain oysters as I'm sure there are more produced here on our prairies than anywhere in the mountains. When the slow season or winter arrives the farmers plot ways of getting together and mountain oysters always draw a very good and diversified crowd. There usually are several non-indulgers and beginners in the crowd. Ones taste buds must be finely tuned and ones inhibitions dulled a little to really enjoy these little delicacies especially for the novice. A few rounds of liquid refreshment usually synchronizes ones thinking and the cooks are pushed into action and kept very busy....They fry these little rascals differently to suit the fads and fantasies of everyone there. These are very tasty but also very rich so one should not over-indulge in these little morsels. It provides a way to get the community together for a very pleasant evening of visiting with neighbors and friends and escape the worries and responsibilities of everyday living. I do hope someone doesn't find an abundance of snails in our area.[226]

(If you are wondering what mountain oysters are, they are male bovine gonads. This is the same town that had a sparrow feed in the thirties.)

ONIDA, 761

The Onida area became the site of an African-American settlement in South Dakota in 1920. Although the black population of the state has always been small, they have made a distinct contribution. The first black person to come to what is now South Dakota was York, a slave given to the explorer William Clark by his father in 1799. York accompanied Clark on the 1804 expedition with Meriwether Lewis. York had a sense of humor and put on quite a show for the Native Americans. A chronicler of the expedition wrote:

> The object which appeared to astonish the Indians most was Captain Clark's servant York, a remarkably stout, strong negro. They had never seen a being of that color, and therefore flocked round him to examine the extraordinary monster, By way of amusement he told them that he had once been a wild animal, and caught and tamed by his master; and to convince them showed them feats of strength which added to his looks, made him more terrible than we wished him to be.[227]

An estimated one of four cowboys was black. African-Americans worked on the steamboats, and some settled in Dakota Territory. Some came as homesteaders after the Civil War while others came with the Gold Rush or military assignment. The Twenty-fifth Infantry, one of four Army garrisons of black soldiers, came from the Mexican border to Dakota Territory in 1880 for service at Fort Randall, Fort Hale and Fort Meade.[228]

The Sully Colored Colony in the Onida area got its start when the Blair family settled northwest of Onida in 1882. Betty Blair attracted other black families to the area as a land agent for King Real Estate. John McGruder of Missouri bought a 1200 acre ranch in 1905, and his success encouraged other African-American families to come to the area. In 1925, there were fifty-eight black people in the area, but that number diminished as they, like many others, became discouraged by grasshoppers, drought and worsening economic situation. By 1950, only one African-American family remained.

ORAL

It's a long way from a ranch in Oral to a New York City stage, but Jarrod Emick has arrived and is thriving. The actor performed while a student at South Dakota State University and left in 1990 to seek the stage in other places. A role in a touring production of "Les Miserables" led to other opportunities. Emick was in the Chicago production of "Miss Saigon" before moving to New York to perform in the same play. His next role was that of young Joe Hardy in the Broadway revival of "Damn Yankees." At age 25, Emick was honored with a 1994 Tony Award for best featured actor in "Damn Yankees." Then, the young actor went home to vacation on the family sheep ranch near Oral. Emick has received acclaim in leading publications, including the *Wall Street Journal* which stated, "Mr. Emick is an ingenuous, appealing Joe with a powerful singing voice." "*U.S.A. Today* called him "the outstanding theater newcomer of 1992." You're going to hear more about this fellow from Oral! [229]

ORDWAY

The parents of Hannibal Hamlin Garland homesteaded near Ordway in 1881. When he couldn't find a teaching job, 21 year-old Hamlin Garland took a train from Iowa to Dakota Territory to visit his newly settled parents. In 1883, Garland homestead-ed in McPherson County, six miles west of his father's claim, and worked in his father's store while building his cabin and making necessary improvements to secure his claim. Hamlin Garland mortgaged his holding for $200 when he left to study literature in Boston in 1884. He didn't have enough money for a college course but studied daily at the Boston Public Library. He became an instructor at the Boston School of Oratory and began writing, publishing a review in 1885 and a poem in 1886 which brought him $25. When he returned to Dakota Territory in 1887 and again in 1889, Garland's mother's health was failing, and he felt the bitterness of the harsh realities in the lives of settlers, many of whom were losing hope after drought and

Pasqueflower

misfortune. The people and experiences of Ordway were etched in Garland's mind as he returned to the East and wrote short stories in the attic room where he lived. These stories written for *Harper's Weekly* in 1887 were published collectively as *Main-Travelled Roads* in 1890. Boomtown of those stories was based on Ordway in Dakota Territory. Many critics were shocked by the depiction of the harshness of life on the plains, its difficulties and drudgery. Garland had become a reformer and preferred to call his style "veritism," that is, realism combined with social purpose. He worked to promote a social agenda both through his writing and his participation in the Populist Party. At the age of 56, Hamlin Garland wrote the autobiographical *A Son of the Middle Border,* which was followed by *A Daughter of the Middle Border,* winner of the Pulitzer Prize for biography in 1922.[230]

PARKER, 984

The *New Era,* the Parker paper of May 14, 1861, began, "The cooings of the prairie chickens sound beautiful these still spring mornings. . . What are the officers of our county agricultural soci-ety doing toward holding a fair this fall? Come gentlemen, the pre-sent year augurs the best of any in the history of Dakota for grains and vegetables. . . "

The pleas were heard, and the Turner County Fair now takes place in Parker each August. FFA'ers and 4-H'ers have thoughts of purple ribbons as they bathe and groom their animals. Participants hope the animals will behave when the judges scrutinize them in the ring. Other kinds of entries are displayed elsewhere with rib-bons attached. You can see breads, pies, cakes and cookies in addi-tion to needlework, vegetables, photography and more. The lure of midway rides and hawkers calling, "Try your skill!" tempt the young crowd, while others play bingo or visit with friends. Plate suppers are sold by a local church which satisfies soul and stom-ach. What could be more fun on a summer day?

PARKSTON, 1572

Major Robert Dollard came to the area and took a soldier's homestead and timber claim eight miles northwest of the present Parkston. He later wrote, "The whole face of the country was blackened by the fires that had swept over it and the only sign of life, aside from our party, was a few antelopes that kept at a safe distance and a flock of ducks that paddled nearby in one of the numerous basins of the south branch of Twelve Mile creek. The air was quiet and all around was the most perfect condition of peace I have ever experienced."[231]

PARMELEE

Parmelee, like many other towns, underwent a series of name changes. It was originally called Cut Meat for a nearby creek named, Wososo, meaning "Cut Meat." In 1916, the town took the Sioux name, Wososo. Five years later, in 1921, the name was changed to Parmelee, honoring early settler Dave Parmelee.[232]

The first name perhaps originated with the Sioux practice of cutting up strips of meat to dry or with the government issue of meat to Native Americans at the present site of the town. When the government first issued beef, the cattle were turned loose on the prairie to be hunted like buffalo. Later, Native Americans shot the cattle in a corral and then skinned and dressed the carcasses which were loaded on wagons. The meat was cut up and "jerked" (dried) to preserve it.

PEEVER, 195

Those who enjoy frog legs might want to explore the Peever area which has a history of a large frogging operation. Some croakers live in that area today. In the roaring twenties, the frogs were scooped from the sloughs, crated up and sent to the East Coast. The going rate for the frogger was twenty cents per pound, and on some days, they shipped as many as 23 crates.

PHILIP, 1077

The Silent Guide Monument marks a waterhole which never failed. Early sheepherders built a crude marker to designate its location. In range feuds between the sheep and cattle ranchers, the marker was often torn down, only to be rebuilt. "It was customary for cowboys to express their contempt for sheepherders by roping the monument and toppling it over whenever they happened along."[233] At one point, a brave sheepherder mounted the crude stone monument with a rifle and challenged any who tried to oust him. The monument was permanently rebuilt in 1924 through public subscription.

PICKSTOWN, 95

Today, the ruins of the chapel and the cemetery are all that remain of Fort Randall, an historic outpost established on the Missouri in 1856 to assert military control on the Northern Plains. The government sought to restrain the Native Americans and bring order to the Black Hills Gold Rush of the 1870's and the Dakota land boom of the 1880's. The fort quartered four companies of soldiers and had six buildings for officers' quarters. Other structures included guardhouses, a hospital, bakery, storehouses, pumphouse, two laundries and an ammunition magazine.

After many years of flooding of the Missouri River, Congress passed the Flood Control Act of 1944 which provided six dams, four in South Dakota, to control the Missouri River. Gen. Lewis A. Pick of the Army Corps of Engineers and W. Glenn Sloan of the Federal Bureau of Reclamation formulated the far-sighted Pick-Sloan plan, a system of dams and reservoirs on the upper Missouri River, primarily to provide flood control. South Dakota gave up more than 530,000 acres of prime farm land, but benefited from flood protection, power and water for irrigation, municipal and recreational uses.

Pickstown developed as residences were needed for workers on the Fort Randall Dam begun in 1946. The dam generated power in 1954 as the first of four dams constructed in South Dakota to tame the mighty Missouri River. The Gavins Point, Fort Randall, Big Bend and Oahe Dams created a series of lakes which are enjoyed for recreational purposes and, at the same time, help to control water levels on the Missouri River.

PIEDMONT

Evidence of Barosaurus was found in the slopes of Piedmont Butte. These animals of approximately 50 tons were among the longest dinosaurs and breathed through a single hole in the top of their skull.

Piedmont has a population of 500, plus or minus a few. We tend to assume they are a town, but they are not. Residents have chosen not to be a town or city, voting against incorporation in 1908 and again in 1993.

PIERPONT, 173

After the town was platted, claim holder E. C. Marsten filed the application for a post office. He wanted to be postmaster but was a Republican and was certain President Grover Cleveland would appoint a Democrat. A friend accepted the appointment with the understanding that Marsten would handle duties. The village was incorporated in 1900, and the 1926 *History of Day County* said of Pierpont, "The citizenry constitute the very best."[234]

PIERRE, 12,906

Get it straight right now; it's pronounced "Peer!" Pierre was a well kept secret until it received publicity as #12 of the 100 best small towns in the country.[235]

To capture some of the local flavor, an historic marker was placed in the downtown area near the state capitol. It says:

PIERRE WAS A COWTOWN

Yes sir, Mister, Pierre was a cowtown. Why they built the sidewalks two feet off the ground to keep the cows from splattering 'em up. The stockyards ran longside the river for half a mile and three ferries were busy night and day in the shippin' season fetching cows over from the holding grounds, where cattle from as far away as Montana were funneled into the railhead at Pierre.

Yes sir, Pierre had 14 saloons in which cowpokes could wet a whistle and it was cows that kept Pierre awake. . . with their endless bawlin' enroute east. Why one year more cows clumb aboard the cars here than ever happened elsewhere. . . Yep sonny, put it down, Pierre was a cowtown. West river ranchers wintered here and the brand books of 1901 and prior listed 75 brand owners with over 200 brands. . . .[236]

PINE RIDGE, 2596

Pine Ridge is the largest village on the Pine Ridge Reservation, land relegated to the the Oglala Sioux. They were encouraged to farm on land poorly suited for that use and had no farming tradition, factors which impact the economy today. Shannon County, in which Pine Ridge is located, has the highest percentage of poor people in the nation with 63.1 percent of its population below the poverty level, according to U.S. census information for 1990. However, Oglala leaders and others have not given up and are working toward a brighter tomorrow. In 1993, Loren and Patricia Pourier of Pine Ridge were among ten minority business owners honored at a White House ceremony.

The best known native son of Pine Ridge, Billy Mills, was a gold medalist in the 1964 Tokyo Olympic Games. Mills, whose story was told in the movie "Running Brave," won the 10,000 meter event with a time of 28 minutes and 24.4 seconds. Mills lives in Sacramento, California, but returns to visit his family in Pine Ridge and to provide inspiration to young Lakotas. Mills says running taught him to pursue excellence.

PLANKINTON, 604

At Plankinton's Grain Festival in 1891, people came from far and wide to see a building covered with grains and grasses which proclaimed, "Dakota Feeds the World!" Other midwestern communities had similar harvest celebrations, and Plankinton abandoned the idea in 1892, the year of Mitchell's first Corn Palace celebration.

Early Plankinton resident, Isabella Todd Diehl came from Scotland to marry Martin Diehl who had seen her picture in the home of her uncle. Isabella and Martin corresponded, and he asked if she would marry him if he sent a ticket for her passage. They were married March 2, 1881, and moved to a claim he had filed in Dakota Territory, taking a train to Mitchell and hauling their goods 18 miles to Plankinton. A kind neighbor taught the 29 year-old Isabella how to grow and prepare vegetables that were strange to her. They dried corn and pumpkin slices which were threaded on a heavy cord, and Isabella learned to bake bread, johnny cake and flapjacks. Homesickness and loneliness tormented her until the birth of Henry, the second white child born in the county. Another son and a daughter were born to them, and the farm and family prospered. Six years after their marriage, Martin was killed by lightning. The funeral was in the Quaker Church, and the Masons who came in full regalia to provide Masonic rites were denied participation by the Quakers. Martin Diehl was buried in the Quaker Cemetery, but several years later his wife had his remains moved to the Plankinton Cemetery. At that time, he also received Masonic honors denied earlier, and his casket was opened at the Masonic Hall for viewing by his sons. To everyone's surprise, Martin's body was remarkably well preserved, and it was theorized that the lightning somehow acted as a preservative.

Before her husband's death, Isabella had been to town only a few times and had never driven a team or carried on business. As she struggled to cope with her three young children and learn the business of farming, Martin's relatives demanded payment of a $300 loan for the land. Four years after her husband's death, Isabella Todd Diehl moved into Plankinton where she found work to support her family.[237]

PLATTE, 1311

The local fire company averted danger when they boycotted the second Firemen's Picnic Association gathering in Platte in 1908. The respectable people of Platte, solid church-going citizens of Dutch origin, said the first such gathering had brought together "the worst gang of pluggers, grafters, thieves and prostitutes that ever assembled in one spot."[238]

PLUMA

Situated between Lead and Deadwood, Pluma gets lost in the golden glitter but has a colorful story of its own. On a night in 1877, Bandit Sam Bass and his gang held up the Cheyenne-Deadwood stage containing 11 passengers and $15,000. The shotgun fired at the stage driver caused the horses to bolt and foiled the hold up attempt.

POLLOCK, 379

Sandhill cranes stop at the nearby Pocasse National Wildlife Refuge during their spring and fall migrations. Their flyway follows the Missouri River, and the sandhills rest and feed before flying to their next stopping point. These noisy birds let you know when they are around. Their call is a long, loud, rolling hollow rattle: garoooooooooooooo! They are gray in color and have a lower and more broken call than the larger but rare whooping cranes which are white with black wingtips. A few whoopers occasionally fly with the sandhill cranes.

POLO

St. Liborius Church is unique in South Dakota, with its Spanish style architecture. The stucco structure of mission design was built in Polo under the leadership of Father Pothmann who had been a missionary in Mexico and southern states. St. Liborius is now served by a nun in residence as the pastoral administrator and a priest who comes from Faulkton on Saturday nights to celebrate mass for more than 90 farm families. After Mass, they gather in the dining hall for food and fellowship. Of her work in Polo, Sister Mary Myles Schwahn says, "I love my work in rural ministry. . .There's no place I'd rather be."[239]

PORCUPINE

Pine trees on the top of Porcupine Butte near Wounded Knee Creek give the mound the appearance of a crouching porcupine. The community takes its name from the nearby butte.

Stories linger about a hard drinking and tough, raw-boned Irishman, Mike Condon, who came into reservation country in 1919 to work with the McKeon outfit. "Mike was not afraid of the 'devil himself' and commanded the respect of the cowhands and sheepherders, yet he had a heart of gold and would give the shirt off his back to help anyone in real need."[240] Condon lived in a sheepwagon out in the hills where he trapped coyotes to safeguard the sheep, and his wagon was covered with drying pelts which he sold. The sheepherder liked Porcupine and its residents so much that he moved to town when his company was taken over by the Matador and he lost his job. He ran a Porcupine filling station where he especially enjoyed dispensing ice-cream cones to children.

PRAIRIE CITY

In this area, you can see strange sandstone formations in a variety of shapes which were formed as ground water seeped through sand dunes and carried dissolved silicates to cement the sand into these natural sculptures. This happened about 80 million years ago as dinosaurs were disappearing and flowering plants were coming on the scene.[241]

PRAIRIE VILLAGE, 0

Prairie Village is an incorporated municipality without a population. This place, where the past is preserved for the future, contains more than 50 buildings which were relocated to Prairie Village for restoration. At the summer Jamboree, one can see hundreds of tractors when the oldtimers compete and show their stuff. A big attraction is the steam driven carousel with its hand-carved horses, perhaps the only operational steam carousel in the United States. You can ride around the village on a coal-fired steam locomotive and recall the good old days.

PRESHO, 654

> Wal Partner, in 1862 when the Civil War was being fit [sic] and Dakota Territory took in everything south of Canada to the Rocky Mountains, the legislature gave a ferry license across the Old Muddy down at Yankton to J. S. Presho. Come 1872 they were casting 'round for a name to call a great big new county they were carving out. . .Someone said Presho and that was it. . .we've been growing by jerks and slow motion since, a peddling cattle and shipping hay. . . .[242]

The first bank went into operation eight minutes after the first town lot went up for sale in 1905. With two barrels supporting a plank and a six-shooter to protect the cash, business began. It was a round-the-clock operation to accomodate the rush of homesteaders.

PRINGLE, 96

Pringle got off to a "rocky" start, originally called Point of Rocks and then just Rocks in 1886. Finally, it became Pringle in honor of the man who owned the water rights in 1890.

The Cold Spring Schoolhouse built of logs in 1887 served as school, church, dance hall and meetinghouse. One man, who helped build it, attended school there, was married there and with his wife celebrated his 50th wedding anniversary in the same building. Both the marriage and the log building, which can be visited today, were made to last.

PUKWANA, 263

Homesteader Miss Richards led a campaign to name the town Pukwana, a word from Longfellow's "Hiawatha" which, in Chippewa, means "smoke of the pipe of the Great Spirit."[243]

The Pukwana area has long been a center of hospitality. General George Custer and his troops stopped at the Nelson Roadhouse on the way to the Black Hills in 1875, and the establishment served many more travelers in the gold rush days that followed.

Hospitality still prevails in Pukwana. One traveler wrote, "The last time I was there I didn't pay for my Coke in a Main Street cafe - the woman running the place said it would be silly to break a twenty for just a coke."[244]

QUINN, 72

In its early years, Quinn was a lively business community in ranch country. The Current History Club and a band and orchestra enriched the life of the community. Ball teams provided good entertainment, especially when they beat the Boston Bloomers, an acclaimed touring team of women. A favorite story from Quinn is that of "Bachelor John" who ran bases with his pet pig behind him.[245] You just can't beat the stories that come from a town such as Quinn, even though today, the population is getting thin!

RAMONA, 194

Swiss settlers from Minnesota scouted out parts of Dakota Territory and named Lake Badus for a mountain peak in their homeland. They staked claims on the lake northeast of Ramona, and the pioneer colony, known as Ligia Greischa, formed a cooperative, sharing all goods in common. These hard-working Swiss broke the land in 1878 and built sod houses, since lumber had to be hauled from the nearest railway point 75 miles away. The sod buildings were a blessing; they survived an 1879 prairie fire which devastated the community. A colony house was built to provide a store, amusements, and rooms for newly arriving colonists, but it burned in 1884 and was not rebuilt. The parish of these Swiss Roman Catholic folk was reinforced by Irish Catholics from the the Nunda area. St. Anne's Church was built in 1884 in the Vernacular-Gothic style, that is, a plain frame, and can be visited today.[246]

RAPID CITY, 54,523

Rapid City was known as "Hay Camp" when it came into existence in 1876, soon after the presence of gold became known. Gold seekers trespassed on land belonging to Native Americans by treaty agreement. The government ordered white people out of the Black Hills and placed troops at strategic points to prevent entry, without success.

Compensation for that land is still an issue today. The Black Hills trust fund contains $350 million dollars of principal and accrued interest which the Bureau of Indian Affairs wants to distribute to tribal people. The Sioux have not accepted relinquishment and therefore are unwilling to receive money for the loss of the sacred Black Hills.

The Chapel in the Hills, is a replica of the Borgund Church in Laerdal, Norway, built in 1050 and one of the best preserved and most beautiful of the 30 Norwegian stave churches still in existence. The Stavkirke replica with its unique architectural styling and ingenious pegged construction is typical of Norwegian churches of the Middle Ages. Intricate woodcarvings, which include hand-carved Apostle's heads, crosses and dragon heads, decorate the unique chapel. The Chapel in the Hills was built west of Rapid City in 1968-1969 to house the Lutheran Vespers Radio Ministry with funds provided by Arndt E. Dahl as a memorial to his parents. Vesper services are held nightly in summer for those who wish to pause for worship. Many weddings take place in the stave church, and tourists visiting on the Fourth of July in 1993 were happily surprised to find South Dakota's Governor Walter Dale Miller there for his wedding to Pat Caldwell.[247]

RAUVILLE

"Three strikes and you're out!" - well, not always. Rauville was begun in 1888 and "discontinued three times and re-established twice, still standing with two elevators and a filling station." Hang in there![248]

RAYMOND, 96

The Associated Press reported the story of the rumble in Raymond in the fall of 1993. The rumble originated when a retiree moved to Raymond from Phoenix, Arizona, (yes, that's right) and decided community spirit needed a boost. The town had experienced two disastrous fires in 18 months in which they lost a tavern called Beaver's Place and the grain elevator. Bill McKinney had an idea and with help from his wife and friends planned the "Raymond Rumble '93" as a morale booster for the town.

Hats and posters were distributed to promote the rumble, a one-day country good time with flagwaving, a pedal-power tractor pull for kids, a benefit raffle and more. The Presbyterian ladies sponsored a craft fair and offered lunch, and the American Legion auxiliary served up bratwurst and dessert bars in the afternoon. The whole shebang was topped off with a dance in the Legion Hall. McKinney and friends are already planning another "Raymond Rumble." [249]

REDELM

When the railroad came through in 1910 and the town was established, railroad graders saw elm trees along the creek where they camped and named the camp Red Elm. A preference of the railroad for one-word names explains the use of Redelm. The sign on the west end of town says Redelm and the sign on the east end says Red Elm.

> Redelm - Red Elm
> Is it one word or two?
> Even the road signs do not agree
> So we'll leave it up to you.[250]

REDFIELD, 2770

The residents of Redfield had some folks "seeing red" back in the fall of 1884. Old Ashton had been selected as the county seat in 1879, but after the railroad bypassed that town, a six-year fight over the Spink County seat began. Redfield claimed victory in an 1884 election, but the number of votes cast exceeded the number of eligible voters. A group of masked men from Redfield, including a banker and a preacher, went to Old Ashton on a Saturday night, seized a safe and records and hid them in Redfield. The county sheriff organized several hundred men, and the territorial governor sent two companies of the militia to restore order. In 1886, Redfield was legitimately established as the county seat.[251]

Redfield is the "Pheasant Capital of the World." Introduced in the state in 1898, Chinese ringnecked pheasants were released along the James River ten years later. The hardy birds did so well that the state Department of Game and Fish released 7000 birds from 1914-1917. The first hunting season was one day long in 1919 when 200 birds were shot. Pheasant hunting reached a peak in 1945 when 7.5 million of the birds were killed out of a population of 40 million pheasants. Storms, pesticides and increased land cultivation contributed to a decline in the pheasant population, but hunting is still good and attracts an estimated 40,000 out-of-state hunters in addition to South Dakota's hunters. In recent years, approximately one million pheasants have been bagged annually.

RED SCAFFOLD

The colorful name of this remote community has two possible explanations, both based on Native American use of scaffolds to hold corpses, often placed in trees. The Sioux thought the soul could not escape if buried in the ground. Scaffolds allowed the spirits of the deceased to ascend while the remains were claimed by nature. One explanation of Red Scaffold's name told of a body wrapped in a red blanket rather than the customary dark wrap. Another account said two young women killed each other in a fight over a man, and relatives placed their remains on a red scaffold. [252]

Ike Blasingame, who covered many miles of the Cheyenne River Sioux Indian Reservation as a cowboy for the Matador Land and Cattle Company, wrote:

> The burial rites varied, according to who died. A papoose was deerhide-wrapped and buckskin-thonged to a branch of a tree. A squaw usually would be bound to a thick limb, or shoved up on top of a high rock heap. But a chief or warrior got considerable ceremony. His bier was a scaffold among many tree limbs, or a ledge on a tall butte, and there, with his finest robes and furs, his bow and his arrows heaped around him, they left him for the journey to the Land of Happy Hunting. . . Contrary to the "stoical" Indian stories, the loss of one of their tribe caused much grief. But their mourning customs differed from the white man's. [253]

REE HEIGHTS, 91

The Arikara, called "the Rees," lived on the plains before the Lakota (Teton Sioux) moved westward into the area. The Rees were agricultural people who lived in round earth lodges and had one-and-a-half acre garden plots on which they grew corn, pumpkins and squash. The Teton Sioux moved into the area and waged a 40 year conflict with the Rees who moved northward to present North Dakota. Near Ree Heights, the Lakota killed some Rees for stealing horses.

In 1959, evidence of a "buffalo jump" was unearthed in the Ree Heights area. The buffalo kill site, used before the arrival of horses on the plains, had steep bluffs over which the Native Americans chased the buffalo. The area contains a layer of buffalo bones more than a foot deep and other evidence that this locale served as a "kitchen" area where the slaughtered buffalo were processed for food and other uses.

RELIANCE, 169

Herron was the original name, but because postal officials thought it would be confused with Huron, the town was named Reliance when founded in 1905. Widow Cooper ran a hotel located on Main Street until she went to her claim one weekend and returned to find the establishment moved to a side street. Mrs. Cooper's daughter, Purllue Cosgrove, helped her mother at the hotel which was so busy that they had to add a bunkhouse for railroad workers. One could rely on being well fed at the first hotel in Reliance.

> In spite of people thinking that the times were hard, the meals were always large and hearty. The meals were served family style, beginning with a big bowl of homemade soup, followed by roast meat, potatoes, gravy, vegetables, and all kinds of pickles, relishes and coleslaw. To top off this "light" meal they were served with a fourth of a pie apiece, an eighth of one kind and an eighth of another kind.[254]

RENNER

The historic Renner Lutheran Church is testimony to the faith that the early Norwegian settlers brought with them from their homeland and which lives on in their descendants today. The Nidaros Church, originally located north of Renner, was organized in a sod house in 1868. The congregation took its name from the area near Trondheim, Norway, the homeland of many parishioners. Pastor Sando came in 1873, agreeing to serve the congregation for $200 a year plus bed and board for himself and his horse. Provision of 75 bushels of oats for the horse was important since Pastor Sando depended on the horse for transportation to 17 other sites where he also led worship.

The Nidaros congregation constructed a church building, used a short time before it was destroyed by a storm in 1878. A modest structure with simple interior and plain furniture replaced the original. The Nidaros parish grew and developed into four congregations, one of which is the Renner Lutheran Church where people worship today in the "old church" which was relocated there.

The parish history tells of Gustav Solem, a young man who brought sparrows to his finger by whistling. Solem died of scarlet fever at the age of 17. Accounts state that on the warm March day of his funeral in 1904, the doors of the church were opened for the service, and "suddenly, birds swept into the sanctuary and perched on Solem's coffin."[255]

REVA

After the defeat of Custer at Little Big Horn on June 25, 1876, the Native American camp split into small bands, moving toward the Black Hills where they could obtain food. Many then went northward to the Reva area which held 700 or 800 Indian lodges in early September. In the Battle of Slim Buttes, U.S. soldiers led by General Crook surprised and destroyed a smaller camp of 37 lodges located about ten miles east of the large encampment. The Indian leader, American Horse, was fatally wounded, and his followers surrendered. After taking supplies and dried meat which provided their first decent meal in a month, Crook and his soldiers burned the village. Crazy Horse and his men came to the scene and attacked but were driven off, marking the end of the great army that Crazy Horse had commanded at Little Big Horn.

REVILLO, 152

Of the name, one lamented:

> In the mere matter of name the new town was to be seriously handicapped. Had those responsible given thought to the case they might have forseen the difficulty of taking seriously a town named Revillo. The name lacked distinction - it had no relish of salvation in it, no smack of accomplishment. Even before I had come to years of discernment the blank poverty of this name smote upon my soul. It seemed a pity, with the wealth of and variety of names available, that a title so tasteless should have been taken.[256]

To make matters worse, the site was poorly chosen, and, "Main Street of Revillo in the early days was nothing but a swamp, and when a team of horses came to town, they usually got stuck in the mud and would have to be pulled out."[257]

RICHLAND

In 1862, soldiers and settlers built Fort Brule "as a protection against renegade and hostile Indians." Some settlers had been scared off by hostilities in August of 1862 but returned with the fort there to provide some security. A granite block today marks the site of Fort Brule which was abandoned in 1868 and dismantled in 1873.[258]

RIDGEVIEW

Ridgeview was once part of the largest ranch operation in South Dakota's history. The Diamond A had 50 to 80 cowboys and held one-and-a-half million acres of land under lease from 1907 to 1914. An old cowboy, Kirk Myers, still living in the area, worked for the Diamond A in 1933 and 1934 and remembers it as the best time of his life. Fortunately, some of Myers fantastic stories have been recorded.

> "Dago Kelley, he never changed (his underwear) anyway, summer or winter," Myer laughed. "All he done was as they wore out, he took them off and put new ones on. Hell, he never changed! And he never took his overshoes off after November. And Christ almighty," as Myers continued in his sartorial review of Dago Kelley, "that Scotch hat, he never took it off!". . . According to Myers, about the worst offense a Diamond A cowboy could commit that would get you chapped (licked with a pair of chaps while held down) is being flatulent during meal time around the chuck wagon. Since beans were a staple, it must have been difficult, but. . .even cowboys realized there was a time and place for everything.[259]

As the days of the open range came to an end, the life of the cowboys changed. The Diamond A, however, survived until 1939, and during the years of its operation, many thousands of cattle wore its brand.

ROCHFORD

Almost a ghost town, Rochford is quiet these days. But it was not always so. As reported in *The Black Hills Miner* published in Rockerville, Dakota, Sunday, March 9, 1879 under "Rochford News Items":

A party of Chicago capitalists will be here soon.
A number of new houses are being erected at Tigerville.
The Manville mill will soon be put in operation.
M.H. Kendig will put in a crop of grain at Pactola this year.
Both of the Rochford Justices have had their hands full during
the week.
Tigerville and the country 'round about is said to be filled
with prospectors.
As spring approaches travel increases. The tide is setting in
this way stronger than ever.

ROCKERVILLE

Rockerville was in the national headlines for a decade when
miners sought gold. Their tents and shacks dotted the area. In
the first two years of its existence from 1876 to 1878, $350,000
worth of gold was removed from the area. As the historical
marker states: "It was 1880 when the great ditch from Spring
Creek, with its 14 miles of twisting, turning side hill canal and
high flumes brought water to Rockerville's fabulous placers. Up
to then, a man with a barrel of water used repeatedly, and his
little rocker, had made Rockerville a place where a man might
make a quick dollar or lose his shirt." By 1882, in terms of the
yield from the mines, Rockerville was a million dollar town.[260]

ROSCOE, 362

The story is told of a Russian-German who traveled by train
across northern South Dakota for the first time: "As the train
made its stop in the town of Roscoe, the conductor stepped into
the unfortunate traveler's car and shouted the name of the town
in husky railroad fashion. The man heard 'Raus da!' ('Get out
of here!') and obediently stepped off the train. It pulled away
without him."[261]

ROSEBUD, 1538

Many tribes of Native Americans once came to the area
including Cheyenne and Arapaho from the west and Pawnee,
Ponca and Kiowa from the south. After the Lakota (Teton Sioux)
moved westward in approximately 1750, they occupied a large
area of the northern plains which they defended as their land.

Old Standby

The Fort Laramie Treaty of 1868 established The Great Sioux Reservation including all of present South Dakota west of the Missouri and more. Chief Spotted Tail and his band of Brule established an agency at Rosebud, first known as Spotted Tail Agency. An act of Congress in 1888 created separate reservations: the Rosebud, Pine Ridge, Cheyenne, Standing Rock and Lower Brule Reservations. The Rosebud Reservation, whose name is taken from the wild roses growing countryside, is home to approximately 8000 Brule today.

Dr. Lucy Reifel grew up in Sioux Falls but moved to Rosebud in 1980. She and her husband, Randy Her Many Horses, wanted their children to have a strong sense of family. Dr. Reifel said, ". . . .They need to know what older people can teach them. Because I had relatives and friends here, I chose to live in Rosebud. . . .Family is what you have forever. . . .That's the strongest tie anyone can ever have. . . ." As a specialist in pediatrics and internal medicine, Dr. Lucy Reifel provides hope and help among her Lakota people as she works to improve the quality of health and life on the reservation. She says, "The answer is education."[262]

ROSHOLT, 408

In spring of 1892, homesteaders made a run for the land in the northeast corner of South Dakota. When the centennial of the territory was celebrated in 1961, 92 year-old Julius Entwiller still owned his original homestead, and he recalled the run for the land:

> April 15, 1892 was the time set for the official opening of the Sisseton Reservation to homesteaders. A company of soldiers had been dispatched to hold back the "Sooners" who might be tempted to cross the line and acquire a choice tract of land before the firing of the starting gun. . . .Soldiers were strung in a thin line south to Browns Valley. At 12 o'clock noon a cannon on the Minnesota side was fired, followed by a volley of rifle shots by the soldiers. The stampede was on! People in hired rigs, buggies, wagons, carts, on foot and horseback set out in a mad rush for free land. On finding a quarter section that was not claimed, the homesteader hurriedly threw up a sod marker on each corner of his 160-acres

as physical evidence of his claim. Many of the settlers started walking to Watertown that very night to file their land claim, fearing that others with less honest motives than their own might file on the land that was rightly theirs.

Entwiller recalled that his team became exhausted as he traveled to Watertown. So he picketed them at a slough, and he walked the rest of the distance to the Land Office at Watertown to file for his homestead.[263]

ROSLYN, 251

On a ridge just off Highway 25, lies a pasture that contains cows, horses, skunks, bears, chickens, deer, a sunbathing pig and more. It is a collection of attractively painted wooden cutouts that a couple has placed in their field for the enjoyment of those passing by. A guestbook in a mailbox by the road indicates that the scene has been enjoyed by many people, some from as far away as Germany.

ROWENA

The railroad brought migrants and stonecutters to the quarries which opened soon after the founding of Rowena in 1888. The first baby girl and boy born in the town were named Rowena and Rowein, respectively. Little Rowena received a baby carriage from the quarry for being the first child born in the town. The quartzite was in demand. Rapidly growing Sioux Falls City used it for paving stones and building blocks. Rowena shared in the growth, and some had hopes of it being the capital of the state. In 1889, one year after its birth, Rowena was a very respectable community containing "20 elegant buildings." *The Larchwood Leader* wrote, "It can but seem that the fairies of old had descended upon the barren wheat fields at night and constructed one of the most beautiful little villages the eyes of man were ever laid upon."[264]

RUNNING WATER

Running Water is a mile as the crow flies from the Nebraska shoreline across the Missouri River but 40 miles by road, so near and yet so far. For many years, the Sally Ann, a nine car ferry, ran across the waters of the Missouri from April to November.

The boat ceased operation in 1984, to the dismay of some who still come to the rivers edge, expecting to find a ferry. There are plans for a South Dakota - Nebraska bridge to span the one mile across the river close to Running Water.

ST. FRANCIS, 815

The St. Francis Indian Mission and School was established over a hundred years ago at the request of Chief Spotted Tail. German immigrant, Father Eugene Buechel, S.J., began teaching in St. Francis in 1902 and was ordained to the priesthood in 1906. He spent his life among the Lakota people and was welcomed into their homes as Wanbli Sapa (Black Eagle). He took over 2100 photos, many of which were included in a photo exhibition, "Crying for a Vision." Father Buechel also published three books in the Lakota language. His card file of over 30,000 Lakota words and translations was edited in 1970 and published as a Lakota-English dictionary. The Buechel Memorial Lakota Museum in St. Francis is a tribute to Father Buechel and the Lakota people he loved.

ST. LAWRENCE, 223

Professor Snoddy opened a training school for teachers in St. Lawrence, but a massive depression forced closing of the college in 1894 after only two years of operation. Snoddy then served as county superintendent of schools. During the Civil War, he had befriended Henry Lew Wallace who later sent Snoddy chapters of a manuscript for criticism and correction. Wallace took Snoddy's suggestion that the story needed a feminine element and could be enhanced with a love story; the book is *Ben Hur*.

ST. ONGE

Some who came to the Black Hills for gold decided to stay and make hay in False Bottom Valley to the north of Deadwood. In the early 1880's, travelers passing through the valley brought the mail to the home of Pitoche St. Onge, a French settler, who became the first postmaster.

A private race track was built on the St. Onge farm in 1888, and as horse racing became a popular attraction, several other tracks were built. St. Onge cowboys are still great competitors in the nearby Belle Fourche Roundup. Horses and cattle remain an important part of area life, and St. Onge comes alive on auction days in late fall and winter when cattlemen gather to sell their livestock. A celebration takes place with hired hands and family when a rancher gets the year's paycheck.

SALEM, 1289

The body of a young man was found in a field near Interstate 90 in March of 1983. It appeared that he died of exposure, and attempts at identification were unsuccessful, local people buried him in St. Mary's Cemetery. They bought a tombstone which reads, "A young man in his 20's found dead Mar. 13, 1983 Buried Mar. 31, 1983 'I am the good shepherd. I know my sheep.' JN. 10:14" Salem people did not forget the stranger and brought flowers to the gravesite every Memorial Day. Ten years later, identification was made through fingerprints, and two brothers and a sister of the young man came to Salem to visit his gravesite. They explained that the 22 year-old was probably hitchiking to visit a brother in Sun Valley, Idaho. They were so impressed with the caring attention given to the remains of their brother by the people of Salem that the family decided to leave that as his permanent gravesite.[265]

SCENIC

John Jacob Astor's American Fur Company operated a trading post northwest of present Scenic at the mouth of Rapid Creek. Thousands of pelts were brought to this post and transported down the Cheyenne River to Fort Pierre by huge skin canoes. A big bang occurred at the trading post in 1832 when a worker knocked a candle into an open 50 pound powder keg. One man was killed, and the ensuing fire destroyed the post.

SCOTLAND, 968

In 1870, Charles Campbell built a trading post and inn on the Firesteel Trail from Sioux City to Pierre. Eventually, more than 100 families of Scottish ancestry came from Canada to settle in the area. They perhaps brought some brewing secrets, too, as

Scotland had a reputation as the bootleg capital of southeastern South Dakota during prohibition. Alcohol is produced in Scotland today, but it is gasohol for fuel use.

SELBY, 707

South Dakota, A Guide to the State, published as a Federal Writers' Project in 1938, described Selby: "At the summit of each ridge a panorama of the immediate sections suddenly unfolds."[266] Quite a drama unfolded on Superbowl Sunday in 1980 when a DC-7 landed in a pasture, and people of the area reported a crippled plane. Officials could scarcely believe their find on the plane from South America. The plane carried a cargo of 12.5 tons of marijuana worth $18 million dollars. It was the biggest drug bust in South Dakota history.

SENECA, 81

From the June 21, 1888, issue of *The Faulk County Time* is the following account of a gathering in Seneca: "A dozen gentlemen with their wives boarded the west bound train for Seneca Friday p.m. From the depot they were conveyed to the residence of Capt. J. Douglas a mile and a half from town, where they were warmly welcomed by the Captain and his wife. During the early evening guests found pleasure in inspecting the Captain's well stocked library, pitching quoits and looking after the farm. After supper Mr. White played the guitar and was joined by others in many a song when the Captain invited his guests to the hall - the second story of a large new barn he had recently completed and had floored the second story in view of its adaptability for 'tripping the light fantastic toe' when not in use for storying hay - where the company was joined by some dozen of the friends and neighbors of the Douglas' and the merry, merry dance held sway til the midnight hour and was supplemented by some of the Captain's grand violin solos; and a solo sung by the young primadonna Miss Jessie. . . .At 1 o'clock the company was called from 'labor to refreshment' and did ample justice to a most sumptuous repast. . . .Some solicitude was entertained by those who remained at Capt. Douglas' till time for the morning train. . . ."[267]

SHADEHILL

This is Hugh Glass country, and a nearby monument commemorates the epic journey of the intrepid hunter and guide. While scouting along the Grand River in August of 1823, he encountered a grizzly and her cubs. Seeking to protect her young, the bear attacked Hugh Glass, who was mauled, bitten and found unconscious. Mountain men gave him as much first aid as they could provide using strips of buckskin. The trading company paid two men $80 to stay with Glass, but after four or five days, they concluded he would not live. Taking his weapons, knife and matches, the mountain men left the critically injured man, reporting to the party that he had died and they had buried him.

Glass recovered consciousness some time later to find himself defenseless and alone, although campfire evidence indicated others had been there. When he tried to move, Glass realized his leg was broken. He managed to tear off some available bear meat with his teeth and ate roots and berries when the meat spoiled. As strength allowed, Glass crawled southward, driven by a fierce desire to survive and motivated by anger toward those who had abandoned him. Glass wriggled and crawled, pulling his injured leg over dirt, rocks and prickly-pear cacti as he struggled to reach Fort Kiowa more than 100 miles away. He drank water at the river and subsisted on whatever he could reach, including grubs, mice and snakes. Somewhere between the Grand River and the Cheyenne River, he fashioned a crutch from a tree branch so that he could stand upright and hobble. At the Cheyenne River, he built a crude raft on which he floated downstream on the Cheyenne and Missouri Rivers to Fort Kiowa, near the present site of Chamberlain, arriving in mid-October. Severely injured Hugh Glass traveled more than 200 miles in two months.

SHERMAN, 66

The *Sioux Falls Argus Leader,* July 21, 1892, reported this news from Sherman:

> About a week ago, Harve Henneger and Martin Erickson of Garretson moved a building from Garretson to this place with the intention of establishing a saloon. About 4 o'clock yesterday morning the intended saloon was turned upside down by a

mob of infuriated Scandinavians of both sexes, there being about as many women as men.

Mr. Henneger, accompanied by attorney Murphy was here today to investigate the destruction of his building, and there is no doubt but that a number of our citizens will be implicated.

SHINDLER

This community close to the historic Blood Run Creek Indian burial site recently became a matter of special interest as plans were made for the 230 acre Spring Creek golf and housing complex. Mounds created by the Oneota culture from the fourteenth to eighteenth centuries may be incorporated into the design of the Spring Creek Country Club. This could provide a special interest on the golf course and at the same time leave the mounds undisturbed.

SINAI, 120

The annual lutefisk dinner is a 50 year tradition. The event attracts Norwegians who smack their lips at the thought of lutefisk and lefsa. The lutefisk is dried fish (usually whitefish or cod). Before cooking, it is soaked in lye, rinsed and soaked in salt water. Butter, salt and pepper, give it most of its flavor. "Ignore the risk; try lutefisk!"

Lutefisk is accompanied by lefsa, a potato flat bread. To make lefsa, potatoes are peeled, boiled and mashed, preferably in good Norwegian company. "Add a little cream, butter and flour, and a lot of Scandinavian tradition, then roll it up in balls, flatten it with a roller and fry it on a grill." Many spread butter and sugar on their lefse, but "some of the real old Norwegians like to eat it rolled up with lutefisk and potatoes." For better or worse, a German who married a Norwegian woman said, with a smile, that she fed him lutefisk and lefse early in their marriage, and he "hasn't been quite the same ever since."[268] Some say there's nothing to get the blood running in January like lutefisk and lefsa. Ufta!

SIOUX FALLS, 100,814

The beautiful falls of the Big Sioux River attracted Native Americans. They camped on Seney Island, drank the crystal clear

The Falls of the Big Sioux River

waters and bathed in a spring-fed pool which they called Minne Waukon, Sacred Water. In 1836, Joseph Nicollet visited the area in his travels with John C. Fremont. An enterprising Iowan, Dr. George Staple, read Nicollet's report in 1857 with an interest in obtaining land for the Western Town Company. They saw the possibility of a #1 city even then, as did a St. Paul land company. Boomers came and were chased out by the Native Americans in 1857, but more land seekers came and helped build Fort Sod. Residents fled when Indians destroyed the town in 1862. After Fort Dakota was built in 1865, settlers returned to Sioux Falls to stay.

Divorce in the early years of the Dakota Territory required an act of the legislature upon recommendation of a committee, jokingly called the "Committee on Internal Improvement." In 1877, the law was revised to list specific grounds for divorce: adultery, extreme cruelty, willful desertion, willful neglect, habitual intemperance, and conviction of felony. Ninety days in the Territory were required to establish residence. Divorce was rare and usually sought by men whose wives refused to accompany them when they came westward. Word of easy divorce in Dakota Territory spread. Dakota divorce lawyers advertised in eastern publications, and Sioux Falls became a divorce mecca. Terms of residence were loosely applied, and false receipts for board or rent sometimes constituted proof of residence. The overall divorce rate in the state was approximately one per thousand of population, and 145 divorces were granted in Sioux Falls in 1908, before the law was changed to require a year of residency.[269]

SISSETON, 2181

French map maker Joseph Nicollet was captivated by the Coteau des Prairies area which he described as "magnificent and indescribably beautiful." Nicollet, a scientist and astronomer, explored at his own expense until the U.S. government appointed him to lead an expedition in 1837. He very accurately mapped the Mississippi watershed.

George Catlin was also impressed by the area which he visited between 1832 and 1839 when he painted and observed life among the Native Americans. Of the Coteau des Prairie, he wrote:

The Coteau des Prairies is the dividing ridge between the
St. Peter and Missouri Rivers. . . .This wonderful feature,
which is several hundred miles in length, and varying from fifty
to a hundred in width, is, perhaps the noblest mound of its
being in the world; it gradually and gracefully rises on each
side, by swell after swell, without tree, or bush, or rock. . . and
is everywhere covered with green grass, affording the traveller,
from its highest elevations, the most unbounded and sublime
views of - nothing at all - save the blue and boundless ocean of
prairies that lie beneath and all around him, vanishing into azure
in the distance, without a speck or spot to break their soft-
ness.[270]

SMITHWICK

Prairie Gem Ranch is a pleasant oasis of many plants and trees
which have done especially well on the plains. Rancher Claude
Barr developed an extraordinary plot by carefully selecting plants
with tolerance for low moisture. He submitted a black and white
pasqueflower photo with a short column of notes to *House and
Garden* magazine in 1932 and was paid $20 for the material. That
was the start of Barr's garden writing and a mail order plant and
seed business which developed as people wrote to obtain the
plants. In 1935, Claude Barr distributed a catalog of plants of the
"high Plains, Badlands, and Black Hills." He continued his cattle
business, but plants were his passion. The self-taught botanist was
well-acquainted with the flora of the region, and in the later years
of his life, he quit ranching to write a book about the plants he
loved. *Jewels of the Plains: Wildflowers of the Great Plains
Grasslands and Hills* was published in 1983.[271]

SOUTH SHORE, 260

South Shore is situated on Punished Woman's Lake where two
nearby boulders represent the young lovers of a Native American
legend. During Harvest Moon in 1773, a fair maiden, Wewake,
and a brave young warrior, Wapskasimuchwah (Big Eagle), fell
in love. When Big Eagle brought gifts to the lodge of her father
and asked permission to marry Wewake, Big Eagle's proposal
was refused. Sadly, the father instead accepted the gifts of
Chemoki (White Tail Wolf), a 60 year-old chief whom he

planned for his daughter to marry. Wewake and her true love tried to escape on a pony but were unsuccessful. The enraged Chemoki killed Big Eagle with a knife and bound Wewake to a tree by the shore where he shot an arrow into her heart. With the bodies of the two lovers on a knoll close by, the angry Chemoki was killed by a lightning bolt as he made a speech calling for the two lovers to be taken the the Land of Ever-Lasting Sorrow. Two boulders represent Wewake and Big Eagle, and a stone representing a repentant Chemoki is at their feet.[272]

SPEARFISH, 6966

The Thoen Stone, believed to be authentic, tells an incredible story of a group of Missourians who found gold in the Black Hills. The piece of sandstone found near Spearfish at the base of Lookout Mountain by Louis Thoen in 1887 was etched by Ezra Kind over fifty years earlier:

> Came to these hills in 1833, seven of us, De Lacompte, Ezra Kinds, G.W. Wood, T. Brown, R. Kent, Wm. King, Indian Crow. All died but me, Ezra Kind. Killed by Ind beyond the high hill got out gold in 1834. Got out all the gold we could carry. Our ponys [sic] all got by Indians. Have lost my gun and nothing to eat and Indians hunting me.

The stone can be seen today in the Adams Museum in Deadwood.

Iron was the metal of interest in the northern Hills, when Spearfish hosted the 75th World Horseshoe Tournament in 1993. The tournament drew participants from 48 states and other countries. Women toss the horseshoe from a distance of 30 feet, and men pitch the two and one-half pound shoe from 40 feet. Twenty-five classes compete with 36 players participating in each class. The best players hit eight out of ten in tournament play, and the clang of metal of shoes hitting stake is music to their ears.

SPENCER, 317

You have to spend time on Main Street to appreciate the unhurried pace of life in Spencer. One building says, "Leisure

Hour Card Club - Welcome." The building isn't used today, and the pitch and whist played at tables there are now just a memory. With a bit of sprucing up, which it looks like someone intended to do, the building could still provide a gathering place for senior citizens and others. Across the street, at the Club House Cafe and Grocery, a welcome mat mounted in the window says, "Forget the dog; beware of the kids!" An arrow to the right points to the door for the store, and an arrow to the left points to the door for the cafe, which is where most of the getting together takes place today. At the north end of Main Street, the old Pontiac garage houses Evelyn's Antiques and Second Hand Store, chock full of items from Spencer's past. Evelyn Bartholow presides over the immense collection which includes more than you can imagine.

SPINK

Johannes Larson, homesteaded in the area in 1867 and opened the first store in 1871. One day in 1876, two men came to the house for a meal and overnight lodging. Mr. Larson was away, but the children served tea to the strangers while their mother milked cows in the barn. The polite men went on their way the next day. Later, Mrs. Larson saw a wanted poster and realized the house guests were Frank and Jesse James. She recalled that they did insist on carrying a heavy saddlebag into the house.

From 1925 to 1947, Myrtle and Lincoln Twedt ran the store begun by her grandfather. In the 1940's, Myrtle Twedt and some friends responded to an ad for one dollar art lessons in Sioux City. She began painting scenes from Spink, including the country store, threshing machines and the blacksmith's shop, "where as a child she was forbidden to enter because of the men's foul language and the horses' dangerous hooves." This "Grandma Moses" of Spink gave away most of her 100 paintings, but some can be seen at the community crossroads today.[273]

SPRINGFIELD, 834

In 1860, settlers built a log school house in Bon Homme, northeast of Springfield. The floorless and dirt-roofed building was the first school in present South Dakota. Ten pupils assembled there in May 1860 for three months of classes with Miss Emma Bradford. (A 1975 replica of the log structure replaced the original destroyed by fire in 1929.) The Territorial Legislature mandated in 1862 that reading, writing, arithmetic, spelling, geography and English grammar be taught in every school district. County superintendents examined applicants for teaching certificates on the basis of character, education and ability to teach. Qualifications of teachers varied widely, and some teachers had classrooms of students who spoke a language other than English.[274]

The instructions to teachers of September, 1872, tell us about the life of teachers of that time:

Instructions to Teachers, Dakota Territory

1. Teachers will fill lamps, clean chimneys and trim wicks each day.
2. Each teacher will bring a scuttle of coal and a bucket of water for the day's use.
3. Make your pens carefully. You may whittle nibs for the individual tastes of children.
4. Men teachers may take one evening each week for courting purposes or two evenings a week if they go to church regularly.
5. After ten hours in school, the teacher should spend the remaining time reading the Bible or other good books.
6. Women teachers who marry or engage in other unseemly conduct will be dismissed.
7. Every teacher should lay aside from his pay a goodly sum for his declining years so that he will not become a burden on society.
8. Any teacher who smokes, uses liquor in any form, frequents a pool hall, or gets shaved in a barber shop will give good reason for suspecting his worth, intentions integrity and honesty.
9. The teacher who performs his labors faithfully and without fault for five years will be given an increase of 25 cents a week in his pay providing the board of education approves.[275]

STAMFORD

What on earth would they have done without her? Minda Fleming Castle Larison (1887 - 1962) came to Stamford in 1912 and was the postmistress, telephone operator and editor of the *Stamford News*. In addition to all of that, she provided entertainment as she sang, accompanied herself on the piano, blew the bazooka and beat the bass drum with her foot. Now, that's a one woman band.[276]

STEPHAN

Father DeSmet, known as the Apostle of the Sioux, visited Crow Creek several times in his missionary work between 1846 and 1867 as he shared the Gospel with Native Americans and baptized them. They welcomed him and served dog, buffalo tongues and ribs, fruit, grains and nuts at a succession of banquets in his honor, providing the "brown robe" with more food than he could comfortably consume. DeSmet honored the chiefs with medals of Pope Pius IX, and they indicated a desire for Catholic missionaries after their meeting with Father DeSmet.[277]

In response to a request from the Yanktonai Sioux and Lower Brule Indians, the government granted 160 acres of land for a mission on the Crow Creek Reservation. A $15,000 donation provided money for the Benedictine mission begun with a small structure which served as school and residence for five boys in 1886. A post office established in 1887 was named for Father Joseph Stephan, then Director of the Bureau of Catholic Indian Missions. Members of the Benedictine order staffed the mission school which had 37 students in 1887. Homestead grants were claimed by benefactors who donated the land to the growing mission. The Benedictines cared for and educated hundreds of Native American children in the boarding school at Stephan for almost a century. Realizing the need for Native American self-determination in the 1970's, the monks turned the operation of the school at Stephan over to the Crow Creek Sioux Tribe.[278]

STICKNEY, 323

Telephone lines came to this part of South Dakota in the first decade of the 1900's. Some old Germans said, "Ach, we don't need dat!" as they considered the newfangled contraption, but most saw the value of a telephone in an emergency. Leonard Andera recalled the nights when, as a 14 year-old in Stickney, he manned the telephone switchboard seven nights a week. During the 6 p.m. to 8 a.m. shift, a bell placed over the bed was supposed to waken him to handle calls. "The emphasis here should be on 'supposed to,' a major reason for my tenure of only about a year."[279]

John Dickson provided glimpses of life of yesteryear in a booklet celebrating of the town's 75th anniversary. His father came to the Stickney area in 1884, and John Dickson recalled preparing for winter by gathering wood and "laying in" a supply of flour and other essentials. Meat was preserved by cooking it well and putting it in stone crockery under a layer of lard. The Majestic range was not only used for cooking, but it provided warmth and was sometimes used as an incubator for newborn animals needing extra care. Before radio and television, families relied on the *Farmers' Almanac* for the weather forecast. The arrival of the medicine peddler broke the monotony of winter when he came in his enclosed horse-drawn wagon with neatly painted sides. After tying up his horses, the peddler took his sample case into the house and shared news as he displayed his wares. He offered flavorings and savories, liniment and laxatives, lotions and potions, cough syrup and cold tablets, and remedies for livestock, too.[280]

STOCKHOLM, 89

The Brown Earth Indian Church in the Stockholm area was built by Native Americans who took homesteads near Yellowbank Creek in 1877. Fifteen to twenty Native American families homesteaded but later sold their lands and moved away.

The Swedes came in 1884 and named the town for the Swedish capital. The Stockholm Cooperative Creamery began in 1896 when pioneers organized at the Brown Earth Church with the slogan, "Stockholm Sticks Together!" The first attempt to sell farmers $25 shares of stock in the cooperative failed, but they soon realized a united effort would result in more money for their dairy products. Because the farmers had no cream separators, they let the milk stand, skimmed the cream from the top and then churned the butter that was traded at the grocery store for prices set by the grocer. With the establishment of the cooperative creamery, farmers sold milk to the creamery, and the buttermaker/manager produced the butter known as "Stockholm's Pride." The effort was truly cooperative. During the early years, each shareholder had to haul ice for creamery use, and if a member didn't do his part, he was fined one dollar per load and received a diminished dividend.[281]

STRANDBURG, 74

"Spika English?" Swedish settlements in South Dakota were few because the Swedes came later than the Norwegians and tended to blend in with the Norskies, who outnumbered them. Strandburg, however, was a Swedish community where the immigrants built a Swedish Lutheran Church and held services in their native tongue. Language blended Swedish and English, and in Strandburg you would have heard phrases such as "spika English," "got a yobb," "maka monni" and "sinja Yankee Doodle." [282]

STRATFORD, 85

Shakespeare's line, "Now my soul hath elbow room," could apply to Stratford, South Dakota. Towns in various places took the name of the English town in which William Shakespeare was born, and some Stratfords in other places stage Shakespearian festivals. Our Stratford has no aspirations of Shakespearian productions, although it has had a cast of colorful town characters over the years. One of the most well known was Pete, the butcher, known far and wide for his carcass skinning ability and the products of his smokehouse. Couldn't you imagine a role for the butcher in "A Midsummer Night's Dream?"

STURGIS, 5330

Some colorful people have come and gone through Sturgis. Annie Tallent, one of the first white women to come to the Black Hills, lived on Main Street. Sturgis was also home to Poker Alice, the cigar-smoking card shark who owned the rowdiest honky-tonk in the state. Poker Alice would have enjoyed the action generated by the Black Hills Classic Cycle Rally which has taken place for more than 50 years. In the late 1930's, "Pappy" Hoel, the local cycle dealer, and some friends got together for a few days of racing at the fairgrounds. That was the start of a tradition attracting more than 100,000 people annually. Sturgis is filled with bikers for a week each August when thousands of cycles fill Main Street.

> It's a rough looking crowd, but don't be fooled. Among the beards, tattoos and fringed tanktops are movie stars, businessmen, diplomats, housewives, policemen and preachers. . . .For a week, they are all "Born To Be Wild," and there's an unspoken truce among all biker types, clubs and factions.
>
> The week is filled with group touring, poker runs, short track races, . . .and big-time concerts. But mostly, they come to party. . . . Altogether, it's a very unconventional convention.[283]

Others come to the Sturgis area for very different reasons. Bear Butte, eight miles northeast of Sturgis is of geologic interest as a 40 million year-old volcano which spewed up lava when internal pressures found a weak spot in the earth's crust. More importantly, Bear Butte is a spiritual place where Sweet Medicine received the Cheyenne people's sacred commandments. Today, members of other tribes also come "to pray, sit in council and seek the visions that can define and direct them as people and spiritual beings."[284]

SUMMIT, 267
This town is the highest point in the Coteau range between the Mississippi and Missouri Rivers, and that sums it up.

TABOR, 403
A society of Chicago Czechs bought 160 acres of land and divided all but 40 acres into 53 residential lots, setting apart some lots for a church, cemetery and school. They did not want to favor any family with use of its name, and called the village Tabor, the Czech word for "camp." Tabor celebrates its heritage with Czech Days each summer, and residents decorate their homes and dress in the colorful costumes of their forebearers. They dance the Beseda and other folk dances and even have a polka mass! This is the place to get kolaches with a variety of fillings. But first, enjoy a delicious Bohemian meal. If you're lucky enough to know a

Czech, you'll be treated to a beer. Everybody and his or her dog comes out for the parade, and if you're not in it, you're watching it. Czech it out!

TEA, 786

When the town was established at the time the railroad came through in 1894, railroad officials proposed to name it Byron, but postal officials nixed the idea since there was already a town of that name. Fifteen men met at the depot one morning to select a new name, continuing on into the afternoon. When the afternoon train arrived, passengers disembarked to look for refreshments saying it was tea time. Weary and out of ideas, the committee meeting to select a name heard "Tea" and took the name seriously. "Beer" was considered since it was a more popular drink among the German settlers, but Tea was chosen by a majority vote.

> Tea for Two
> A gentleman was he
> Who took his love to Tea
> Said she, "I'll think I'll have a beer
> And a sirloin, too, while I am here."
> Said the surprised gentleman, "Well, I'll be. . ."
> "Such an appetite has she!"

THUNDER BUTTE

Picture the Christmas Eve celebration in a school house many years ago as Native Americans gathered to observe the birth of Christ and the tradition of Santa Claus.

> The women, in spite of the heat from the large stove, were all wearing heavy bright colored plaid or striped shawls. Nearly all women, men and children had on beaded moccasins. . .After each speech or talk, given by both older and some younger Indian men, about Jesus and the Spirit of Christmas. . . Old Santa came dressed in furs and feathers. He had on a cap similar to a dunce cap, very high and trimmed with bells. His face was painted in a merry fashion, not like a warrior on the warpath, but with friendly lines masked in yellows and reds. The children left their mothers and flocked to old Santa, shook hands with him and were given candy boxes, bags of nuts, apples and oranges.[285]

TIMBER LAKE, 517

"Timber Lake is South Dakota, unobstructed by bill boards, neon lights, chain stores and fast food....It is a place where lawns are mowed neatly in the summer, and walks are cleaned of snow in the winter. The only risk of letting youngsters run free is that parents may have to stop at three or four houses to find them at suppertime."[286]

TINTON

Prospectors sought tin in the area of "Tintown" in the northern Black Hills. Townspeople sometimes saw phosphorescent lights over the graves of miners who had died violent deaths. Mysterious lights, also seen on the prairie, were the subject of speculation and fascination. Settlers called the elusive and unexplained lights "will-o-the-wisp" and "Elmo's fires." A pioneer reported terrifying bouncing balls of fire which skipped all around him, sometimes close and sometimes distant. One family saw a "burning bush" as they looked southward at night, and the pioneer children often looked to see if the "lights were burning." Attempts to track and identify the source of these apparent fires or lights were unsuccessful. Some think a harmless gas escaped from the ground, invisible by day but luminous at night.[287]

TOLSTOY, 69

> Two bits, four bits,
> A shave above the collar-
> At Bitzer's Barber Shop
> You'll get a hair cut for a dollar!

Harold Bitzer's barber shop served the people of Tolstoy for almost 50 years. Today, the little barber shop with its two chairs and two shoeshine seats can be seen at Prairie Village.

TORONTO, 201

A Toronto boy, the son of the Lutheran pastor, went on to play major league baseball. Even though it happened in 1928, they still recall that Ossie Orwell struck out the immortal Babe Ruth.

The Old Place

TRENT, 211

A former pastor of the Trent Baptist Church has not forgotten a cow named Queenie on a dairy farm in Trent. Pastor Rohn Peterson, conceived of the Arky project, which in its first phase features a hot air balloon designed as Noah's ark, along with T-shirts, caps, stuffed animals and coloring books. The balloon, designed and built by Aerostar International in Sioux Falls, South Dakota, has 28 inflatable animals, one of which is Queenie, the cow. The high flying ark with rainbow overhead is the most complex balloon of its type, the ultimate in "moo-vability." The floating zoo was endangered in a trial run when forced to make an emergency landing on a busy Sioux Falls street due to dying wind and depleting fuel, but the ark was saved.[288]

TRIPP, 664

Some of the sturdy German-Russian homesteaders walked or traveled a hundred miles by ox-cart to get needed supplies before the railroad came in 1886. They were a determined people who moved from Germany to South Russia in search of freedom. When the Russian government changed its policy in 1871, forcing them to use the Russian language and participate in military service, they left Russia and moved to Dakota Territory, bringing old world traditions. "House-barn combinations were popular, and almost every home had a Sommer Kuche (summer kitchen) close by. Also each home had a Lieberherrgottseck (God's corner), where a Bible was kept among baptism, confirmation, and marriage certificates. Pictures of a religious nature were hung on the walls of that corner, which served as a religious focal point for the family." The culinary heritage has endured, and families occasionally enjoy a good meal of spatzele, kase knopfle, fleisch kuchle or bratwurst along with beer or schnapps in Tripp.[289]

TULARE, 244

Tulare was without a cafe, and residents missed a place to enjoy meals and visits. Townsfolk took action and found a building where they set up a cafe. Volunteers cook, wait tables and serve the tasty home-style food which is delivered to those who can't come in. It's service with a smile in Tulare.

TURTON, 76

The village blacksmith traditionally "shot off the anvil" on the Fourth of July in Turton. The anvil was moved out into the street, and a torch at the end of a long rod ignited the gunpowder on the anvil. The deafening explosion occurred at about 3 or 4 o'clock in the morning. If one didn't hear the blast, there was reason to question one's hearing - or sobriety.

Because of the many functions the smithy performed, he was as important to the community as the doctor or midwife. As an ironworker, the blacksmith made the plowshares, fixed the shafts on threshing machines and forged small parts for buggies, wagons, sleighs and other farm equipment. He also replaced boards on wagon boxes. The blacksmith was a wheelwright and farrier; he shod horses and also fashioned bars or plates for teams of oxen. When horseless carriages arrived on the scene, he tried to keep them running, too. As the handiest man in town, the smithy was responsible for the wheels of progress.

TUTHILL

Everything is "ducky" at the the 16,000 acre Lacreek National Wildlife Refuge which provides shelter for ducks, geese, trumpeter swans, sharp-tailed grouse, pheasants and other species. If you are extremely lucky, you might see a whooping crane on its 3700 mile migratory flight between its summer home in Canada and its winter home in Texas and New Mexico. The "whoopers," North America's tallest flying birds, are rare birds numbering only about 200. As scientists studied the birds in an effort to save them from extinction, they removed eggs from nests containing more than one, since the whooping cranes are usually successful in raising only one hatchling. The eggs taken from parental nests were placed in nests of sandhill cranes who hatched the birds and taught them to find food and avoid predators such as coyotes and eagles. That helped the comeback of the whooping cranes whose population dipped to 16 in 1941.

TYNDALL, 1201

Ballooning enthusiast, Jacques Soukup, grew up near Tyndall and was instrumental in the town's role as host of The Sixth World

Gas Balloon and First World Roziere Balloon Championship, September 21-30, 1990. The competition brought contestants from various countries, and the longest flight ever logged in a world hot-air balloon championship was achieved by an Austrian pair who landed their balloon near Stillwater, Oklahoma. Nick Saum of the U.S.A. placed first in the Roziere championship, a long distance competition for specially constructed balloons fueled by helium.

UNION CENTER

For 30 years, nuclear missiles were planted in fields in 150 scattered sites of western South Dakota, including Union Center. Ranchers patriotically tolerated nuclear nuisance when helicopters checking on the facilities caused cattle stampedes. A newborn lamb wiggled inside one fenced site and tripped an alarm. Security guards refused to let the rancher help in the retrieval of his lamb until their attempts to chase it were futile. Rattlesnakes, cottontail rabbits and tumbleweeds set off alarms, too. A rancher triggered an alarm when the mound of hay he was moving swerved into the path of the highly sensitive radar around a silo. Reflecting on the number of gun-toting guards who suddenly appeared that day, the rancher said, "Jimminy Christmas, you'd think I started World War III!" To comply with terms of S.A.L.T., the Air Force proceeded with removal of the missiles. Although the military personnel provided a presence sometimes welcome in remote areas of western South Dakota, the nuisance of the situation will not be missed.[290]

USTA

The name came from the term "Huste," meaning cripple, which Native Americans gave to G. E. (Ed) Lemmon, who covered almost every foot of range land in western South Dakota on horseback. The town of Lemmon, 50 miles north of Usta, is also named for the "Boss Cowman" whose right leg was crushed by his horse in 1871, when he was 14. Lemmon broke the same leg the next year when he went down with another horse. His bad leg, although an identifying characteristic, didn't slow him down during 53 years in the saddle as cowhand, trail rider, wagon boss, range manager and ranch owner.

Ed Lemmon handled more cattle than any other man of his time, bossed the biggest roundup and had the record of 900 cattle cut, roped and branded in a day. The old cowboy had great respect for his cutting horse, Bosler Blue, whom he regarded as the best ever, but Lemmon said it was harder to train a good cutting man than a good horse. As a wagon boss, he worked the second guard from twelve to two in the morning and got up with the cook, crawling into his bedroll 18 hours later after being in the saddle all day. Said Lemmon, "I throve on it."[291] The Sheidley Cattle Company leased 865,000 acres of land on the Standing Rock Reservation and enclosed the area with a three wire fence. As range manager of 53,000 cattle branded L7, Lemmon supervised the biggest fenced pasture in the world, an area bigger than the state of Rhode Island. That's how it "Usta" be!

UTICA, 115

In 1870, a Bohemian trading center known as Ziskov was established in the vicinity of Utica. A number of Czechs settled in an area west of Yankton, and these hard-working and fun-loving people brought an exuberance and a hearty love of life and music. The concertina, an accordion-like instrument of which the Bohemians were fond, provided music for many gatherings and dances.

VALE

A 1974 accident at a missile site in the Vale area was one of the 32 worst nuclear weapons accidents between 1950 and 1980. It wasn't made public until years later. Although it was a close call, the Air Force said there was no leak of radio-active material. Two security system repairmen were inside the silo on December 5, 1964, when they heard the rumble of the retro-rockets.

> According to a Pentagon report, a seven-foot section containing the warhead and re-entry vehicle atop a Minuteman I accidentally was blown off as Dodson (one of the two repairmen) and a colleague checked a fuse on the security system. The warhead never left the silo. But the firing of a re-entry rocket tipped it off its perch. Twice grazing the missile and

once hitting the side of the cone, the warhead plunged 57 feet. It struck support cables, then fell 16 feet farther to the floor, coming to rest horizontally beneath the missile. One estimate said the warhead, probably 1 megaton, was capable of killing 250,000 if exploded over Detroit. A months long investigation concluded the screwdriver Dodson used to jostle a fuse had crossed the wrong wires.[292]

VALLEY SPRINGS, 739

The Jenney family endeared themselves to the community where Reverend Mr. Edward Jenney served as pastor of the Federated Congregational Church from 1916 until his death in 1921 at the age of 78. His wife, Katherine Thrall Jenney was one of the first female graduates of Knox College after the Civil War. After marriage, the Jenneys did missionary work in Macedonia, now Turkey, until malaria forced their return to the United States. Then, Rev. Jenney served several South Dakota pastorates while his wife promoted foreign missions.

The two Jenney daughters, Adeline and Harriet, both educators, joined their elderly parents in Valley Springs and made significant contributions to the life of the community. Adeline M. Jenney was the second Poet Laureate of South Dakota and edited three books of poetry in addition to writing a novel, stories and poems. She was awarded an honorary doctoral degree and continued editing and writing until she was 96.[293]

VEBLEN, 321

The Fairmount and Veblen Railway was completed in 1913 and provided an important connection for the two communities 50 miles apart. Residents wanted the railroad for shipping goods and commodities and became actively involved in doing the work to bring the line to their area. The railroad was known as the "F and V," the "Hay Line" and the "The Snus Line," because Norwegian men used "snus" (tobacco), which American slang picked up as "snoose" for chewing tobacco.

VERMILLION, 10,034

August 24, 1804, Lewis and Clark camped near the White Stone (Vermillion) River. Having heard about a place called

Spirit Mound, they and seven expedition members hiked eight miles to see it. In 1893, Elliot Coues published an account of the Lewis and Clark expedition, telling of the excursion to Spirit Mound:

> August 25th. . . . The heat was so oppressive that we were obliged to send back our dog to the creek, as he was unable to bear the fatigue; and it was not till after four hours' march that we reached the object of our visit. . . .The Indians have made it a great article of their superstition; it is called the mountain of Little People, or Little Spirits, and they believe that it is the abode of little devils in the human form, about 18 inches high and with remarkable large heads, armed with short arrows, with which they are very skillful, and always on the watch to kill those who should have the hardihood to approach their residence. The tradition is that many have suffered from these little evil spirits; among others, three Maha Indians fell a sacrifice to them a few years since. This has inspired all the other neighboring nations . . . with such terror that no consideration could tempt them to visit the hill. We saw none of these wicked little spirits; . . .though we remained some time on the mound to enjoy the delightful prospect of the plain. . .enlivened by large herds of buffalo feeding at a distance.[294]

VIBORG, 763

Viborg residents yielded to temptation when they approved on-sale liquor in 1991 after previously rejecting eight such attempts in over 71 years. In 1993, residents drank a toast in celebration of the Viborg centennial. A wagon train of 22 wagons and 70 riders opened the festivities. Children will long remember a ride home from school in a horse-drawn school bus built for the occasion. Centennial festivities included a parade, road races, white horse patrol, street dance, beard judging, skydiving, church services, tractor pull, barbecue and more. The success of the centennial celebration resulted in a decision to revive Viborg's Danish Festival Days. Danes settled the area of Viborg, once the largest Danish Colony in the United States.

VIENNA, 93

A story of true grit comes from an area native whose father emigrated from Vienna, Austria, and settled in what became

Vienna, South Dakota. When you think you're having a bad day, consider the life of Josephine Wopat Stevens who wrote,

> . . .When I was six years old, my mother passed away. . . .
>
> When I was 14 I had to make my own clothes I wore - even my undies, petticoats and I knit my own stockings, when we needed stockings, that is, as we went barefoot most of the time. . .The shoes were made from pigskin from the hogs we butchered for meat.
>
> When I was 15 my stepmother died. That left us girls, Molly and I, to take over.
>
> When I was 16 I got appendicitis and as there was no one to operate locally, I was shipped to Minneapolis on a stretcher in a baggage car with an ice pack on my side. . . .
>
> By 18 I was my own boss so I sent my name into Aberdeen for a land lottery. I was lucky to get my name drawn and got a quarter of land in the Cheyenne Reservation. I went to the reservation near Eagle Butte and had to build a certain dimension house. . . .
>
> Then we ran out of money, not even enough for a stamp to write home, stamps were 3 cents. . . .
>
> Marie and I went to town to get a job. . . .
>
> After four years of "holding down our claim" we owned 160 acres of prairie grass - so we all left. . . .
>
> I rode back to the old home and hard work. I rode home from Eagle Butte on my horse and led another one. I had to cross the Missouri River on the ferry. That was fun! I lost my Western horses to Glanders disease. . . .we broke a cow to pull a stone-boat to haul our eggs and butter to the highway where a neighbor picked it up to take it to town for groceries as nothing could last on the farm for a year. . . .
>
> . . .We got along.[295]

VIRGIL, 33

Water is and was a precious resource. Settlers sometimes hauled water for miles on a stone boat, a kind of sled used to remove stones from fields. The Doyle family in Virgil "had the only good water near Virgil" and supplied others. A son of the family worked for the railroad but lost his job when he was "falsely accused of hitting a surveyor's stake." The father refused to give the foreman water unless he reinstated the son who had been wrongly fired. The worker was rehired, and the foreman got his water.[296]

VIVIAN

Top ten responses to "What was the *Vivian Wave*?"

     #10: Prairie grass blowing in the wind
     #9: A cowhand ready to lasso a steer
     #8: Breakup of an icejam in Medicine Creek
     #7: I surely don't know!
     #6: Friendly arm movement
     #5: Cold weather front moving in
     #4: A 50's style perm
     #3: Closing time at the bar
     #2: A female Naval recruit from Vivian
     #1: Newspaper of 1906

And the correct answer is: #1! *The Westover Wave* was established in 1904 and became the *Vivian Wave* when the newspaper moved to Vivian in 1906. [297]

VOLGA, 1263

Scandinavians prevail in this town with a Russian name chosen to attract German-Russian immigrants who never came. Some may remember the chapter "Pa Goes to Volga." in Laura Ingalls Wilder's book, *The Long Winter,* which tells of the winter of 1880-1881. The first blizzard came in October, and snow continued to fall until April. Trains carrying desperately needed food and fuel could not get through, and ingenuity was necessary as provisions grew scarce. Ma made "apple" pie of green pumpkins, and the family ground wheat in the coffee grinder. They burned calico in axle grease in a saucer for light while the family twisted hay to burn for warmth. When there was a break in the weather, Pa Ingalls joined six other men on a handcar over the 50 miles of railroad track to Volga, pumping the open-air car in the frigid air and clearing the track where necessary. They succeeded in opening the way for the westward bound train from Volga.

VOLIN, 175

If you're looking for the "Little Town with a Big Heart," this is it! Michael Hill, a potter who moved to Volin, says, "This is just where I wanted to live. It's so nice out here. . . .Maybe it's just the pace of life, the type of people, the land. Everything about it is thoroughly intriguing." A variety of wildlife wanders through the yard of his studio near a spring-fed creek. In those peaceful surroundings, Hill gives form and new life to earthen clay.[298]

WAGNER, 1462

In the vicinity of Wagner, you may hear a beautiful tune coming from the home of a Native American musician. A large man with long braids, Vince Two Eagles, speaks the truth powerfully through music, using traditional flute, guitar and drums. According to Two Eagles, "The drum is the heartbeat of native people." The rhythms and feelings find beat and expression in the music of Two Eagles, who often puts words written by his wife, Gayle, to melody. Two Eagles said, "I want to see the truth, and the truth is sometimes ugly. But people have the power to change it, and that's what we're trying to do with our music - to empower people to think and to change things on their own. The only person you can change is yourself."[299]

WAKONDA, 329

The name meaning "something wonderful" is of Santee Sioux origin. Gene Vognild, who grew up in the Wakonda area, reflected warmly on being born and raised in the town:

> We used to have a saddle club and all my friends and I had our horses and spent a lot of time riding through the hills west of Wakonda - good outdoor time with your friends. . . . I always spent my summers working on the farm and enjoyed farm life. All my friends and everyone grew up on the farm. . . .Farm people are just real wonderful people to deal with and be acquainted with.[300]

WAKPALA

The Standing Rock buttes in the area are holy places in the culture and religion of the Lakota who for centuries have retreated to the buttes in their vision quests.

> Anthropologist Bea Medicine, a Blackfeet Lakota who grew up near Wakpala in the shadow of Rattlesnake Butte, says the

buttes represent the power of Wakan and remind Lakota of their connection to the land. "This is the last stronghold we have with the continent," she says, "The power is there. They give me a sense of place and space, a sense of belonging and being part of a universe that is primarily Lakota."[301]

Dr. Bea Medicine, a Wakpala native, holds earned and honorary doctoral degrees and was an associate professor of anthropology at California State University. In retirement, she moved to the Wakpala area where she continues to write and do research. She said,

> . . . .My main interest though is living as a Lakota. I feel much more a part of the Lakota people than I do of the white man's world.
>
> And I try to live like a Sioux woman. We were grounded in our culture, and I think that's what really helped me. My father always taught us about the Lakota beliefs, the four cardinal virtues: hospitality, bravery, fortitude and wisdom.[302]

WALL, 834

Frank Hart was one of the greatest bronco busters that ever was. One who knew Hart said, "No cowboy ever drew a breath that could outride Frank Hart." Arch Hall told of taking Frank Hart to the untertaker when they thought he was dead:

> Once a bronc threw Frank on the frozen ground while he was riding "slickered" in a blizzard on Lake Flat north of Wall, only Wall wasn't there then. Frank hit the flinty ground so hard it killed him. Cowboys swore he was stone dead. Frank stopped breathing for a half-day. He was so dead the boys loaded him into a buckboard to haul him into Rapid City and the undertaker. Some kind soul noticed Frank's spurs had not been removed and out of respect for their poor deceased pard began taking them off. The boys turned white as ghosts when the tarp covering the body was suddenly thrown back and Frank's rumbling voice said calmly. . . ."Don't touch them spurs and where is the damned fool horse. I'm going to bust him wide open!" A few minute later Frank was back in the saddle to conquer the outlaw once and for all.[303]

Wall Drug signs have been sighted in far away places, including the French Riviera, Antartica, the African Continent and Vietnam during the war years. The well-publicized business draws about 1.5 million tourists into the the town each year. It all began in 1935 when Dorothy Hustead heard the traffic going by her husband's struggling drug store and thought of a way to entice people to stop. Soon, Burma Shave style road signs advertised, "Get a soda. Get root beer. Turn next corner. Just as near. To Highway 16 and 14. Free ice water. Wall Drug." That was the start of a tourist attraction advertised around the world.

WALLACE, 83

In 1911, the late Vice-President Hubert Horatio Humphrey, Jr. was born in Wallace in an apartment over his father's pharmacy. Herb Gilbey helped save the life of young Humphrey when the boy was very ill with pneumonia. Gilbey drove over 500 miles through a blinding snowstorm in his unheated Model T Ford to Minneapolis to get an experimental drug thought to be the only hope for saving seven year-old Hubert Humphrey.

WANBLEE, 671

In 1874, 20 year-old Gus Craven left New Jersey to go West to be a cowboy. He trailed cows from the Kansas railhead to Wyoming and acquired a few heifers of his own. That was the start of the well-known Open Buckle Ranch. Good grazing and availability of water prompted Craven to locate his operation on Eagle Nest Creek. In 1914, the Open Buckle Ranch moved to a site with a fine spring 12 miles northwest of Wanblee with a view of the Badlands and plateaus.[304] Wanblee was named for nearby Eagle Nest Butte, called "Wamblee Hokpila" by the Lakota.[305]

WARNER, 336

A round barn southeast of Warner is one of fewer than three dozen circular barns in the state, all built before 1925. Most were built of concrete blocks and had silos in the center, but the Warner area structure is a polygonal wooden building. George Washington built a similar structure of 16 sides and may have been the first American farmer to have such a barn. The Shakers built round barns which suited their desire for simplicity in design and function. "Historians also think the Shakers built round barns to keep the devil away. Lucifer supposedly avoids buildings without corners in which to hide." [306]

WASTA, 82

The Cheyenne River that flows through the area has been known by many variations of the name. Old Spanish maps called it the Chyanne; it was also referred to as the Chaquiennes, the Shayenne and the Chaquyene. To Lewis and Clark, it sounded like the French word "Chien" (or Dog River). As the second largest tributary of the Upper Missouri, the Cheyenne provided transportion for the fur trade, and trappers shipped thousands of hides and pelts down the river. In spring of 1830, more than 5000 buffalo robes were transported by bateau.

Homesteaders forded the Cheyenne with a team pulling a wagon load of possessions in boxes and salt barrels. One settler stopped at an isolated house to ask directions. Using sign language, a Native American with long black braids pointed the way to Wasta hill, an area landmark. Writing later about his travel through the area as a homesteader, Ernest Bormann wrote,

> This was no smooth highway for me at the time, but a narrow, crooked and steep trail, slippery as soap from recent rains. A scared young man and a couple of sliding horses managed to get down into town. I left my team in the always present livery stable of the Dakota towns of those days, and found the only hotel, where both food and lodging were available. "If you want fine board, ask for sawdust," a sign told me. I settled for meat and potatoes.[307]

WATERTOWN, 17,592

The stones at Stoney Point on Lake Kampeska and Maiden's Island, several hundred yards from the shore, are part of a story. Legend tells of young Sioux braves who wanted to win the heart of a beautiful young woman, Minnecotah. To determine who might win her favor, they competed to see who could hurl rocks and boulders farthest from shore. Because her true love was away,

Minnecotah prolonged the competition. The rocks accumulated to form a stone island. Waves made it difficult to determine distances of boulders hurled, and the competitors grew frustrated. To force a decision, the men placed Minnecotah on the island without food or shelter. A protector in the form of a great white pelican brought fish to the young woman. Finally, her lover returned and canoed to her by night. He swept her into his arms, tenderly placed her in his canoe, and left with her to live happily ever after. The disappointed braves did not know of the arrival of her lover and upon finding Minnecotah missing, decided that the white pelican had been sent by the sun god to transport her to other realms. [308]

WAUBAY, 647

Samuel J. Brown, "South Dakota's Paul Revere," rode in the Waubay area. Born in 1845 at a trading post established by his father, Sam Brown knew the area well and became chief of scouts at Fort Wadsworth (later called Fort Sisseton). When Brown received word that a hostile Indian party was advancing toward the settlements in April of 1866, he wrote a warning to be sent to Fort Abercrombie the next morning. Then, he mounted a horse and rode 45 miles to a scout camp near the present site of Columbia, arriving at midnight. There he learned that the reported hostiles were actually runners carrying a message to Native Americans that President Johnson had signed a peace treaty. Despite a raging storm and a need for sleep, Sam Brown returned to Fort Wadsworth to stop the message to Fort Abercrombie. He lost his way in the blizzard during the night and found his bearings by daylight near Waubay Lakes. By the time Sam Brown rode northward to the fort, he had traveled over 150 miles on horseback in the most miserable of conditions. He was almost frozen upon arrival and had to be lifted from his mount. Sam Brown succeeded in his valiant attempt to prevent bloodshed but remained paralyzed the rest of his life.

WAVERLY

If one wanted an evening out on the town in the late 1800's, chores were done early to make it possible to catch the 5:00 p.m. train to Watertown. At the end of the evening, announcement of approaching departure time alerted patrons at the "Old Met" theater, but the train often waited for latecomers. Since Waverly had no physician, a Watertown doctor took the midnight train to Waverly and made rounds by horse and buggy, before returning to Watertown on the 6 a.m. train. That's service in the 1800's.

WEBSTER, 2017

George Whyte, a VISTA volunteer, came to Webster in the early 1960's, planning to help farmers get started in hog raising. Plans took a turn when Whyte looked at the beautiful quilts made by Native Americans and saw a product with possibilities. His first attempt to market the quilts in New York City and Washington D.C. failed miserably, and Whyte says with a laugh, "If we knew anything about business we wouldn't have started." Whyte's visionary thinking gave birth to Dakotah, Inc. which makes home fashion products sold today by major retailers across the country. Much of the inspiration and many of the designs come from people of the nearby Sisseton Wahpeton Dakota nation. Many work as cooperative members for Dakotah which has provided not only income but pride. Dakotah, Inc., employs about 350 at its plants in Webster, Sisseton and Veblen but has a hard time keeping up with orders.[309]

WENTWORTH, 181

Puzzling and unusual designs in fields in Great Britain were eventually explained as a great hoax. In 1969, a Wentworth farmer employed a strategy similar to that used in creating the mysterious designs in British fields. He disked a field to create a message that could be read from the air. "Hi, Nixon" was seen by President Nixon during a visit to the state.

WESSINGTON, 265

In 1993, Wessington, a farming community of 265 people, ran an ad in the Mother Earth News that said, "WANTED MOTIVATED FAMILY looking for child oriented community. Small business opportunity welcomed. Homes/buildings available. Innovative K-12 school. Excellent hunting, fishing. 605/458-2249. Boxholder, P.O. 167, Wessington, SD 57381." The responses were surprising, and one of the earliest came from a San Bernardino, California, family who decided to move after seeing videos of the town and exploring possibilities. Said one of the happy new residents of Wessington, "This is like a little piece of heaven here. You couldn't pay me enough to go back to California. . . Everybody here waves to you, and everybody cares about you."[310] Wessington is attracting interest and was featured on national television in September 1993.

WESSINGTON SPRINGS, 1083

Farmer Ed Bult was working in his wheat field in the summer of 1993 when he "spied a huge brown cat lying in a nearby alfalfa field." Then, he saw a smaller cat, presumably a cub. Skeptics raised their eyebrows at the report and thought maybe Bult was dreaming while spending long hours on his John Deere tractor. Bult called the county sheriff, "thinking that maybe a lion had escaped from a circus or that it was somebody's pet." The description fit that of a mountain lion, a shy, secretive animal which feeds on smaller wild animals, including deer. Wildlife officers were very interested, but they never caught sight of the big cat. Mountain lions are rare east of the Missouri River, although they are sometimes sighted in the Black Hills.[311]

WHITE, 536

White had more action than it wished on a day in May in 1969 when the students of South Dakota State University promoted a "Whip to White Day," after hearing about a North Dakota "Zip to Zap Day." When over 600 students came to a party to wind up the semester in White, students outnumbered townspeople and caused more mayhem than the residents wanted. A second annual "Whip to White Day" was publicized, but residents quickly discouraged the idea which, fortunately for the people of White, fizzled.[312]

WHITE LAKE, 419

The people of White Lake are to be applauded for their leadership in showing sensitivity to racial concerns. In 1993, they changed the name of their high school team from the Indians to the fighting Wolverines. While many saw nothing derogatory in playing proudly as the Indians, others understood that because animal names are often used for teams, the Native American mascot identity caused offense.

Some Native American elders wonder why they should be called Indians as the result of Columbus' confusion in thinking he was in India. Agnes Ross said, "Oh I hate to use the word, Indian, but I do. I guess it is the way people understand best. But really, we are the Dakota people."[313]

WHITE RIVER, 595

Early settlers created their own entertainment in the first years on their homesteads. Everyone contributed to Sunday dinner gatherings, and afterwards, the men usually played baseball. Threshing time, birthday celebrations and the Fourth of July also brought people together.

Jessie Ilgenfritz described community activity:

> . . .There was always something to look forward to. Often it was a dance at the house of one of the neighbors. They set most of the furniture (there wasn't much) outside, to make room in the little 10 x 12 shack for the dancers. If there happened to be another room, the babies and small children were parked in there. Usually there was someone in the crowd who was able to play a fiddle, banjo or accordion. If nothing else was available, a mouth harp or a comb would serve the purpose.[314]

Homesteaders in White River sometimes joined Native Americans in dances in the log Indian dance hall down by the river. The big octagon-shaped building had a flag pole in the middle, and at the celebrations, a kettle of dog soup hung in the center of the building. Cups were attached to the pole for those who wished to partake of the soup. The Native Americans wore their finest beaded buckskin clothing, and some of the women wore black dresses decorated with valuable elk's teeth. The men sat on benches lining the wall and smoked their pipes while the women sat on the ground in a circle, smoking cigarettes. Faces were painted with bright red and blue paint, an unusual sight for a white newcomer. These gatherings broke the ice for Native Americans and settlers as they danced together and formed friendships.[315]

WHITE ROCK

Old-timers remember the boulder in White Rock, from which the once lively town took its name. The boulder disappeared from the scene, and the town almost vanished, too. In 1980, eight residents lived in White Rock when Steve Burgess moved there, and he remained as the others left. When it became too quiet, Burgess played his guitar or listened to the radio, with his dog for company, while he watched the snow pile up on winter days. He gained a neighbor when Californian Rudy Rodriquez moved to White Rock in 1993, and a few more followed. Although there were seven residents at last count, White Rock remains a quiet place where one can enjoy the solitary, reflective life.

WHITEWOOD, 891

The pretty town of Whitewood, situated among aspen and birch, became the respectable successor to Crook City, a roaring town of Gold Rush days, now a ghost town a mile-and-a-half away. At one time, Crook City had a population of almost 3000 and was the temporary seat of Lawrence County. The dusty main street was filled with an assortment of colorful characters, including drifters, prospectors, gamblers, cowpunchers, bullwhackers and tenderfeet. In the year of Crook City's founding, it was reported that, "On the Fourth of July 1876, the day began with gun play but it was decided not to bury the dead until after the races were over."[316] When the railroad came through, surveyors decided that the railroad could never make the grade from Crook City to Deadwood. So, tracks were laid about a mile away, where Whitewood sprang into being.

WILLOW LAKE, 317

A new resident had these observations about life in Willow Lake:

> Willow Lake is a dusty little town in the eastern part of the state, 45 minutes from anything resembling a large town. We have one little store, Jan's Clover Farm, the R & H Cafe, a bank, post office, school, bar, recreation center, grain elevator, meat locker, two beauty shops and about a half dozen buildings dotting main street which have long since lost their usefulness.

Retired

On a windy day, dust clouds waft in the air, clinging to freshly laundered clothing and sticking to anything in its path. They tell me it was once a growing, bustling town.

Willow Lake, South Dakota, is not on the cutting edge of our society. There are no fashion districts. We will never be cited as the place where trends begin. Tourists visiting the United States will not pick Willow Lake as a stop on their itinerary. But Willow Lake, like so many little towns dotting the Great Plains of South Dakota, has a rich natural resource in its people. For a land which offers hot, and often dry summers and cold, blustery winters, these people are determined to make the land come alive in their spirit of making room, their caring and their vision.[317]

WILMOT, 566

The train depot was a hub of activity at the turn of the century when Wilmot was an important trade center.

> At train time the (Wilmot) depot was an exciting spot: reporters from the two newspapers checking the coming-and-going of passengers; the postmaster with his two-wheeled push-cart for mail; two hotel-men, each with his cart to pick up the smaller bags for their over-night guest. - The train-service was important, being practically the only means of travel to Sisseton and return the same day. Grocery and fruit salesmen came, working part of the town during switching-time, with two long blasts from the whistle warning that the train was about to leave. Drygoods and shoe salesmen came, with 5 or 6 large trunks of samples, staying two or three days, showing their wares, and taking orders for future delivery. Then to Browns Valley via team and heavy buckboard from the local livery barn, carrying the salesman and his trunks, as well as the driver. In these days, the small town supplied all the needs of their trade territory, which was quite sharply defined as the half-way distance to the nearest town in any direction.[318]

WINFRED, 54

In September of 1994, to reduce cost of government, Winfred residents voted to cease to be a town. The 1994 budget was $16,000 for insurance, street lights, salaries, fire hall expenses and road repairs. As of 1995, Winfred will be governed by

Winfred Township, which most residents think will be fine. Of 45 registered voters, 29 voted to unincorporate and 5 voted against dissolution of the town.[319]

WINNER, 3354

The first weekend of pheasant hunting season in October brings a flurry of activity to Winner. Hunters fly in from all over the country with their dogs, and nonresident hunting licenses are in demand as 40,000 out-of-staters come to hunt in South Dakota each year. Motels are booked a year in advance, and all rental cars are reserved. Friendships develop between hunting parties and the families who host them yearly. Farmers typically charge $50 to $100 per day, depending on the services provided and the number of birds brought in from the field.

The state has many good hunting areas, and good natured rivalry develops between communities vying for the distinction of "pheasant hunting capital." The story is told of a radio announcer touting the virtues of Redfield (200 miles from Winner) as the pheasant capital and calling a Winner resident to ask why that city claimed the title. "Why that's easy," said the resident, "The flock is so big around here it reaches clear up to Redfield."[320]

WITTEN, 87

A Witten teacher, Ruby Bennett Williams, wrote about the night spent with nine students at East Banner School during a blizzard in January 1952. When the storm began in the afternoon, five of the children were able to go home, but the others had to stay overnight at the schoolhouse. The teacher lived at the school in winter and made a supper from supplies on hand. The children looked forward to playing games and spending the night together, but when the heat went out, the fun lessened.

> About ten o'clock my first, second and third graders were getting pretty sleepy so they crawled into bed with their caps, coats, mitten and overshoes on. I put a heavy blanket over them and they soon went to sleep. Then one by one the others, who thought they could stay up all night, crawled under the blanket to keep warm. My seventh graders took turns. Before morning

there were eight on the bed. . . .Along about 5:30 a.m. the chidren started moving around. But they soon crawled back on the bed as the floor was so cold. For breakfast we had two cookies apiece and all the water we wanted to drink. . . . Duwayne Maas, age 13, decided he could follow the fence to his place about a mile away. I hated to see him go but he said he might as well go as to freeze in the school house. It was about noon when I finally let him go. Then I worried about him until I heard his name over the WNAX radio station that he had arrived home safely and they asked for someone to come to our aid. . . .About 2:30 p.m. Mr. Slim Schwinler arrived after having walked three miles to the school house and we were all glad to see him. He had brought some scarves to tie over the chidren's faces and some twine to tie the children together so no one would get lost. We decided to go to the Maas place. Mr. Schwinler asked every child if they wanted to try going and if just one had said no he would not have started out. The Maas place was about a mile southwest of the school. Before we got half-way there four of the children were crying and we all had our turn falling down. I do not believe we could have gone much farther. . . . Mrs. Maas had a very nice supper for us and we were all hungry. We spent the night there. After it was all over Mr. Schwinler said, "Happy Birthday, Mrs. Williams," and that's one birthday I won't forget.[321]

WOLSEY, 442

A Grand Ball traditionally marked the opening of a new hotel in the West. Although the Wolsey Hotel was not very grand, an opening ball took place during the holidays. A large, cast-iron stove in the center of the dining-room and another in the office heated the "so-called hotel." Around the exterior, a three-foot high bank of manure held in place by boards helped to insulate and provide heat as it decayed. Wolsey had no saloon; so party-goers brought their own beverages, and the proprietor sold Tom and Jerry on the side. The building was filled to capacity with locals and visitors from Huron. When it was almost time for the last dance of the evening, everyone able to stand was out on the floor. "The caller was shouting 'Alamand left, Forward and back, Swing your partners,' etc., when one of the graders, a big bohunk, swung his long-legged Norwegian partner against the redhot stove, knocking it over, breaking her leg and setting the building on fire."[322] Pandemonium prevailed, and in the end, there was a pile of smoking manure on the scene of the Wolsey Hotel.

Richard Sears, the first railroad station agent in Wolsey in 1882, had unclaimed C.O.D. shipments at the station. At the suggestion of a jewelry company which had shipped some of the goods, he sold the articles on commission. This success in merchandising led to a small mail order business. Two years later he left Wolsey and with a partner organized Sears, Roebuck & Company.[323]

WOOD, 73

One early resident reminisced:

> Those farm days near Wood have their share of memories, too. The sweet sharp song of a meadowlark on a fencepost; fleecy white clouds with every fold and billow plain against the deep blue sky; the wind, sometimes just rattling the cottonwood leaves, sometimes pushing against you hard; mouthwatering wild plums hanging ripe from the trees along the creek; distant coyote howls mingled with pulsing tom-toms in the night; endless miles of hard crusted snow for me and my sled; digging blue-white caves in the big drifts; building shaky rafts that almost sank in the swollen creek after the thaws; dad showing me how to make willow whistles; sneaking up on prairie chickens with a .22, trapping for rabbits and catching a skunk!; gathering hailstones to make ice cream.[324]

Mrs. A.K. Wood, who came from Culpepper, Virginia, and married the man for whom the town was named, liked the friendliness of the area. Her daughter said,

> In fact, it was nothing unusual to find a note on the kitchen table in the morning saying, "Thank you for the breakfast, we were passing through." Travelers knew they were welcome, so had stopped to help themselves. She liked the Indians, too. She was the only white woman on the reservation and when she brought Mary Gray home, a little baby girl with golden curls, the Indians were fascinated. She was a great curiosity. Many a time Mrs. Wood would be working in the kitchen and

have the feeling that someone was watching. Only to realize that it was a squaw with her nose pressed to the window pane. She would take Mary Gray out for them to see and touch, as if she were a doll. . . .We never locked our doors. Never had any keys in the keyhole so that in the winter snow drifted through and made a pyramid of snow on the floor inside.[325]

WOONSOCKET, 766

The *Mitchell Gazette* of October 5, 1893 stated, "In cereals, South Dakota easily leads the world, and the 'corn belt' is well up in the vanguard. Twenty-three varieties of wheat, all raised successfully in the 'corn belt' are on exhibition." C.W. Post proposed building a cereal factory in Woonsocket if the town would give him land, but community leaders were skeptical. Mr. Post took his idea elsewhere, eventually establishing Post Cereal Corporation in Battle Creek, Michigan.

WORTHING, 371

It may seem like an unlikely place, but Worthing offers a unique dinner-theater experience at The Olde Towne Theater. In a no frills setting, intimate theater takes place in what was once the old furniture store. Less adventuresome folks might raise their eyebrows, but it is a place to relax and enjoy an evening of entertainment without hassle. There is no worry about getting lost, tipping the valet, big city crime, or several lanes of traffic. Main Street offers diagonal parking in front of this not-like-New York theater. After the show, you can conveniently step through the connecting doorway into the cozy neighboring establishment for libations. A few doors down, a country band plays for dancing at the American Legion Hall. That's "Saturday Night Live" in Worthing!

WOUNDED KNEE

Wounded Knee speaks of the tragedy of misunderstanding in a poignant way. Although the pain of a bloody hour 100 years ago is still felt today, it strengthens our resolve to promote reconciliation.

In 1889, news of a new Messiah came to the Native Americans at Pine Ridge. A Paiute Indian named Wovaka, better known as Jack Wilson, had fallen asleep during the total eclipse of the sun on January 1, 1889, and said he was taken up to a beautiful heaven but sent back to earth with a message. The message Jack Wilson proclaimed was, in part:

> Grandfather (meaning himself, the Messiah) says when your friends die you must not cry. You must not hurt anybody or do harm to anyone. You must not fight. Do right always. It will give you satisfaction in life.
>
> Do not tell the white people about this. Jesus is now upon earth. He appears like a cloud. The dead are all alive again. I do not know when they will be here, maybe in the fall or in the spring. When the time comes there will be no more sickness, and everyone will be young again. Do not refuse work for the whites and do not make any trouble with them until you leave them. When the earth shakes, at the coming of the new world, do not be afraid, it will not hurt you.
>
> I want you to dance every six weeks. Make a feast at the dance and have food that everyone may eat. Then bathe in the water. That is all. You will receive good words from me some- times. Do not tell lies.[326]

The altered message that came to the Sioux, according to histo- rian Doane Robinson, was:

> . . .There was a man near the base of the Sierras who was the Son of God, who had once been killed by the Whites, and who bore on his body scars of the crucifixion. He was now return- ing to punish the whites for their wickedness, especially for their injustice toward the Indians. With the coming of the spring of 1891 he would wipe the whites from the face of the earth and would then resurrect all the dead Indians, bring back the buffalo and other game . . . He had before come to the whites, but they had rejected him. He was now the God of the Indians . . .[327]

As the Sioux held dances, officials became increasingly uneasy, but there was no evidence that the Native Americans planned war- fare, despite their many grievances. Many were opposed to the treaty of 1889 which broke up and diminished the Great Sioux Reservation. Agricultural failures of 1889 and 1890 caused a short- age of rations and hunger. A new and ineffective agent at Pine Ridge who "proved to lack tact, judgment and courage" worsened the situation. The Native Americans did not respect the official who resorted to calling in military forces, the first time government troops had been brought to the reservation.

The presence of 3000 troops made the Native Americans uneasy, and 700 warriors fled to the Badlands, "awaiting developments to know whether to come in and surrender or to continue to retreat."[328] As confrontation developed, a Catholic priest brought military leader General Brooke and Lakota chiefs together for a December 6, 1890, meeting which ended in a feast and Indian dance, although there was no real resolution of issues. The government troops were clearly in a position of power and planned to send peaceable Big Foot's band back to their village on the Cheyenne River, a distance great enough to remove them from the hot spot. On the morning of December 19th, 1890, troops of the 7th Cavalry attempted to disarm members of Big Foot's band before taking them to the railroad, although these Minneconjous had not demonstrated hostility. The weapons search provoked excitement and distress in the Indian camp. Yellow Bird, a medicine man, blew an eagle bone whistle and urged resistance, telling the Native Americans to wear their sacred "ghostshirts" which would protect them. "A young Indian, said to have been Black Fox, from Cheyenne River, drew a rifle from under his blanket and fired at the soldiers. . .In a few minutes, 200 Indian men, women and children, with sixty soldiers, were lying dead and wounded on the ground. . . There can be no question that the pursuit was simply a massacre where fleeing women with infants in their arms were shot down after resistance had ceased. . ."[329] Although authorities differ on the numbers of people killed at Wounded Knee, all agree that it was a tragedy.

YALE, 128

Stop and visit, and then you can proudly say, "I went to Yale!"

YANKTON, 12,703

When Elizabeth "Libby" Custer accompanied her husband's regiment to Dakota Territory in spring of 1873, a late spring blizzard raged in Yankton. The soldiers, more concerned about warmth than appearance, improvised leggings and wrapped themselves in scarves. Yankton residents welcomed the soldiers warmly, and Mrs. Custer wrote about a ball there:

> . . . those Western people were generous about lamps, as they are about everything else, and the hall was very bright. The ladies had many trials in endeavoring to make themselves presentable. We burrowed in the depths of trunks for those bits of finery that we had supposed would not be needed again for years. . .There were but few young girls, but that night must have been a memorable one for them. All the town and even the country people, came to the ball. The mayor and common council received us, and the governor opened the festivities.[330]

ZELL

An Austrian immigrant owned most of the land around Zell and was eager to establish a German speaking community of Roman Catholics. When a train bringing newcomers arrived at Redfield, he greeted them with, "Bist du Catalisher?" and encouraged those of similar background to settle in Zell.[331] A remarkable group of nuns obtained land for their order by homesteading at Zell and doing all of their own work to "prove up."

As the town grew, it became a shopping center for the area in the late 1800's. Because travel of 50 miles with a team of oxen might require five days, shopping trips were made once or twice a year. Settlers "made do" until they could purchase needed provisions. Letters were folded and sealed with a drop of wax if there were no envelopes. When kerosene was unavailable for lighting, resourceful pioneers lit a rag or a wick stuck in lard. Ground roast corn or a brown beverage of barley with a bit of ground chicory substituted for coffee. Dried sunflower leaves replaced tobacco. Butter sometimes greased wagon wheels. Grain sacks provided articles of clothing, including mittens and footwear. Ingenuity prevailed.

They Were Able

Pasque-crowned, green-kirtled Spring with a promise
    Met our people that April day,
As their oxen stopped their weary plodding
    At a stream they could trace on their claim's survey.
Here was spread of the virgin prairie,
    With hardly a tree for comfort or shade;
Not a sign of a trail in any direction,
    Except the faint one their own wagons had made.
The moment they turned from the deep-rutted stage route
    They had broken all ties with the world they had known.
Here were their homestead' dream acres unharrowed-
    The future was theirs, they were now on their own;
Yet they brought to this task a joy from the old home,
    With its strength and commitment to meet problems and fears;
With their Bibles and hymnals a clear way they charted
    Which should guide and give meaning to all of their years.
Their week by week prayer hours in some pioneer kitchen-
    With The Book on the table - nail kegs for seat stands -
Brought refreshment and purpose; so -though money was scanty -
    They erect a church - a faith-piloted band.
The community they fashioned is now meeting the challenge
    Of horizons more shrouded, more hard to assay,
Have men, today, faith, vision and courage
    To build for the future as truly as they?
Adeline M. Jenney

Prairie Poets III., (Minneapolis, Minn.: *Pasque Petals*
and The S.D. Poetry Society, 1966), p. 19.

ENDNOTES

1. P. J. DeSmet, *Western Missions and Missionaries* (Shannon, Ireland: Irish University Press, 1972), p. 73.

2. *South Dakota Magazine,* Sept.-Oct. 1992, p. 4.

3. Variations of "Thank God for Small Towns" have appeared in various publications. See *Dakota West,* Vol. 10, (South Dakota Cowboy & Western Heritage Hall of Fame, 1984) p. 27. In *On the Road with Charles Kuralt,* the newsman attributed the piece to Shelton, Nebraska, newspaper editor, Douglas Duncan, who perhaps adapted the material.

4. *South Dakota Magazine,* Nov.-Dec. 1993, p. 14.

5. Bernie Hunhoff, *South Dakota Magazine,* Sept.-Oct. 1993.

6. Randy Hascall, "Cold Doesn't Stop Florida Biker," *Argus Leader,* Nov. 9, 1993

7. Mike Hughes, "Actress finds S.D. people good as gold," *Argus Leader,* May 9, 1993.

8. Dennis Gale, "Prairie Academy fights declining enrollment," *Argus Leader,* Aug. 1, 1993.

9. Chuck Cecil, "Stubble Mulch," *Moody County Enterprise,* Aug. 25, 1993.

10. Mildred Soladey, *Hanson Heritage,* (1963), p. 51.

11. Luther Standing Bear, *My People the Sioux,* (New York: Houghton Mifflin, 1928), p. 235.

12. Fred N. Dunham, *A History of Jerauld County,* (Wessington Springs, S.D.: 1963), p. 15.

13. *Alpena Centennial Flashback,* excerpts from the *Alpena Journal* compiled by Joyce Webb, (1983).

14. Tom Lawrence, "Researcher give critters jobs as Weed Eaters," *Argus Leader,* Aug. 25, 1994.

15. Bernie Hunhoff, "Our Four Corners," *South Dakota Magazine,* Nov.-Dec. 1993, p. 30.

16. *Argus Leader,* Nov. 17, 1985.

17. Brenda Wade Schmidt, "Wanted: movers and shakers," *Argus Leader,* Jan. 26, 1994.

18. Tom Lawrence, "Sold on South Dakota," *Argus Leader,* May 26, 1994.

19. Reprinted in Robert F. Karolevitz, *Douglas County: The Little Giant,* (Armour, S.D.: Douglas County Historical Society, 1983), p. 54.

20. Mildred Schrag quoted in Linda Hallstrom and Maricarrol Kueter, eds., *Country School Days,* (Dallas, Texas: Taylor Publishing Co., 1987), p. 185.

21. Qtd. by Bernie Hunhoff, "Round Barns of South Dakota," *South Dakota Magazine,* Jan.-Feb. 1993, p. 21.

22. Dagny Hinderaker, *Where We Live,* (Watertown, S.D.: *Watertown Public Opinion,* 1978).

23. Mike Trautman, "Witnesses say Olson gave pot immunity," *Argus Leader,* Sept. 28, 1993.

24. Dana Harlow, *Prairie Echoes,* (Aberdeen, S.D.: 1961), p. 176.

25. John E. Miller, *Looking for History on Highway 14,* (Ames, Iowa: W.W. Norton & Co., 1993), p. 14.

26. Centennial Book Committee, *1882-1982, 100 Years of Progress,* (White Lake, S.D.: 1982), p. 270.

27. Cullen Murphy, "The voice of a community: Life as a small-town editor," *U.S.A. Today,* Aug. 4, 1993.

28. *Argus Leader,* July 18, 1993.

29. Miller, *Looking for History on Highway 14,* pp. 37, 42.

30. Donald L. Prestbo, ed., *Baltic Centennial, 1881 - 1981,* p. 26.

31. Gary Lee Jerke, *Bancroft, South Dakota,* (De Smet, S.D.: 1971), pp. 17-23.

32. Brown County Museum and Historical Society, *Brown County History,* (Aberdeen, S.D.: Brown County Museum and Historical Society, 1980), pp. 50-52.

33. Leland D. Case, *National Geographic,* Oct. 1956, pp. 479-509.

34. The Pioneer Club of Western South Dakota, *Pioneers of the Open Range,* (Midland, S.D.: 1965), p. 8.

35. Go-Getters Extension Club, *Party Potpourri,* (Beresford, S.D.: 1981), p. 40.

36. Jane N. Hunt, ed., *Brevet's South Dakota Historical Markers,* (Sioux Falls, S.D.: Brevet Press, 1974), p. 98.

37. Joseph Nicollet, *Nicollet on the Plains and Prairies: The Expeditions of 1838-39 With Journals, Letters, and Notes on the Dakota Indians,* translated and edited by Edmund C. Bray and Martha Coleman Bray, (St. Paul, Minn.: Minnesota Historical Society Press, copyright 1976), p. 161.

38. Ernest Thompson Seton, *Life Histories of Northern Animals,* (New York: Charles Scribner's, 1909), p. 300.

39. Bernie Hunhoff, "Where the Buffalo Roam," *South Dakota Magazine,* Mar.-Apr. 1993, p.15.

40. Chuck Raasch, "Coming in from the Cold War," *Argus Leader,* Nov. 21, 1993.

41. Deuel County History Book Committee, *Historical Collections of Deuel County,* (1977), p. 56.

42. Harlow, *Prairie Echoes,* pp. 63, 206, 212, 280.

43. Esther Shane, ed., *Echoes of an Era,* (Bridgewater Centennial Committee, 1980), pp. 145-146.

44. Robert Goldberg and Gerald J. Goldberg, *Anchors: Brokaw, Jennings and the Evening News,* (New York: Carol Publishing Group, 1990), p. 39.

45. Joseph Nicollet, *Nicollet on the Plains and Prairies: The Expeditions of 1838-39 With Journals, Letters, and Notes on the Dakota Indians,* translated and edited by Edmund C. Bray and Martha Coleman Bray, (St. Paul: Minnesota Historical Society Press, copyright 1976), pp. 89-90.

46. Northeastern South Dakota Tourism Association, *Glacial Lakes and Prairies,* (Watertown, S.D.: 1993), p. 48.

47. Charles Arneson, ed., *Hamlin County 1878-1979,* (Hamlin Historical Society, 1979), p. 38.

48. David Holden, *Dakota Visions,* (Sioux Falls, S.D.: Center for Western Studies, 1982), p. 116.

49. Archer Gilfillan, *SHEEP: Life on the Dakota Range,* (1929; Boston: Little, Brown and Co., 1936).

50. Edmond Mandat-Grancey, *Buffalo Gap: A French Ranch in Dakota, 1887,* Translated by Phyllis Gorum; Keith Cochrane, ed. (1889; Hermosa, S.D.: Lame Johnny Press, 1981), p. 17.

51. *Ibid.,* pp. 9, 10.

52. Kevin Woster, "Prairie pit stop packs 'em in for tasty daily specials," *Argus Leader,* June 14, 1993.

53. John Hopkins, "Book casts Sitting Bull in new light," *Argus Leader,* Sept. 12, 1993.

54. Herbert Hoover, *American Indian Leaders,* R. David Edmunds, ed.,(Lincoln, Neb.: University of Nebraska Press, 1980), p. 152-174.

55. Yankton Area Chamber of Commerce Bicentennial Committee, *Black People in South Dakota History,* (Yankton Area Chamber of Commerce Bicentennial Committee, 1976), p. 26.

56. Oscar Micheaux, *The Conquest,* (1913; College Park, Md.: McGrath Publishing Co., 1969).

57. Brookings County History Book Committee, *Brookings County History Book,* (Brookings, S.D.: Brookings County History Book Committee, 1989), p. 279.

58. *South Dakota Magazine,* July-Aug. 1991, p. 9.

59. *Blunt Advocate,* Oct. 13, 1883, qtd. in *Hughes County History* (Office of the County Superintendent of Schools, Hughes County, 1937), p. 141.

60. Stu Whitney, "A legend who delivers," *Argus Leader,* July 3, 1994.

61. Eric D. Hohman, "Ski Jumping on the Bluffs of the Sioux River," paper presented at the Dakota History Conference, Augustana College, Sioux Falls, S.D., June 3, 1994.

62. *South Dakota Place Names,* Compiled by Workers of the Writers Program of the W.P.A. in South Dakota. (Vermillion, S.D.: University of S.D., 1941).

63. Lynn Nelson, interview, Aug. 21, 1994.

64. Carl Tideman in Mrs. Walter Hellman, *Blizzard Strikes the Rosebud,* (Pierre, S.D.: State Publishing Co., 1952), p. 45.

65. Leif I. Fjellestad, *Early History of Miner County,* A thesis submitted for Master of Arts Degree, U.S.D., (1931; Sioux Falls: Center for Western Studies, 1981), pp. 41-43.

66. Arneson, *Hamlin County,* p. 41.

67. Kevin Woster, "Farmers to once again enjoy barn-to-home phone capability," *Argus Leader*, Oct. 21, 1993.

68. *South Dakota Place Names,* p. 53.

69. Ardyce Samp, "Dillenger & S.D.," *South Dakota Magazine,* Jan.-Feb. 1993, p. 11.

70. S. Goodale Price in *Lawrence County,* Mildred Fielder, ed., (Lead, S.D.: Lawrence County Centennial Committee, 1960), p. 49.

71. *Ibid.,* p. 58.

72. John J. Bingham and Nora V. Peters, *A Short History of Brule County,* (1947), pp. 56, 57.

73. L. E. Weeldreyer in *South Dakota: Our Towns,* Vol. III, (Dallas, Texas: Taylor Publishing Co., 1987), p. 72.

74. Paul Higbee, "Survivor's School," *South Dakota Magazine,* Mar.-Apr. 1994, pp. 37-43.

75. Northeastern South Dakota Tourism Association, *Glacial Lakes and Prairies,* (1993), p. 18.

76. Tom Lawrence, "Clark residents keep alive tale of Little Fellow," *Argus Leader,* May 31, 1994.

77. Mrs. Paul Zimbelman, in Hellman, *Blizzard Strikes the Rosebud,* pp. 46-48.

78. *Argus Leader,* Apr. 24, 1982.

79. Mary Taggart Hammon in Diamond Jubilee Committee, *Colome Diamond Jubilee: 1908-1983,* (Winner, S.D.:1983), p. 175.

80. Harlow, *Prairie Echoes,* pp. 238, 239, 379.

81. Karolevitz, *Douglas County: The Little Giant,* p. 146.

82. Hunt, ed., *Brevet's South Dakota Historical Markers,* p. 221.

83. *Pioneers of the Open Range,* p.100.

84. C. H. Ellis, *History of Faulk County, South Dakota,* (1909; Aberdeen, S.D.: Faulk County Historical Society, 1973), p. 228.

85. *Ibid.,* p. 441.

86. Tim Giago, *Notes from Indian Country,* Vol. 1, (Keith Cochrane, 1984), p. 376.

87. Leland Case, "Back to the Historic Black Hills," *National Geographic,* Oct. 1956, p. 498.

88. *South Dakota Magazine,* Mar.-Apr. 1989, p. 35.

89. Lawrence Welk with Bernice McGeehan, *Wunnerful, Wunnerful,* (Englewood Cliffs, N.J.: Prentice-Hall, Inc., 1971), p. 98.

90. *South Dakota Place Names,* p. 57.

91. "All You Need to Know About Apple Pie," *Quick 'N Easy Country Cooking Magazine,* Oct. 1993.

92. Leander Richardson qtd. in Lloyd McFarling, *Exploring the Northern Plains,* (Caldwell, Idaho: Caxton Printers, 1955), p. 350.

93. Kevin Woster, "Owner convinced ghost roams through halls," *Argus Leader,* Sept. 8,1993.

94. George Armstrong Custer qtd. in Mc Farling, *Exploring the Northern Plains,* p. 319.

95. Karolevitz, *Douglas County: The Little Giant,* p. 57.

96. Hunt, ed., *Brevet's South Dakota Historical Markers,* p. 65.

97. Peggy Schelske, *South Dakota: Our Towns,* Vol. 3, (Dallas, Texas:Taylor Publishing Co., 1987), p. 54.

98. *Argus Leader,* July 11, 1993.

99. The Book and Thimble Club, *Proving Up, Jones County History,* (Murdo, S.D., 1969), p. 83.

100. Thomas L. Riggs, *Sunset to Sunset,* qtd. in *South Dakota's Ziebach County, History of the Prairie,* (Dupree, S.D.: Ziebach County Historical Society, 1982), p. 12.

101. James M. Robinson, *West from Fort Pierre,* (Los Angeles: Westernlore Press, 1974), p. 124. Note: The number of buffalo calves is given as 5 in this source and 8 in Doane Robinson's *Encyclopedia of South Dakota.*

102. Agnes Ross, interview, Feb. 2, 1993.

103. Egan Centennial Committee, *The Centennial of Egan, South Dakota,* (1980), p. 6.

104. Audrae Visser, Brookings County History Book Committee, *Brookings County History Book,* pp. 282, 283.

105. James Buehler, *Dakota Pioneer,* qtd. in The Centennial Book Committee, *Farmington, Emery, Clayton,* (Freeman, S.D., 1984), p. 3.

106. *Farmington, Emery and Clayton,* p. 2.

107. *South Dakota Magazine,* Aug.-Sept. 1987, p. 50.

108. Fjellestad, *Early History of Minor County,* pp. 38, 39.

109. Ernest Sutton, *A Life Worth Living,* (Pasadena, Cal.: Trails End Publishing Co., 1948), pp. 188,189.

110. Leon W. Jenks, *The First 100 Years of Ethan,* (1983), p.17.

111. Lincoln County History Committee, *The History of Lincoln County,* (Canton, S.D.: 1985), p. 75.

112. Hunt, ed., *Brevet's South Dakota Historical Markers,* p. 256.

113. Mildred Soladey, *Hanson Heritage,* p. 88.

114. Business Research Bureau, University of South Dakota and the Historical Preservation Center, *Historic Sites of South Dakota,* (1980), p. 33.

115. Ellis, *History of Faulk County,* p. 76.

116. Mike Barondeau "Fuel of the Thirties," *Onaka Diamond Jubilee Remembrances,* (1982), p.109.

117. David Kranz, "Cafe of Higher Learning Closes," *Argus Leader,* June 25, 1993.

118. George Catlin, *North America Indians, Being Letters and Notes on Their Manners, Customs, and Conditions, Written During Eight Years' Travel Amongst the Wildest Tribes of Indians in North America, 1832-1839,* qtd. in Lloyd McFarling, *Exploring the Northern Plains,* pp. 46, 47.

119. Chuck Cecil, "Stubble Mulch," *The Moody County Enterprise,* Aug. 25, 1993.

120. Terry Woster, "Living in a Dying Town," *Argus Leader,* July 18, 1993.

121. *South Dakota Magazine,* Jan.-Feb. 1994, p. 31.

122. Larry Baton, *Minneapolis Star and Tribune,* June 8, 1984, qtd. in Lady Helpers Society, *History of Buffalo County,* (Gann Valley, 1985), p. 284.

123. *Garden City, South Dakota, History,* (Clark, S.D.: 1987), p. 3.

124. *Armour Chronicle-Tribune,* July 1902, qtd. in Karolevitz, *Douglas County: The Little Giant,* pp.143-144.

125. Karolevitz, *Douglas County: The Little Giant,* p. 144.

126. *Historical Collections of Deuel County,* p. 66.

127. Tom Lawrence, "A Rare Event in Goodwin: First election in 41 Years," *Argus Leader,* June 22, 1994.

128. Frances Densmore, *Teton Sioux Music,* (Washington: Bureau of American Ethnology, 1918), Bulletin 61, p. 66, qtd. in Ernest L. Schusky, *The Forgotten Sioux,* (Chicago: Nelson-Hall, 1931), p. 6.

129. Don Doll, "Vision Quest: Men, Women, and Sacred Sights of the Sioux Nation," an exhibition at the Civic Fine Arts Center, Sioux Falls, S.D., Sept. 2 - Oct. 23, 1994.

130. *Historic Sites of South Dakota,* p. 73.

131. William Rohrer in Hellman, *Blizzard Strikes the Rosebud,* p. 54.

132. Randy Hascall, "Couple: Ghosts haunt our home," *Argus Leader,* Oct. 31, 1993.

133. Karolevitz, *Douglas County: The Little Giant,* p. 60.

134. *Ibid.,* p. 60.

135. Miller, *Looking for History on Highway 14,* p. 134.

136. *Hartford Centennial,* p. 155.

137. William S. Mc Feely, *Grant, a biography,* (New York: W.W. Norton & Company, 1981), p. 317.

138. Francis Paul Prucha, *Indian Peace Medals in American History,* (Madison, Wisc.: State Historical Society of Wisconsin, 1971), p. 65.

139. Harold H. Schuler, *The South Dakota Capitol in Pierre,* (Pierre, S.D.: State Publishing Company, 1985), p. 19.

140. Micheaux, *The Conquest,* pp. 62, 63.

141. Montana Lisle Reese, ed., *South Dakota, a Guide to the State,* (1938; New York: Hasting House, 1952), p. 234.

142. The Hyde County Historical and Geneological Society, *Hyde Heritage,* (Pierre, S.D.: State Publishing Co., 1977), p.12.

143. *South Dakota Place Names,* p. 69.

144. Harlow, *Prairie Echoes,* p. 352.

145. *Ibid.,* p. 424.

146. *Ibid.,* p. 129.

147. *Hyde Heritage,* p. 37.

148. *Ibid.,* p. 616.

149. Tina Feyereisen, interview, Aug. 29, 1994.

150. *Brown County History,* p. 163.

151. Hoven Jubilee Historical Committee, *75 Years of Progress,* (1958), pp. 29-33, p. 39.

152. Fjellestad, *Early History of Miner County,* p. 39.

153. Kevin Woster, "Bald Eagle Enjoys Solitude," *Argus Leader,* July 8, 1993.

154. Hurley Historical Society, *From Covered Wagon to Compact Car, Hurley 1883-1983,* (Hurley Historical Society, 1983), p. 32.

155. Sutton, *A Life Worth Living,* pp. 196, 197.

156. Carson Walker, "Ammunition Graveyard," *Argus Leader,* Sept. 18, 1994.

157. Qtd. in John Gunther, *Inside U.S.A.,* (New York: Harper & Brothers, 1947), p. 246.

158. Big Foot Historical Society, *Reservation Roundup,* (Shannon County, S.D.: undated), p. 38.

159. Elliot Coues, *History of the Expedition under the Command of Lewis and Clark,* vol. 1., (New York: Francis P. Harper, 1893), pp. xxvi, xxvii.

160. Randy Hascall, "Irene memorial honors area veterans," *Argus Leader,* Aug. 20, 1993.

161. Rod A. Janzen, *Perceptions of the South Dakota Hutterites in the 1980's,* (Freeman, S.D.: Freeman Publishing Company, 1984), p. 6.

162. Madonna Wortman Alley qtd. in *Country School Days,* Hallstrom and Keuter, eds., (Dallas, Texas: Taylor Publishing Co., 1987), p. 16.

163. Nettie Kunz Hauck in *Daughters of Dakota,* Vol. 1, Sally Roesch Wagner, ed., (Carmichael, Cal.: Sky Carrier Press, 1989), pp. 17, 18.

164. *A Century in Review, City of Elk Point, South Dakota,* (1959), p. 21.

165. *Centennial History of Jefferson, 1859-1959,* (1959).

166. Kathleen Norris, *Dakota: A Spiritual Geography,* (New York: Ticknor & Fields, 1993), p. 161.

167. Doane Robinson, *Encyclopedia of South Dakota,* (Pierre, S.D.:1925), p. 638.

168. Mrs. Kenneth Painter in Hellman, *Blizzard Strikes the Rosebud,* p. 97.

169. Hunt, ed., *Brevet's South Dakota Historical Markers,* p. 274.

170. Quoted in Centerville Centennial Book Committee, *Centerville: Our Home Town,* (1983), p. 303.

171. Barbara Miller, ed., *The First 100 Years in Codington County,* South Dakota, (Watertown, S.D.: Codington County History Book Committee, 1979), p. 70.

172. Tim Giago, *Argus Leader,* July 17, 1993.

173. Mel Antonen, "Fans feel S.D. touch at Oriole Park," *Argus Leader,* July 13, 1993.

174. William R. Lewis, *A Historical Momento: Lake Preston,* (Lake Preston, S.D.:1979), p.16.

175. *Alpena Centennial Flashbacks,* p.10.

176. Quoted in Marshall County Historical Society, *Marshall County,* (Dallas, Texas:Taylor Publishing Co., 1979), p. 202.

177. G. E. Lemmon, *Boss Cowman,* ed. Nellie Snyder Yost, (Lincoln, Neb.: University of Nebraska Press, 1969), p. 309.

178. Randy Hascall, "Musical drive-in," *Argus Leader,* July 7, 1994.

179. Bob Keyes, "Irritable? Bored? Get out of there," *Argus Leader,* Jan. 24, 1993.

180. Steve Young, "One church celebrates, one closes," *Argus Leader,* June 28, 1993.

181. *South Dakota Historical Collections,* Vol. X, (Pierre, S.D.: State Dept. of History, 1920), p. 392.

182. James Audubon, *Audubon and His Journals,* vol. 1, Maria R. Audubon, ed., (New York: Charles Scribner's Sons, 1900), pp. 516, 517.

183. Mick Garry, "The Man Behind the Trigger," *Argus Leader,* July 11, 1993.

184. P. E. Tyrrell, ed., *Pioneer Days in Lake County,* The Karl E. Mundt Historical & Educational Foundation (Madison, S.D.: Dakota State College, 1980), p. 60.

185. *Ibid.,* 59.

186. *Brown County History,* p. 140.

187. Mrs. Paul Palmer qtd. in *Brown County History,* p.142.

188. *Brown County History,* p. 140.

189. Candy Hamilton, "Project unites Indian, white on the job," *Argus Leader,* Feb. 18, 1993.

190. Reese, *South Dakota, A Guide to the State,* p. 298.

191. *Ibid.,* p.190.

192. Anson Yeager, "It's time to sort memories of Christmases in S.D. past," *Argus Leader,* Dec. 19, 1993.

193. Helen Graham Rezatto, *The Making of the Two Dakotas,* (Lincoln, Neb.: Media Publishing, 1989), p. 196.

194. John Gunther, *Inside U.S.A.,* p. 237.

195. *Seventy-five Years of Progress,* Mc Laughlin Golden Jubilee;1909-1984, (1984), p. 30.

196. Dwight Coursey, *Aberdeen-American News,* September 18, 1945, qtd. in Harlow, Prairie Echoes, p. 289.

197. Bernie Hunhoff, "Midland Spells Relief," *South Dakota Magazine,* Feb.-Mar. 1987.

198. Holden, *Dakota Visions,* p. 111.

199. Hellman, *Blizzard Strikes the Rosebud,* pp. 10, 119.

200. Sutton, *A Life Worth Living,* p. 218.

201. Randy Hascall, "Long swim begins," *Argus Leader,* May 1, 1993, and "River Swim Completed," *Argus Leader,* May 10, 1993.

202. Holden, *Dakota Visions,* p. 41.

203. Heidi Bell, "Youthful drum group captures top prizes at powwows in region," *Argus Leader,* July 17, 1994.

204. "Over the Fence," *Argus Leader,* Feb. 3, 1993

205. Bernie Hunhoff, "Roy Houck's Triple U Ranch," *South Dakota Magazine,* Mar.-Apr. 1991, p. 14.

206. Kevin Woster, "Orton enrollment now down to one," *Argus Leader,* May 30, 1993.

207. Quoted in Robert Schutt, *The Corn Palace Story,* (Mitchell, S.D.: 1976), p. 7.

208. Doane Robinson, *Encyclopedia of South Dakota,* p. 635.

209. *Ibid.,* p. 636.

210. *Ibid.,* p 637.

211. *Ibid.,* pp. 637, 638.

212. Mrs. Howard Richter in Hellman, *Blizzard Strikes the Rosebud,* p. 100.

213. Erma Zoss quoted in *Country School Days,* Linda Hallstrom and Maricarrol Kueter, eds., pp. 237, 238.

214. *South Dakota Magazine,* Sept.-Oct. 1993, p. 33.

215. Winifred Angel Ziemann qtd. in Sally Roesch Wagner, ed., *Daughters of Dakota,* vol. 2, *Stories From the Attic,* (Yankton, S.D.: Daughters of Dakota, 1990), p. 112.

216. Case, *National Geographic,* Oct. 1956, p. 507.

217. Mildred Fielder, *Hiking Trails in the Black Hills,* (Aberdeen, S.D.: Northern Plains Press, 1973), p. 35.

218. Reese, *South Dakota, A Guide to the State,* p. 256.

219. The Roberts County Centennial Committee, *Roberts County History,* (1989), p. 61.

220. Karolevitz, *Douglas County: The Little Giant,* pp. 122, 123.

221. *Argus Leader,* Oct 21, 1993.

222. Blanch Kaufman qtd. in Winifred Reutter, ed., *Mellette County Memories,* (White River, S.D.: Mellette County Centennial Committee, 1961), p. 31.

223. Tom Lawrence, "A touch, and the smell, of Norway comes to Sinai," *Argus Leader,* Jan. 26, 1994.

224. *Contemporary Sioux Painting,* Catalog of exhibition sponsored by the Sioux Indian Museum and Crafts Center (Rapid City, S.D.: Tipi Shop, Inc., 1970).

225. *South Dakota Magazine,* May-June, 1989, p. 47.

226. Mike Barondeau, *Onaka Diamond Jubilee Historical Book,* p. 100.

227. Coues, *History of the Expedition Under the Command of Lewis and Clark,* p. 159.

228. Yankton Area Bicentennial Committee, *Black People in South Dakota History,* (1977).

229. Ann Grauvogl, "S.D. native enjoying rise to stardom," *Argus Leader,* March 27, 1994.

230. Lora Crouch, compiler, *Hamlin Garland,* (Sioux Falls, S.D.: Dakota Territory Centennial Commission, 1961).

231. *The Monthly South Dakotan* qtd. in Karolevitz, *Douglas County: The Little Giant,* p. 9.

232. *South Dakota Place Names,* p. 86.

233. Reese, *South Dakota, a Guide to the State,* p. 241.

234. L. G. Ochsenreiter, *History of Day County,* (Mitchell, S.D.: Educator Supply Co., 1926), pp. 107 - 108.

235. Crampton, *The 100 Best Small Towns in America,* (New York: Prentice Hall, 1993).

236. Hunt, ed., *Brevet's South Dakota Historical Markers,* p. 150.

237. Ella T. Wilson, *Department of History Collections,* Vol. 33, pp. 109, 110; also Sally Roesch Wagner, ed., *Daughters of Dakota,* vol. 2, (Yankton, S.D.: Daughters of Dakota, 1990), p. 115.

238. *Delmont Record* qtd. in Karolevitz, *Douglas County: The Little Giant,* p. 100.

239. Donna Schaefers, "Polo church stands tall despite loss of a priest," *Argus Leader,* Jan. 13, 1994.

240. George Malone qtd. in *Reservation Roundup,* p. 43.

241. Holden, *Dakota Visions,* pp. 147, 148.

242. Hunt, ed., *Brevet's South Dakota Historical Markers,* p. 163.

243. Orah M. Glass, *History of Pukwana and Vicinity,* (1970), p. 3.

244. Paul Higbee, *South Dakota Magazine,* May-June 1991, p. 54.

245. *Proving Up,* p. 27.

246. *Historic Sites of South Dakota,* p. 57.

247. *Hardrock,* Vol. XXXXI, #4, Mar.-Apr. 1975, A publication of South Dakota School of Mines and Technology.

248. *Glacial Lakes and Prairies,* p. 32.

249. *Argus Leader,* Oct. 6, 1993.

250. *South Dakota's Ziebach County,* p. 83.

251. Herbert S. Schell, *History of South Dakota,* (Lincoln, Neb.: University of Nebraska Press, 1961), p.130.

252. *South Dakota Place Names,* p. 245.

253. Ike Blasingame, *Dakota Cowboy,* (New York: G. P. Putnam's Sons, 1958), p. 68.

254. Lyman County Historical Society, *Early Settlers in Lyman County,* (Pierre, S.D.: State Publishing Co., 1974), pp. 147, 148.

255. Steve Young, "Church book chronicles pioneer life," *Argus Leader,* August 21, 1993.

256. Celda Lundin, *Revillo: A Century on the Prairie* (Milbank, S.D.: 1984), p. 4, qtg. Will Dillman, *A Human Life,* (Excelsior, Minn.: Record Office, 1934).

257. *Ibid.,* p. 16.

258. Hunt, ed., *Brevet's South Dakota Historical Markers,* p. 179.

259. Todd David Epp, "Good & Bad of the Diamond A," *South Dakota Magazine,* Nov.-Dec., 1993.

260. Hunt, ed., *South Dakota Historical Markers,* p. 268.

261. Kent Hyde, "Tale of Two Tongues," *South Dakota Magazine,* Mar.-Apr. 1989.

262. Don Doll, "Vision Quest: Men, Women, and Sacred Sights of the Sioux Nation," an exhibition at the Civic Fine Arts Center, Sioux Falls, Sept. 2-Oct. 23, 1994.

263. Ralph Anderson, "Reservation Run," in Roberts County Centennial Committee, *Roberts County History,* (1989), p. 99, 100.

264. Wayne Fanebust, *Where The Big Sioux River Bends,* (Sioux Falls, S.D.: Minnehaha County Historical Society, 1985), pp. 311, 312.

265. *Argus Leader,* June 8, 1993.

266. Reese, *South Dakota, A Guide to the State,* p. 353.

267. Qtd. in *History of Faulk County,* p. 459.

268. Kevin Woster, "Watertown crew rolls out the lefse," *Argus Leader,* Oct. 12, 1993.

269. Doane Robinson, "Divorce in Dakota," *South Dakota Historical Collections,* Vol. XXI, (Pierre, S.D.: State Dept. of History, 1924), pp. 268-280.

270. George Catlin, *North America Indians, Being Letters and Notes on their Manners, Customs and Conditions, Written During Eight Years' Travel Among the Wildest Tribes of Indians in North America, 1832-1839,* Vol. 2, (Edinburgh: John Grant, 1926), p. 232.

271. Claude A. Barr, *Jewels of the Plains,* (Minneapolis, Minn.: University of Minnesota Press, 1983), p. xiv.

272. Reese, *South Dakota, a Guide to the State,* p. 338.

273. *South Dakota Magazine,* July-Aug. 1992, p. 14.

274. J. Leonard Jennewein and Jane Boorman, eds., *Dakota Panorama,* (Dakota Territory Centennial Commission, 1961), p. 172.

275. Hallstrom and Kueter, eds., *Country School Days,* p. 8.

276. Esther Serr, "Commentary on the Belvidere Cemetery," *Proceedings of the 19th Annual South Dakota History Conference,* H. W. Blakely, ed., (1988).

277. DeSmet, *Western Missions and Missionaries,* pp. 45 and 105.

278. *Hyde Heritage,* pp. 38 - 42.

279. *South Dakota Magazine,* May-June 1989, p. 40.

280. *Stickney, South Dakota, 1905-1980,* (Stickney, SD: *Stickney Argus,* 1980), p. 85.

281. Stockholm Centennial Commitee, Steve Misener, chr., *Stockholm, South Dakota: 1884-1984,* (1984).

282. August Peterson, *History of the Swedes Who Settled in Clay County, South Dakota, and Their Biographies* (Swedish Pioneer and Historical Society of Clay County, South Dakota, 1947), p. 2.

283. *Summer '93 Magazine,* (The Black Hills, Badlands & Lakes Asso. of South Dakota,1993), p. 18.

284. Kevin Woster, "Bear Butte soothes spirits of Indian visitors," *Argus Leader,* July 4, 1993.

285. *South Dakota's Ziebach County,* p. 96.

286. Bernie Hunhoff, "Colors of the Butterfly," *South Dakota Magazine,* Mar-Apr. 1989, p. 42.

287. Harlow, *Prairie Echoes,* p. 220.

288. Brenda Wade Schmidt, "Balloon man," *Argus Leader,* Oct. 15, 1993.

289. The Tripp Study Club, *A Touch of Tripp,* (Tripp, S.D.: 1976), p. 5.

290. Chuck Raasch, "Coming in from the Cold War," *Argus Leader,* Nov. 21, 1993.

291 Lemmon, *Boss Cowman,* p. 245.

292 Chuck Raasch, "Nuclear accident near Black Hills among worst," *Argus Leader,* Nov. 22, 1993.

293 Centennial Book Committee, *Valley Springs Centennial,* (1978), p. 3.

294 . Coues, *History of the Expedition Under the Command of Lewis and Clark,* vol 1., pp. 85 -87.

295. *A History of Southern Clark County and Spirit Lake, South Dakota* (1976), p. 117.

296. Mildred Mc Ewen Jones, *Early Beadle County, 1879 to 1900,* (Huron, S.D.: 1961), p. 46.

297. *Proving Up,* p. 110.

298. Ann Grauvogl, "You're invited to shattering reception for exhibit," *Argus Leader,* Nov. 23, 1993.

299. Bob Keyes, "Two Eagles," *Argus Leader,* April 8, 1993.

300. Argus Leader, June 14, 1993.

301. Todd Epp, "Spirits soar at buttes," *Argus Leader,* Oct 10, 1993.

302. Don Doll, "Vision Quest: Men, Women, and Sacred Sights of the Sioux Nation," an exhibition at the Civic Fine Arts Center, Sioux Falls, S.D., Sept. 2-Oct. 23, 1994.

303. Arch Hall "Frank Hart Termed Best Bronc Buster," *Reservation Round-Up,* pp. 56, 57.

304. Hunt, ed., *Brevet's South Dakota Historical Markers,* p. 238.

305. *South Dakota Place Names,* p. 99.

306. Bernie Hunhoff, "Round Barns of South Dakota," *South Dakota Magazine,* Jan.-Feb. 1993, pp. 19, 20.

307. Ernest G. Bormann, *Homesteading in the Badlands,* (Stickney, S.D.: 1971), p. 22.

308. Reese, *South Dakota, A Guide to the State,* p. 338.

309. John Manasso, "Dakotah Inc. saves northeastern S.D. with jobs, growth," *Argus Leader,* Dec. 26, 1993.

310 . Terry Woster, "Family finds 'heaven' in Wessington," *Argus Leader,* July 28,1993.

311. Kevin Woster, "Mountain lion sightings reported," *Argus Leader,* Nov 5, 1993.

312. *Brookings County History Book,* p. 301.

313. David Kranz, "Vanishing Indian culture worries retiree," *Argus Leader,* Nov. 14, 1993.

314. Jessie Ilgenfritz in Reutter, ed., *Mellette County Memories,* p. 31.

315. *Ibid.,* p. 27.

316. Reese, *South Dakota, A Guide to the State,* p. 246.

317. Carola Van Heukelom in *South Dakota Magazine,* Jan.-Feb. 1990, p. 26.

318. Elmer Foss, "Business and Transportation," *Roberts County History,* p. 101.

319. *Argus Leader,* Sept. 14, 1994.

320. Bert Popowski, *South Dakota Brags,* (Custer, S.D., 1953), p. 10.

321. Ruby Bennett Williams in Hellman, *Blizzard Strikes the Rosebud,* p. 23.

322. Sutton, *A Life Worth Living,* pp. 215, 216.

323. Reese, *South Dakota, A Guide to the State,* p. 237.

324. Richard Kerlin in Reutter, ed., *Mellette County Memories,* p. 38.

325. Virginia Kirk Wood in Reutter, ed., *Mellette County Memories,* p. 90.

326. Robinson, *Encyclopedia of South Dakota,* p. 861.

327. *Ibid.,* p. 860.

328. *Ibid.,* p. 866.

329. *Ibid.,* p. 878.

330. Elizabeth B. Custer, *Boots and Saddles,* (New York: Harper and Brothers, 1885), pp. 16-22.

331. Ellis, *History of Faulk County,* p. 381.

Cottonwood (Haakon) ....Cow country
Creighton (Pennington) ....Old Finnegan
Cresbard (Faulk) ....Old settlers
Crooks (Minnehaha) ....Name play
Custer (Custer) ....Crazy Horse Monument
Dakota Dunes (Union) ....New development
Dallas (Gregory) ....Lawrence Welk's players quit
Dante (Charles Mix) ....Dante's "Inferno"
Davis (Turner) ....Country place
Deadwood (Lawrence) ....Early Deadwood; Seth Bullock
Deerfield (Pennington) ....Custer expedition in Floral Valley
Dell Rapids (Minnehaha) ....Pink quartzite city
Delmont (Douglas)....................When the residents were hopping
DeSmet (Kingsbury) .... Laura Ingalls Wilder
Dimock (Hutchinson) ....Star; small town loyalty
Doland (Spink) ....Home of Hubert Humphrey
Draper (Jones) ....The real Prairie Home
Dupree (Ziebach) ....Fred Dupris saved the buffalo
Eagle Butte (Dewey) ....Eagles
Eden (Marshall) ....This must be paradise.
Edgemont (Fall River) ....Flint Hill
Egan (Moody) ....Early ordinances
Elk Point (Union) ....Lewis & Clark
Elkton (Brookings) ....Funny money; helicopter
Emery (Hanson) ....Emery House
Enning (Meade)....................................Ornithominus
Epiphany (Hanson) ....Father Kroeger's remedies
Estelline (Hamlin) ....Early school teacher writes home
Ethan (Davison) ....Woman abandons family
Eureka (McPherson)............................Commodity capital
Fairburn (Custer)..Agate
Fairview(Lincoln)...........................Spared from being Iowans
Faith (Meade) ....All about Faith
Farmer (Hanson) ....Longevity
Faulkton (Faulk)........................The Picklers and their mansion
Firesteel (Dewey) ....Firesteel fuel
Flandreau (Moody).. Breakfast Club
Florence (Codington) ....Healing waters
Forestburg (Sanborn)...........................Melon mecca
Fort Pierre (Stanley) ....Steamboats on the Missouri
Fort Thompson (Buffalo) .... Santees brought to Fort Thompson
Frankfort (Spink) ....All because of an error in Washington

Frederick (Brown) ....Finns; cooperatives
Freeman (Hutchinson) ....Schmeckfest
Fruitdale (Butte) ....Number 3 on "Best of the Rest" list
Fulton (Hanson) ....Return to small town
Gann Valley (Buffalo) ....The jolly giant of Gann Valley
Garden City (Clark) ....A pretty name
Garretson (Minnehaha).......................................Jesse James
Gary (Deuel) ....Cattle drive on Main St.
Gayville (Yankton) ...."Hayville"
Geddes (Charles Mix) ....Sports rivalries
Gettysburg (Potter) ....Medicine Rock, Civil War association
Goodwin (Deuel) ....Where life is low key
Green Grass (Dewey)...Sacred pipe
Greenwood (Charles Mix) ....Native American commune
Gregory (Gregory)......................................Lottery ticket story
Grenville (Day) ....Poles settle in
Groton (Brown) ....Flax seed mill
Grover (Codington) .... WWI vets left to strains of band music
Hamill (Tripp)...Cattlemen
Hammer (Roberts) ....Arrival of the railroad
Harrisburg (Lincoln) ....Ghosts in house
Harrison (Douglas) ....Early flight
Harrold (Hughes) ....Abundance of bachelors
Hartford (Minnehaha) ....Women's husking contest
Hayes (Stanley) ....Wild west town
Hayti (Hamlin)...Tying hay
Hecla (Brown)....................................Schense quadruplets
He Dog (Todd) ....An Indian chief, Sunka Bloka
Henry (Codington)...Hunting camp
Hermosa (Custer) .... "Wyatt Earp" movie location
Herreid (Campbell) ....About Governor Herreid
Herrick (Gregory)......................Oscar Micheaux's description
Hetland (Kingsbury) ....Romance developed in dugout
Highmore (Hyde)...World War I events
Hill City (Pennington) ....Mining fraud; fossil feud
Hisega (Pennington) ....Origin of name
Hitchcock (Beadle) ....Camp meeting; circuit rider
Holabird (Hyde) ....A promising town
Holmquist (Day) ....Three houses the same
Hosmer (Edmunds) ....Oodles of noodles
Hot Springs (Fall River) ....Mammoth site
Houghton (Brown)..................Sand Lake National Wildlife Refuge

Hoven (Potter)...Cathedral of the Prairie
Howard (Miner) ....Election fraud
Howes (Meade)..David Bald Eagle
Hub City (Clay) ....A Swedish smorgasbord
Hudson (Lincoln) ....Bank robber biked away
Humboldt (Minnehaha) .... Senator Pressler's home town
Hurley (Turner) ...."One of the most promising towns"
Huron (Beadle)..Where the West begins
Ideal (Tripp) ....The name says it all
Igloo (Fall River)..The igloos
Interior (Jackson) ....Badlands town; the wild man
Iona (Lyman) ....Lost member of Lewis and Clark party found
Ipswich (Edmunds) ....The Yellowstone Trail
Irene (Clay, Turner, Yankton) ....Centennial celebration in 1993
Iroquois (Kingsbury, Beadle) ....The Hutterites of Pearl Creek Colony
Isabel (Dewey) ....Early school days
Java (Walworth) ....Coffeetown; Pioneer woman
Jefferson (Union) ....Grasshoppers
Junius (Lake) ....A rocking place reported in New York
Kadoka (Jackson) ....Outhouse races
Keldron (Corson) ....A place of Hope
Kenel (Corson)...........................Fort Manuel; death of Sacajawea
Kennebec (Lyman) ....Mystery money
Keyapaha (Tripp) ....Snow goose
Keystone (Pennington) ....Mt. Rushmore
Kimball (Brule)..Carrie Nation's visit
Kranzburg (Codington) ....Prairie fires
Kyle (Shannon).........................Tim Giago remembers life in Kyle
Ladner (Harding) ....Getting away from it all
Lake Andes (Charles Mix) ....Lake Andes National Wildlife Refuge
Lake City (Marshall).......................Buried treasure, Ft. Sisseton
Lake Norden (Hamlin) .... Ball park remembered
Lake Preston (Kingsbury) ....The great pathfinder
Lane (Jerauld) ....Thirst is more terrible than drink!
Langford (Marshall) ....A golden event
LaPlant (Dewey)..Cattle outfits
Lead (Lawrence) ....Gold at the Homestake
Lebanon (Potter) ....Cedars of Lebanon
Lee's Corner (Buffalo).............................Crow Creek massacre
Lemmon (Perkins) ....Named for cowboy; Kathleen Norris
Lennox (Lincoln) ....Drive in band concerts
Leola (McPherson) .... All about rhubarb

New Effington (Roberts) ....That a way, Effie!
Newell (Butte) .... "The Russians are Coming"
New Holland (Douglas) ....Dakota Dutch
New Underwood (Pennington) ....Home of cowboy Governor
Nisland (Butte) ....Green grow the gardens
Norris (Mellette) ....Social affairs
North Sioux City (Union) ....A Gateway city
Northville (Spink) ....Major league baseball player, Deacon Phillipe
Nunda (Lake) .... "Ignore the risk; try lutefisk!"
Oacoma (Lyman) ....Untapped manganese deposits
Oelrichs (Fall River) ....Black Hills and Canadian Trail
Oglala (Shannon) ....An archeologist's find
Okreek (Todd) ....On the canvas of Godfrey Broken Rope
Oldham (Kingsbury) ...."Oldham's burning"; Social(ist) Hall survived.
Olivet (Hutchinson) ....Miracles of Jesus pageant
Onaka (Faulk) ....Mountain oysters
Onida (Sully) ....African-Americans in South Dakota
Oral (Fall River) ....From Oral to the New York stage
Ordway (Brown).........................Boomtown of Hamlin Garland
Parker (Turner) ....County fair
Parkston (Hutchinson) ....Aftermath of a prairie fire
Parmelee (Todd) ....Cut Meat
Peever (Roberts) ....Froggin' business
Philip (Haakon)..............................Silent Sheep Monument
Pickstown (Charles Mix) ....Fort Randall
Piedmont (Meade) ....Barosaurus
Pierpont (Day)..Political maneuvering
Pierre (Hughes) .... "Pierre was a cowtown"
Pine Ridge (Shannon) ....Home of Oglala; native son Billy Mills
Plankinton (Aurora) ....Grain Fest; Isabella and Martin Diehl
Platte (Charles Mix).......................Fireman's Association Picnic
Pluma (Lawrence) ....Holdup of Deadwood-Cheyenne Stage
Pollack (Campbell) ....Lake Pocasse National Wildlife Refuge
Polo (Hand) ....St. Liborius Church
Porcupine (Shannon) ....Irishman Mike Condon
Prairie City (Perkins).............................Sandstone formations
Prairie Village (Lake) ....Town without a population
Presho (Lyman) .... Bank sprung up
Pringle (Custer) ....On the Rocks
Pukwana (Brule) ....Hospitality still prevails
Quinn (Pennington) ....Where the action was
Ramona (Lake)...Swiss colony

231

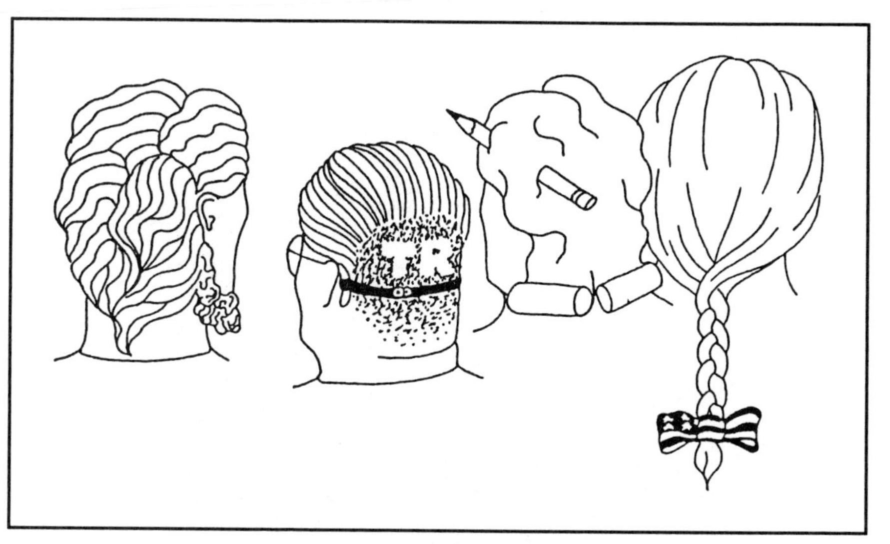

Behind the Scenes at Mount Rushmore

The Vander Lugts in Earlier 1977 South Dakota Days

ABOUT THE AUTHOR

Before they married in 1964, Joyce Dalebout jokingly told Karel Vander Lugt, that she would move anywhere with him, with the exception of Kansas and Nebraska. The Great Plains became part of their life when the Vander Lugts moved to South Dakota in 1968, after having lived in Michigan and the Washington, D.C. area. Karel and Joyce were soon wearing comfortable denims and feeling at home. The Vander Lugt children, Ellen and Bill, were born in Sioux Falls where the family has lived for over 25 years. The four Vander Lugts have enjoyed camping and exploring the state together. The photographs in the book were taken by Karel or Joyce on those outings. Joyce enjoys the changing seasons and says she welcomes the first snowflakes of winter as much as the first spring flowers. Karel and Joyce have backgrounds in science, and both of their children are English majors whose editing skills have been put to use. Joyce worked in medical and dairy microbiology research and has since turned her curiosity to the *BEHIND THE SCENES in South Dakota* project which was conceived during a year away. Karel spent a 1991-1992 sabbatical leave at Cornell University where Joyce attended lectures in history and other subjects. Living away from the state brought a fresh and appreciative perspective of the people and places in South Dakota.

ThinkPrint Publishing Company
Box 89604
Sioux Falls, South Dakota 57105